A B Y S S I N I A

W9-CSY-570

Lake Rudolf

⋏ **L. Paradise** (1923-1927)
Mt. Marsabit

*Kaisoot
Desert*

K   E   N   Y   A

*Lorian
Swamp*
(1932)

Archer's Post
● Chobe Hills

Eauso Nyiro R.

S   O   M   A   L   I   A

●
Isiolo

● Meru

⋏*Mt. Kenya*

● Garissa

● *Nyeri*

⋏● Naivasha

*Masai
Mara*

Nairobi
●

Athi

Tana River

*Serengeti
Plain
(1926)*

⋏ *L. Amboseli*

N

Mt. Kilimanjaro ⋏
● Arusha

● Voi

● Mombasa

INDIAN OCEAN

N   I   K   A

I MARRIED ADVENTURE

THIS BOOK BELONGS TO

Osa Johnson

I MARRIED ADVENTURE

The Lives and Adventures of Martin and Osa Johnson

WILLIAM MORROW AND COMPANY INC.
NEW YORK

Library of Congress Cataloging-in-Publication Data

Johnson, Osa, 1894–1953.
    I married adventure : the lives and adventures of Martin and Osa
Johnson / Osa Johnson. —Rev. ed.
      p.   cm.
    ISBN 0-688-08687-X
    1. Johnson, Martin, 1884–1937.   2. Johnson, Osa, 1894–1953.
    3. Photographers—United States—Biography.   4. Nature photography.
    5. Wildlife cinematography.   I. Title.
    TR140.J63J64   1989
    910'.92'2—dc19
    [B]   88-37299
                                                                  CIP

Printed in the United States of America

First Revised Edition

1 2 3 4 5 6 7 8 9 10

BOOK DESIGN BY PATRICE FODERO

With all my love,
I dedicate this book
to the memory of my husband,
whose work will be an everlasting monument
to his heroic dreams and indefatigable spirit.

*Foreword*_____

Here, in a story about everywhere else in the world, is romantic Americana that will one day be history. These pages are themselves adventure. Here the watchmaker's boy from Independence out in Kansas meets the Santa Fe engineeer's daughter from Chanute, plain people from the prairies. Against that homespun background is woven a life and career filed with exotic color.

Many a story is called a saga. This is one—in all the meaning of that word from the language of Martin Johnson's Scandinavian forebears. Martin was as born to adventure road as Lief-the-Lucky, and when Osa married Martin she married his destiny, too. It was to be always a-going, always a-seeing. Home was to be a schooner in the South Seas, a raft in Borneo, a tent on safari, a hunt in the black Congo, sometimes a dash of Paris, interludes of an apartment on Fifth Avenue—but always a place to be going from.

No matter where or how, through it all, the telling is no mere travelogue and picture album, but rather the intimate tale of their two lives—boy and girl from Kansas, pushing their horizons into far places. The bigger story is of their life, sometimes to be read between the lines, and not quite so much of the world they went to see as of the hearts they took with them.

The American Museum of Natural History with its great

halls of exhibits and its laboratories has also a great invisible collection of careers in the lives of those who have been associated with its projects, intangibles of tradition. To this Martin and Osa have contributed richly. And this is set down by one who has broken bread with them by the campfires of safari.

—F. TRUBEE DAVIS
President, American Museum of Natural History
New York

January 1940

Editor's Note _____

I would like to offer assurance to all Johnson fans that the romantic adventure story of Martin and Osa Johnson remains intact. There are minor changes in the spelling of names, there are a number of different photographs, and some chronological adjustment has been made to render the story more accurate in terms of data which have surfaced since the final editing (not Osa's) of the original publication.

In my resolve not to tamper with *I Married Adventure*, I have left untold, as did Osa, the problems posed by Martin's long battle with diabetes. In Martin Johnson's carefully created "never negative" image of "Mr. and Mrs. Martin Johnson," there was no room for what was then considered a debilitating illness.

The editing of the book could not have been done without the help and encouragement of many people. The staff of the Martin and Osa Johnson Safari Museum, Barbara Enlow Henshall, Patricia Miles Hutinett, and Mary C. Hutinett have searched, listened, read, given advice, corrected errors, typed, and retyped, all so this book could be finished. Without Mrs. Henshall's expertise, the photographs used in the book could never have been found and identified.

To honorary trustees C. Jackson Selsor and Kenhelm W. Stott, Jr., go special thanks. Mr. Selsor's careful study of the manuscript has been invaluable. Mr. Stott, general curator emeritus of the San Diego Zoo, author of *Exploring with Martin and Osa Johnson,* and a noted authority on the life and works of the Johnsons, has given generously of his time and expertise in support of this project.

—SONDRA UPDIKE-ALDEN
Editor

Chapter 1 _____

In light of the placid expectation that because I was born in
Chanute, Kansas, I would grow up, marry, raise a family, and
die there, I find it amusing to recall a certain hot September
day of my seventh year, when I asked my father for ten cents.
It was early morning and he was just on his way out the back
screen door, his oil-blotched denim work coat over his arm.
Pausing, he put down his carefully packed bright tin dinner
pail and looked at me.

Ten cents was a lot of money in those days. As a brakeman
on the Santa Fe, all my father earned was a dollar and a quarter
a day. Ten cents would buy a pound of round steak or a gallon
of kerosene, or a peck of potatoes, or two yards of calico—yes,
or even a hank of wool sufficient for one of the many socks
that emerged by some sort of magic from the bright, clicking
needles in Grandma's workworn hands.

Ten cents. My father pushed back his cap and looked toward
my mother. She smoothed her clean, faded apron and considered me. I urged quickly that they needn't give me another
thing for a whole year, not even for Christmas.

Grandma eyed me gravely and wondered what the children
of today were coming to. When she was my age there were
worries about food and clothing and firewood, and even wolves;
and hurried flights from marauding Indians. Why, when she
was my age, she hadn't even seen ten cents. And as for presents, she remembered a doll her mother had contrived for her
out of a knobbed stick and a bit of bright cloth. Ten cents.

1

I knew that my request was beyond all reason and almost beyond explanation, and, as if haste could make up for logic, I told breathlessly of a young traveling photographer to whom Babe Halloran, my bosom friend, had taken her baby brother, and to whom I felt I ought to take mine. Vaughn, being three, wasn't a baby exactly, but certainly he'd never be any younger. And, I hurried on, it was something that would have to be done right away because tomorrow the photographer was leaving Chanute and going back to Independence. That's where he lived and went to school, I added, feeling vaguely the need of something to give weight to my plea and stability to the young traveling photographer.

A smile twitched at my father's mouth.

"Oh, back to school," he said.

"High school," I replied with dignity. "And the pictures he takes are the cutest you ever saw, and only ten cents for a whole dozen."

Williams' Opera House was over on Main Street, four blocks away. The young photographer, according to Babe, took his penny pictures in a vacant storeroom upstairs. With the ten-cent piece clutched in one of my hands and Vaughn's hot fist in the other, we started out, and not until then did I begin to worry about the success of the venture. Suppose the pictures were no good after all.

The red-brick walks sent up wavy lines of heat. Even the dusty elms seemed to drip heat, and my hair lay on my neck warm and heavy as freshly pulled taffy. Vaughn dragged his copper-toed shoes through the thickest dust along the way, and by the time we reached Williams' Opera House and climbed the long flight of dark stairs, my temper was very nearly the equal of his.

Tacked on the door was a large, glossy white card, with one word lettered boldly in black. Its message, brief and doubtless simple, was nevertheless mysterious to me. "Studio" was what it said. I opened the door and pushed Vaughn, howling with protest, before me.

A tall, thin young man with a black cloth over his head and a gray rubber apron covering him from knees to chin stood behind a camera. Peering at us briefly, he said, "Sit down, you

kids, and be quiet," then went on taking the picture of a smiling pink-and-white baby girl. There were no chairs, so we sat
on a pasteboard box, which promptly collapsed. Vaughn's face
was smudged and streaked with tears, and, moistening my
handkerchief with my tongue, I did my best to restore him to
the shining cleanness that had been his when we left home.

The smiling little girl was carried off at length by her proud
mother, and I wondered vaguely whether, with all my pride in
my little brother, it wasn't a pity he had been born a boy.

The young man took something out of the camera, put
something back in, then turned and spoke to me for the first
time. "All right, little girl, his hair's all right. Leave him alone
and tell him to go sit on that chair."

Well, nothing that has happened to me before or since has
equaled the humiliation, struggle, and pure anger of that next
fifteen minutes. The young photographer had his ideas of how
the picture should be taken, I had mine, and Vaughn wanted
none of any of it. And then something happened that was quite
beyond my experience and to this day has me puzzled whenever I encounter it. They looked at each other, these two, and
then effortlessly and without a word reached some sort of pact
that completely excluded me. Off came the broad white embroidered collar, the hair which I had smoothed at regular intervals from the moment we left home was tousled deliberately,
and just as the picture was snapped, Vaughn grinned.

The photographer laughed and said, "That's fine, young fellow. This'll be good." Then, to me, something about, "Ten cents,
please, little girl, and you'll have to come back for the pictures
this afternoon. I'm leaving Chanute in the morning."

I looked at him and picked up the discarded white collar; I
looked at Vaughn, now a perfect angel of sweetness and good
intention; then I paid the ten cents in a voiceless rage and left.
The name of that young itinerant photographer, I learned some
eight years later, was Martin Johnson.

Martin was born October 9, 1884, in Rockford, Illinois, where
his father was foreman of the stem-winding department of the
Rockford Watch Company. A new ambition stirred in John
Johnson with the birth of a son. Instead of merely working at

a job, he would build a business which in later years his boy could share. Word came of the railroad that was being laid through the rich farm lands of Kansas and of a newly assembled town in Saline County. A likely spot for a little jewelry store, he reasoned. Mrs. Johnson, who knew of his ambition, agreed wholeheartedly, and her careful saving provided the money necessary to make such a move, with the result that the spring of 1885 saw them established in that raw and thinly settled community named Lincoln Center.

This move was not as foolhardy as it appeared, for the section of the country which John Johnson had thus chosen as a home and for a new venture into business was, in part at least, familiar to him.

Brought to America from Sweden when just a baby, he spent his younger years as a newsboy in New York and Chicago. At fourteen, tales of the untamed frontier so stirred his adventurous spirit that he headed west, where he worked at odd jobs. After adding to his height and weight, John Johnson figured, rightly, that he could do better with a regular job and so began hauling buffalo hides and supplies for the army. Due to either his job or his ability at poker, young John did manage to save some money, and after this period of his life he married the fine and understanding girl who was to become Martin's mother.

When he set out for Lincoln Center, Kansas, in 1885, Martin's father knew exactly what to expect. The streets were unpaved, and the business section was a huddle of as-yet-unpainted stores. Wisely, he rented the one adjoining the newly erected Salina Savings Bank, gave it three coats of paint against the hot Kansas sun, and put in a modest stock of jewelry, actually little larger than would make a fine display in the brightly polished front window. Lincoln Center was heartened by the appearance of a jewelry store on its dusty main street, and the farmers around as well as the people in town gave John Johnson their business instead of going to the county seat at Salina.

And while all this was going on, the small boy who had inspired it found life good in and about the spotless white house on Second Street, two blocks from the Johnson jewelry store.

School for the first year or two offered no serious problem beyond having to sit in a stuffy room long hours every day with a lot of girls and other boys. The lessons were repetitious and therefore dull; the droning recitations put Martin to sleep; and the girl in the seat just in front of him wore purple plaids, smelled of strong soap, and had a coarse, black braid which swept his slate pencils onto the floor and broke them. Martin didn't like that. Her ears were pierced, and she had little pieces of toothpick in them to keep the holes open. He didn't like that either. Then when she appeared with little rings in place of the toothpicks, he felt relieved somehow in the pit of his stomach, but he didn't like the rings either. He maneuvered for a different seat, but where you sat in school seemed as fixed and nailed down as the seats themselves, so, shamelessly, he played hookey at least once a month.

His father taught him to swim when he was five, and every Saturday morning found him up early, barefooted, and off in bibbed blue overalls and wide-brimmed straw hat to explore the infinite wonders of the Saline River. Ben Marshall and the Everett boys usually went with him on these expeditions, and the Reese brothers, whose father owned the mill, made up a noisy, lusty six. They took paper bags of lunch, packed the night before, and fishing poles and bait according to the season. The Saline River, except at flood time, was an orderly stream, and so the boys liked best that spot at the foot of the mill where a cataract tumbled and gave the sound and feeling of danger to a place that in reality was as safe as a wooden washtub. The willows spread grateful shadows on the sloping bank, and the mill, built of native yellow stone, bulked large and solid and was, Martin knew, one of the biggest buildings in the world—anyhow, bigger than anything in Lincoln Center. Darkly cool inside, it had the sweet, clean smell of ripe crushed wheat and a ghostly powdering of white that drifted and clung even to the highest spiderwebs, and often went home with him on the seat of his blue denim overalls.

An amiable youngster, Martin nevertheless had definite likes and dislikes. Routine of any sort was an abomination, and chores, whether cutting wood, hoeing the garden, mowing the lawn, or even going to the store, fell into this category. He figured it out, however, so that everybody was happy, his mother included. Gathering up old bottles, for one thing, he'd pile them in his wagon, haul them to the river and wash them carefully, then haul them to the drugstore on Main Street and sell them for half a cent apiece. Or he washed the windows of the bank, the grocery, and the hardware store for a nickel apiece. Then, with perhaps thirty cents in his pocket, he would pick up one or both of the Everett boys and pay them twenty cents to do general chores for his mother. They were happy to have the twenty cents, his mother was happy to have the chores done, and Martin was twice happy in having dodged the chores and in gaining possession of the ten cents remaining in his pocket.

Martin was ten when his sister, Freda, was born. He didn't like the name Freda, so he called her Tom, and he was very proud of her. He was especially pleased the day she started to walk, but it bothered him to see her fall down, so he put casters on an old cane-bottom chair, removed the seat, and, with an arrangement of straps, fastened Freda in so that her feet touched the floor and she couldn't fall down even if she wanted to. This might have been the forerunner of the somewhat less clumsy contrivance in use today.

My husband's life seems always to have had a clean and clear design. With perfect instinct for selection, he always knew what he wanted to do and did it, regardless of consequences to himself. It was as simple as that, and as unconfused.

For this directness, both of impulse and thought, his mother and father deserve much credit. Their part in Martin's achievements was neither obvious nor greatly considered.

That his body was sound and his instincts right was taken for granted; his failure to distinguish himself in school according to the system of the day left them, wisely, undisturbed. From his Swedish father, Martin inherited a keen mechanical sense and a Viking's love of adventure. From his mother, whose forebears had fought in both the Revolutionary and Civil wars, came the urge to push back new frontiers.

There was always much of the little boy in Martin, and it showed itself in his delight in pure nonsense, his excitement sometimes over small rather than large achievements. Often I would look up at him, and for all his six feet one, which was nearly eleven inches more than I boasted, I could see in him the small boy he must have been. I think my greatest delight on some of our long safaris was to hear about those little-boy days, when, stimulated every now and then by a gentle prod from me, he would conjure up a thin, taller-than-average lad with curly yellow hair and sea-green eyes born just nine years before I was.

Driving all night, as we often did in Africa, with all of our resources and hopes of success staked on outdistancing the dreaded rains, dodging pig-holes, anthills, and sleeping rhinos, we would make a game of comparing dates. When he first ran away in Lincoln Center, for instance, I was first seeing the light of day in Chanute. I shall always love the memory of his mother for her rare understanding of her only boy on that night when he first decided to leave home. He had failed to pass his grades and had been marked "poor" in everything but geography. Worse, he was being put back into the sixth grade. There was nothing to do, he decided, but to run away. During supper that night he managed to slip some of the food off his plate into a paper bag, and, when he thought no one was looking, he left by the back door. He stopped at the pump for a drink, and there, to his astonishment, his mother overtook him, carrying an old carpetbag packed with his things. Giving it to him, she wished him a cheerful good-bye and sent him on his way. Martin got as far as a cave which he and his friend Ben Marshall had dug in the railroad embankment, crawled in, then crawled out again and ran straight home, where he was received without surprise or comment.

Thanks to Martin's mother, the return to school and the lower grade the following day was completely without embarrassment. He had his mother's and his father's support; their belief in him at a time when his pride in himself and his confidence might have suffered a damaging blow helped to keep intact a free, courageous, and imaginative spirit. His almost excessive love for animals turned the neat backyard of the Johnson home into a sort of cemetery, not only for the occasional cat or dog that happened to die in the neighborhood but for wild squirrels, turtles, rabbits, mice, sparrows, canaries, pigeons, and even a four-foot bull snake killed by some of the boys up the street. All were given a place marked out with

orderly precision in the Johnson flower garden. It was not until
the headstones inscribed by Martin with appropriate epitaphs
began to crowd the rose bushes that the vacant lot next door
was suggested as an extension, if not a more suitable place for
this boyish challenge to oblivion. In no sense was there anything morbid about all this. It was rather that Martin's percep-
tions were acute, his sympathies alive, and his imagination
active. A squirrel, for instance, wasn't vaguely just another of
an undetermined number of lively and impudent rodents. Each
was an individual—one with perhaps a tuft of hair missing from
his left shank, another with a scar across his nose, another
with a finer and longer tail or with more audacity, cleverness,
or drollery, as the case might be. And out of this keen awareness, it seems to me, grew his interest in the camera, his determination to learn and master all its possibilities, his ardent
wish to capture all he could of living things in its lens.

At the beginning of the nineties, Lincoln Center was the
unfortunate target of some of nature's more afflictive moods.
Damaging droughts, frightening floods, and ruinous pests im-
poverished this section, which depended almost entirely upon
agriculture for its existence. John Johnson saw that it would
take years for the country to reach again its former level of
prosperity. So, in the spring of 1895, he moved his business
and his family to Independence, Kansas, a small town in the
southeast corner of the state, and it was from here that Martin
started out on some of his larger adventures. Martin was just
eleven years of age when the move was made, and he was
distinctly unhappy about it, for apparently he'd lost everything
and gained nothing. The boys, the mill, the places where he
used to go fishing and swimming—all were left behind, and
here he was in school again, and as far as he could see all
schools were exactly alike. They even had the same smell of
disinfectant, varnish, and chalk dust. Then, wholly unexpectedly, there developed a new and absorbing interest, and day
after day he sat reluctantly at his desk and thought about it,
and the voice of his teacher became a meaningless drone. His
father, on opening the new jewelry store in Independence, had
acquired the exclusive sales agency for Eastman Kodaks and

supplies. Martin helped him unpack the first boxes to arrive on an eventful Saturday morning, and told himself with a deep inner excitement that here was something he wanted to know about—know all about.

Experiment followed on experiment, and it is certain that more stock was wasted than was sold over the counter in those first few months of Martin's awakened thirst for knowledge. Instead of being annoyed by these raids on his valuable photographic stock, Mr. Johnson encouraged them by building a darkroom in the back of the store and supplying Martin with all the books to be had on the subject. These Martin promptly took to school with him, further distracting his mind from his studies and exasperating his teachers.

Unless there was an element of novelty in an undertaking, Martin was not interested. On one occasion, however, his efforts to dodge a rather tiring as well as boring chore did not work out so well. On washdays, Martin was expected to get up earlier than usual, often before daylight, and to carry enough water from the well to fill the boiler and tubs, a task that he heartily disliked. Using every bit of his considerable powers of persuasion, he eventually coaxed his father to buy a hand-powered washing machine, which then was being extensively advertised as a labor-saving device. When it arrived, Martin found to his disgust that not only was he obliged to carry just as much water as before, but to furnish the hand power as well.

Mr. Johnson continued to cherish the dream that some day his son would take over the prosperous little jewelry business. To this end he exerted every effort to teach Martin to buy and sell rings and watchfobs, to repair watches and clocks, and to polish silver—but without success. Martin's horizon was far beyond the plate-glass window of his father's store.

One morning, just before Christmas, Martin was leaving for school when his father said, "Martin, I want you to come straight over to the store this afternoon. There's a lot of new Christmas stuff to unpack."

Martin, now knowing what awaited him, dawdled on the way, engaging in a halfhearted snowball fight that carried him finally and reluctantly to the door of his father's store. In the back room, he took off his coat, cap, muffler, and mittens, blew on his cold, wet fingers, reached for the unwieldy nail-puller, and went to work on the big boxes.

The first one was filled with cuckoo clocks trimmed with wooden lace. He tried but failed to visualize the places they came from. Interlaken! Lausanne! Montreux! What strange names. He tried tentatively to pronounce them but gave it up at once. The letters and numerals on the box and in the old Swiss newspapers used for packing had a distinctively and intriguingly foreign look. It was that way with the French and Italian newspapers, too. All used the Roman alphabet, just as they did in Kansas, and yet there was something fascinatingly different about the letters.

Another box of Christmas novelties was from Nuremburg, Germany. The newspapers in these boxes were printed in letters that had the look of Sunday-school texts. Next was a box of glass from far-off Venice, in which he found a newspaper printed with odd-shaped letters wholly new to him.

He went with it to his father and interrupted the sale of a wedding ring, but John Johnson didn't know whether the printing was Russian, Greek, or Turkish; it might be all or any of them.

Martin always saved the boxes from the Eastman Company until the very last. Often he would wait until after supper to open them, and that gave him time without interruption to inspect each camera down to the last screw. Iris, shutter, and lens—all were subjected to a careful scrutiny and became a part of his store of knowledge as well as part of the stock on the orderly shelves.

The snapshots sent by the Eastman Company as specimens fascinated Martin quite as much as the cameras themselves. Usually there was a liberal sprinkling of scenes of foreign lands. Maybe, he conjectured, these are from those same places where the newspapers came from. After that, Martin might be seen at almost any time taking pictures of the town hall, the bank, the corner drugstore, and the new hotel. Underexposed, over-developed, poorly printed, light-struck, and badly composed, they were, Martin decided, pretty bad. And for that matter, he concluded in justice to himself, as he compared his photography with that from across the world, Independence might be a pretty big town, bigger than Lincoln Center, but its buildings, civic and otherwise, weren't much to brag about.

It was about this time—he was just thirteen—that Martin read of the circus in Kansas City. Pictures of some of the animals and performers appeared in the Independence papers, and since he had never seen a circus, the whole thing proved too much for him. Packing a small but strong wooden box with camera, tripod, plates, and films, and emptying his iron bank of its seventy-eight cents, he dropped from the window of his bedroom at two in the morning and made his way down to the Santa Fe freight yards. Here he climbed into the open door of an empty boxcar and promptly fell asleep. He awoke several hours later to find himself in Topeka. He arrived in Kansas City that night to find the circus had left town. Martin had then to content himself with taking pictures of the colored circus posters; and he had likewise to think about getting home. Too many cream puffs and peanuts made him violently ill. His father, notified by a kindly brakeman, found him curled up in a corner of the Santa Fe freight yards and took him home.

Chapter 2 _____

"I'm going to travel and make money doing it," Martin announced to his parents some three weeks after vacation had started.

"That's fine, Martin, that's fine," his father answered characteristically. Then, a little anxiously, "How are you going to do it, son?"

"Take pictures." Martin was confident. "A penny apiece. County fairs. Volume business."

John Johnson's thoughts wandered to his jewelry store, one of the finest in the state, and to his fast-fading hopes that one day his son would take it over. Then, a little dubiously, he eyed the equipment on which Martin had worked hard and secretly for the past three weeks. It consisted of a rickety buckboard and the piebald pony Socks; an old camera and tripod together with developing fluids and trays bought from Hannah Scott on the installment plan; an ambitious number of plates out of the Eastman stock in the store; and an old tent. This last was lined with black cloth. How much labor had gone into it Mr. Johnson could only guess.

"That's my darkroom," his son explained proudly.

Martin was fifteen, going on sixteen. John Johnson sighed and, as the strange contraption rattled off down the road, thought of his own youth.

"Anyhow," he smilingly said aloud to Martin's mother, "one thing we don't have to worry about in Kansas these days is Indians."

The first letter from Martin was postmarked Neodesha, Kansas. After two or three weeks a letter from Fredonia informed them that he was well except for spots in front of his eyes—was it his stomach and what should he do about it?—and that he was going on to Altoona. The next letter was to the effect that a spell of rain had almost ruined his equipment, but that he was going on to Chanute, where he would open a gallery. Somebody had told him that no photographer was there at the moment. "And," he asked, "don't you think this is a good idea?"

Arriving in Chanute, Martin found Mr. Williams, who owned the opera house, about the only person who would rent him a room and take a chance on collecting the rent later. This turned out to be a storeroom, cluttered and dusty, but it had a fine skylight and, almost equally important, a washbasin with running water. Martin took the room on the spot. Elatedly, he cleared a place for work, carried his equipment up the long stairs, hand-lettered some announcements, and, after pasturing Socks with a genial farmer on the edge of town, settled down to wait for business. This was in the middle of August, and hot as only a Kansas August knows how to be. Martin remarked some years later that in all our years together in Africa he never suffered from the heat as he did in that practically airtight cubicle over Williams' Opera House in Chanute.

His patrons, mostly of the grade-school age, came in just sufficient numbers to let him hope he was establishing a business; he even dreamed of becoming as important to Chanute as Hannah Scott was to Independence. The fear of missing a customer, however, kept him a virtual prisoner in his oven-like cell. The old tent with its black cloth lining still served as his darkroom, and night usually found him developing the plates that had been exposed during the day. Some "prop" cushions were kicked together in a corner and that was where he slept, though often with wistful visions of his comfortable bed and clean, cool sheets at home.

Business picked up, and it seemed to Martin that he was doing very nicely indeed. He was even saving money. But a new problem arose when his materials ran out and he had to pay cash for more. This was a very different matter, he found, from drawing on his father's stock at will, and on Hannah Scott's on credit. His money was almost gone. He made several valiant efforts at producing cabinet pictures and charging ten cents apiece, but here his equipment failed him utterly. And then— whether it was the heat or nature tardily rebelling at his too-steady diet of watermelon, peanuts, and cream puffs—his stomach went back on him. Reluctantly he began to wonder whether it wouldn't be a good idea to go home—yes, and maybe even go back to high school again.

The last penny picture Martin took in Chanute was of a hot, cross little boy who came with his sister, equally hot and cross, and there was an argument over a white, starched, embroidered collar.

Martin had dreaded the return home. Grimy, almost ragged, and hollow to his heels with hunger, he could think of no way to justify himself. Naturally, he knew of his father's hope to have him learn the jewelry business and eventually to take over the store, and he also knew that because of his failure to buckle down, his father had had to hire some help.

Martin sighed when he remembered all these things. What was the matter with him anyhow? Why couldn't he do the thing that was expected of him, the right thing? It seemed to him that surely his parents would reproach him this time—gently, of course—and point out that from now on he had better consult them about his plans. What he found, however, was a sympathetic sort of casualness that left no room at all for embarrassment over the outcome of his initial trek. There were no questions or reproaches anywhere, either spoken or implied.

And, of course, there had been that other notion of his, now vanished, in which he had pictured himself returning grandly bearing gifts. All he had been able to manage was a little gingham parasol for Freda. It was bright pink, and the wooden handle smelled of shellac.

"It cost thirty cents," he said. "I could have bought one for twenty-five cents, but while I was about it I thought I might as well get a good one."

His father eyed Martin's lean, lank figure, but commented only on the fact that he sure was growing to be a tall fellow;

must have added at least an inch since he left. His mother, saying nothing, hurried a plate of ham and eggs before him. Freda pulled a chair close and looked at him in pure, unmixed admiration because he had gone away, traveled far, and come safely back with a parasol.

The next few months showed a concentration of effort which, by all odds, should have succeeded in anchoring Martin to Independence for life; at least such was his worthy intention. Promptly after school every day he would appear for work at his father's jewelry store.

The girls at school began to take note of Martin, a rather better-than-average-looking youth, and even consulted his mother about giving a surprise party for him on his birthday. It seemed to Mrs. Johnson that this was a very nice idea indeed, and she entered wholeheartedly into the pleasant conspiracy. There was much secret cake-baking and chicken-frying, and all went well until the very evening of the party, when, just as he was entering the strangely quiet house, one of the girls giggled. Martin gave one startled look, wheeled about, leaped the fence, and was off in the direction of the river.

Here, tied to an overhanging limb, was a raft which he and some of the gang had rigged up. A houseboat, they called it, though the structure was little more than an oversized box nailed none too securely to the center crosspieces. It was raining by the time Martin got there, so he crawled into the little shelter, fastened the door securely against any of the crowd that might follow him, curled up on the old blanket with which the place was furnished, ate some stale cookies, and went to sleep.

The rain became a downpour, and Martin's impressions of what happened next were somewhat mixed, but he found himself bumping around in the once-snug box, and found further that if he didn't get out in a hurry he'd probably drown. Finally, kicking his way free, he swam to shore and from there saw what was left of his houseboat carried in odd bits and pieces down the swollen river. He also saw the end of his half-formed plans to spend the next summer on that raft, taking pictures while he drifted down the river, perhaps clear to the Mississippi.

Martin was rarely seen without his camera. He took pictures of his class individually and as a group, and nearly everyone in school had yielded indulgently at one time or another to posing for an informal snapshot. Neither party nor picnic was considered a success without Martin's pictorial record of the occasion, and with an eye to business he garnered a few dollars here and there selling the prints. Picnics were his special delight. He liked the challenge of light and shade under the trees down by the river, and groupings and composition claimed his earnest attention.

One bright, warm Saturday that fall, with camera and tripod lashed to the handlebars of his bicycle, Martin led a party to a spot several miles out of town beside a clear stream. There were shoebox lunches of fried chicken, deviled eggs, and cake. This, Martin decided, was a nice life indeed.

Propped lazily against the trunk of a tree, he sank his teeth into a big piece of chocolate cake and thought about girls. He was both pleased and embarrassed when they showed a preference for him. He liked the big brown eyes of one, but her hair was coarse and reminded him of another girl with a long, dark braid who had once sat in front of him at school. The little blonde was all right—pretty enough, he guessed—but she giggled too much and agreed with everything he said. The girl with the red hair was cute in her way, had pretty hands, and was graceful, but he suspected her of a bad temper. Martin couldn't help thinking it was too bad one couldn't make a composite, using the good points of maybe half a dozen of them.

The trend of the day was on the sentimental side, and Martin, in the mood—objectively, at least—took some pictures of a sweetly tender nature. One couple, cheek to cheek, peeped coyly at the camera over a low-hung bough. Another stood in embrace before a weeping-willow tree. A young lady sat on a tree stump while a young man, intently ardent, knelt at her feet. Undeniable was the influence of those colored slides used in "nickel shows" to illustrate the popular songs of the day.

On developing the plates, Martin was gratified to find a distinct improvement in his skill as a photographer, and after making a few prints he carefully filed the negatives. Several months later found him working in the little darkroom which he had rigged up at home, and whatever he was doing required the most careful and exacting performance. It had its amusing side, too, for his mother, at the door with his nightcap of bread, jam, and milk, heard a sudden shout of laughter.

At morning recess the next day, the schoolyard was static with huddles of shrieking students; there were more huddles in the halls and cloakrooms. At the approach of a teacher, each huddle sobered instantly and dissolved. Late that forenoon, Martin was called too the office of the principal.

"Martin," that gentleman said sternly, "it has come to my attention that you have been distributing photographs around the school—photographs that are indecent!"

"Indecent, sir?"

"So I have been told. Indecent and ridiculing the faculty. What have you to say for yourself?"

"Well, I made some photographs, but—"

"Let me see them, please."

Martin pulled from his pocket what appeared at first glance to be ordinary snapshots, but the principal, eyeing them closely, saw the very proper instructor of algebra cheek to cheek with the comely new Latin teacher. He saw every gentleman member of the faculty paired off with a lady member in what, without quibble, was an attitude of love. And, lastly, he saw himself on one knee in an attitude or ardor before the lady teacher of English 4-B.

"I only thought they were—well, sort of funny," Martin ventured lamely.

"Funny! Indecent, that's what they are, and I demand that you collect every print you gave out and bring them here to me!"

This Martin did during the noon hour, taking them at once to the principal's office. There was an ominous silence as they were torn in bits. Then the principal spoke.

"Martin Johnson, by this performance you have disgraced not only yourself but the entire school, and it is clear that we can no longer tolerate your presence here. You are expelled, sir."

Martin felt suddenly hollow inside. His mouth was dry.

"I meant no harm, sir. It was all in fun. If you'll give me

another chance, I'll—for my father's sake, I mean—I'll do anything."

"Your father is a fine man, and my sympathy goes out to
him for having an idle, mischievous wastrel for a son. How you
will end up, only the good Lord Himself knows. There is nothing more to be said, sir. Good-bye."

Trudging homeward with his books, Martin couldn't have
said just what his feelings were; they were too mixed. To quit
school was one thing, to be expelled was another, and there
was a sick feeling someplace deep inside that was part defiance, part shame. Then, with a fresh surge of indignation, he
asked himself how those composite snapshots of his were any
worse than the comic valentines the kids bought at the five-
and-ten and sent to teachers every year. He was also indifferent and yet plagued by a sense of failure: How was he going
to make his father and mother see that he meant no harm?
Lately they had been so confident of him, so proud.

Arriving home, he heard his mother busy about the kitchen.
Slipping in the front door, he went upstairs to his little darkroom and there carefully destroyed the few remaining prints
and all the negatives of his too-successful attempt at composite
photography. This done, he sat down and tried to think things
out. He was through at school—no doubt of that! And then
another thought struck him that left him cold: This whole thing
might reflect not only on him but probably on his father too.
The best thing would be to go away. Yes, there was nothing
else left to do.

That same afternoon saw him at the railway station, where
he asked information about schedules and fares—one way—to
New York, San Francisco, Philadelphia, Chicago—any distant
locale, as distant as his funds would permit. He found that his
savings would take him to Chicago with a dollar and two cents
left over.

This time it was a little more difficult for John Johnson to
convince his wife that it was all right for Martin to leave home.
Mrs. Johnson felt that she should have questioned him on the
night before. Perhaps she could have saved him all this. But
John Johnson, out of a wisdom that had something to do with
his own boyhood, said that saving a boy was not the way to let

him grow strong. He had to follow his own bent and suffer his own consequences. And then he assured her that since Martin didn't have much money, he'd soon be glad to come home again, that he probably wouldn't be gone more than a few months.

And so, the following morning, with his father and mother giving what passed for a cheerful consent, and with the only outward tears those shed by his young sister, Martin said good-bye to Independence.

Chapter 3

Martin's last glimpse of the town in which so much of his boyhood had been spent was of the high school, and he made a
vow that they'd be sorry some day for the way they had treated
him. He'd show them that he wasn't worthless and an idler
and a wastrel or whatever it was the principal had called him.
He might even make a name for himself somehow, and maybe
a fortune besides. He'd show his father and mother, too. A lump
rose in his throat as he thought of them. They had never asked
to be shown.

Huddling down in the dusty, red-plush seat of the day coach,
he looked out at the bleak, wintry Kansas landscape and made
himself think about Chicago. He tried to visualize the Loop,
the elevated, the tall buildings. The lake, too, a hundred miles
or so wide. He guessed it would be cold in Chicago in the dead
of winter, and he wondered where he'd sleep, how he'd live.
He fingered the dollar and two cents in his pocket—he had
refused his father's offer of help—and felt a little relieved. With
that and the big box of lunch his mother had packed for him,
he'd get along fine for a day or two.

A couple of traveling salesmen occupied the seat just in
front, and he heard them say something about the Chicago
LaSalle Hotel. That might be a good place to get a job, he
thought—for the winter, anyhow. He recalled the few times he
had been to the Booth Hotel in Independence. Salesmen taking his father there for lunch had included him every now and
then, and he had liked to sit in the lobby and watch strangers

20

arriving with baggage, others leaving. It always gave him the feeling that he was part of their larger world. He grinned then as he thought of the big and realistic painting of an African lion that hung in the lobby. Someone had had the idea of putting vertical wooden bars in the heavy frame, and the effect was of a very fierce lion hanging in a cage on the wall. Foolish as the whole idea always seemed to Martin, nevertheless the picture had seemed a sort of symbol of adventure.

Chicago was fully as cold as Martin had expected it to be. He went straight from the train to the LaSalle Hotel and applied for a job. Next he found himself in pillbox hat and brass buttons—a bell-hop. He liked the smart, often foreign-labeled luggage it was his job to carry in the wake of beautifully dressed men and women; he liked the quiet air of sophistication, the ease with which these people lived a large and full life. What he didn't like was the unreasonable demands his job imposed upon him. Knowing hotel boys' problems and sympathizing with them, he always, in later years, tipped far more than the customary amount, and sometimes more than he could afford.

He wrote home with some attempt at regularity. His father always answered promptly and encouragingly, and one of these letters contained the mild suggestion that perhaps some wholesale jewelry concern would give him a job, and might even give him an opportunity to learn engraving. As an apparent afterthought, John Johnson included at the bottom of his letter the name and address of a fine Chicago firm.

Following his father's advice, Martin applied for a job and was engaged on the spot at a surprisingly good wage. It wasn't until many years later that he discovered the reason for this. His father, it seemed, had bought from the company something over a thousand souvenir spoons as an inducement to give his son a job.

Martin's talent for freehand drawing made engraving easy, and in a comparatively short time he had mastered its technique. And, as was the way with him—once a thing was mastered and its challenge gone—his interest was also gone. At lunch with some of his fellow employees one day, he talked idly of the foreign lands he would like to visit, and a discussion was started as to how far a person could travel and on how much. Martin searched his pockets and took out a total of $4.25.

"If I wanted to," he said thoughtfully, "I bet I could go to London and back on that."

There were hoots of derision from his coworkers, the bet was taken on, and in another week Martin was in New York on the first leg of his journey across the Atlantic.

His family received a letter from him a few days later, written grandly from the Waldorf-Astoria. He had availed himself of a desk in a corner of the lobby and some embossed writing paper, and the impression the letter gave at first glance was that he was stopping at New York's most fashionable hostelry, and that in the same magnificent style he would soon be on the high seas bound for England. A P.S. on the reverse side of the letter, however, added that he was to take twenty-eight horses, worth $250 each, to Liverpool.

Martin landed in Liverpool barefooted and wearing a hastily contrived suit of gunny sacking. The sturdy shoes and good wool suit in which he had expected to step ashore were stolen from him the night before the boat docked. There had been four bloody fights with as many sailors in his efforts to recover these habiliments of respectibility and comfort, and just as he had his hands on them, a fifth sailor entered the salty bit of hazing and heaved shoes and suit overboard. Martin spent the night under the bridge.

Liverpool, London, Brussels, washing dishes, loading cargo, mopping floors, he found that often he had to fight for his jobs and then fight to keep his money after he had earned it. Stowing away on a cattle boat, he returned to New York City.

Once more Martin came home. He had sent no word, and as the train pulled into the station at Independence and he swung himself down the steps of the day coach, there was no one on the platform to meet him. This was the way he had wanted it. A cluster of people waiting in the shade for the northbound train glanced at him but without recognition. Harry St. John, one of the boys with whom he had gone to school, was among them, as was Charlie Kerr, the plump, jolly druggist, mopping his face as usual with a big white handkerchief.

Cutting across lots, Martin became aware of the almost forgotten Kansas heat. His hands were moist and grimy, and on second thought he guessed his face was grimy, too. And then,

of course, there was that day's stubble of beard. No wonder the
people hadn't recognized him. A sharp pebble found the hole
in the bottom of his shoe, and he let go with a bit of profanity
that belonged more on the docks of Liverpool than in Independence.

Over the tops of the dusty trees he saw the bell tower of
the high school and remembered his vow not to return to Independence until he had made a name for himself, and a fortune. Anyhow, a small fortune.

He glanced down at his battered canvas suitcase; the frayed
cuffs of his trousers also caught his eye. No, he reflected wryly,
he didn't exactly have the look of a conquering hero, but he
was heartened by the knowledge that his family would be glad
to have him home anyway.

He saw the familiar white house through the trees and
quickened his stride. It was just dinner time, the midday meal
in Kansas. His father would be home, Freda too, and the two
would be sitting at the kitchen table and his mother putting
good food in front of them.

Circling the house, he went through the dusty alley and in
the back gate, past the old barn and along the brick walk, then
very quietly up the steps of the neat back porch. Here he
knocked on the screen door, and then stood back a little.

"Sorry to bother you, lady," he said as his mother appeared
at the door, "but could you give a poor bum a cup of coffee?"

His mother sat down and cried, his father declared a holiday for himself, and Freda, now twelve and in the eighth grade,
did the same.

They watched him in silent awe as he bent to wash his
hands at the sink, then crossed to the table, towering high above
them. It just wasn't possible that he could have grown so much,
they said. Martin, with his knees once more under the kitchen
table and a big dish of stew before him, said he thought they
were all wrong about that. They had just forgotten how he looked
before he went away. In his familiar bedroom, later, where
everything was just as he had left it, he thought he would get
out of his travel-worn suit and into some of his old clothes, only
to find that he must have gained nearly four inches in height
and nearly as much in width.

John Johnson had a call from the store telling him that one

of his best customers had sent a phonograph to be fixed; something was wrong with the spring, and he wanted it right away. Mr. Johnson was as close to profanity as it was possible for him to be. Today of all days. Why, the only thing you could do when one of those big springs got out of order was to send the machine back to the factory.

Martin said maybe he could fix it. His father shook his head. There wasn't a man born with enough strength in his hands to fix one of those springs. Martin said he'd still like to try it. A few minutes later he was striding into the jewelry store with his father. Quickly shaking hands with Dr. Brann and Opal Conrad, and brushing aside their exclamations of surprise at his unexpected return, he went to the familiar back room where the phonograph stood. Carefully, he studied the problem to find the best method of putting back into place the powerful coiled band of steel.

Dr. Brann brought various tools that he thought might help. But Martin shook his head, and taking the coil in his hands, he first tested its resistance, then began winding it firmly and smoothly into place. Twice the lawless coil sprang alive from his hands, whipping and cutting its way free.

Grimly eyeing the mass of tangled steel on the floor, Martin picked up a rag, wiped the sweat and blood from his palms, and began again.

"You just can't give up the first time on anything," he told his father, who looked on helplessly and voiced incoherent protests against the attempt. Dr. Brann said testily that no man ever had been able to get one of those coils in place with his bare hands, and why was he so suddenly set on doing it?

Martin couldn't have told why. He smiled his brief thanks to Opal for the clean cloth she brought him and again began winding the coil. Pressing, winding, pressing, winding—the coil seemed suddenly to resign itself to an acknowledged master and slipped quietly into place.

Wiping the sweat from his forehead and hands, Martin chanced to look at his father, and what he saw in the kindly, sensitive face brought more of a catch to his throat than any he'd known in years. Someday, somehow, he swore, he'd merit that pride.

Martin, at the age of three, with his mother and father

Osa's mother and father, William H. and Belle Leighty

Eight-year-old Osa in a party dress

Martin, as a boy, already dreaming of adventure

Martin on board the *Snark*

The crew of the *Snark* at Penduffryn. Left to right: Tehei, Wada, Charmian and Jack London, Martin, Ernest, and Henry

Martin proudly poses in front of the Snark No. 2, one of the two theaters he operated in partnership with Charley Kerr in Independence, Kansas.

Mr. and Mrs. Martin Johnson after their marriage, on May 15, 1910

MARTIN JOHNSON
The Traveling Companion of
JACK LONDON
And Scenes From His Wonderful
South Sea Island Travelogues

Advertisement broadside used by Martin Johnson on the vaudeville tour

Two of the stage costumes Osa wore when performing with Martin's travelogues

"Hawaiian" costume designed by modest Kansan for his wife

"Hawaiian" costume designed by Osa

The Londons and the Johnsons reminisce at the London home, Valley of the Moon, California. The Johnsons at that time were touring the Orpheum circuit.

Seasoned travelers now, the Johnsons wait with their luggage on a train platform.

Chapter 4_____

Two months passed, and Martin tried with everything that was in him to adapt himself to the confining routine of his father's jewelry store. He sat on the high watchmaker's bench, a glass screwed in his eye, his movements restricted to a finger or two, his vision, if not his thoughts, narrowed down to an escapement pin or the hairspring of a lady's watch. He designed monograms and made, in the bowls of spoons, freehand engravings of the city's most important buildings. He got the knack of handling phonograph springs, and wondered at his own and his father's pride over the first one he had fixed. He sold engagement rings, wedding rings, and silver baby cups, and secretly and ashamedly he was miserable.

That he was of interest to the younger set of the town for a while because of his vagabonding was of no consequence to him. He couldn't even be persuaded to talk about those four years. His only impression was of great masses of humanity, dependent on one another, defeating one another, and of men's struggle, often cruel, for supremacy over other men. He wouldn't care if he never saw another big city as long as he lived.

Several times his father had felt him out about expanding the business. He broached the subject again one chilly evening in the fall. They had locked up the store for the day and were on their way home for supper.

"We could rent the vacant store next door and carry the finest supply of photographic stuff in the whole state." He paused. "What do you think, Martin?"

"Uh, yes. Sure. Sounds like a fine idea."

"You see, I was thinking—as long as you don't like fiddling around with watches and things—"

"Its just that I'm no good at it. Anybody can see that."

"Well, photography's your line. I thought we could have a fine darkroom at the back, too. Do developing. You take charge of the whole thing."

"That sounds great."

"And I was thinking we could have a new sign made to go clear across both stores, and it would say Johnson and Son."

"Johnson and Son. That sounds good."

"I think so. A regular partnership, and fifty-fifty on the profits."

"Oh, no. I couldn't take what I didn't earn."

"You'd earn it, Martin, don't worry. Why, people who never go near a jewelry store, except maybe at Christmas time or weddings, would be coming in from your side of the store to buy souvenir spoons, baby pins, and things."

"Well, I guess I hadn't thought about that part of it."

Mrs. Johnson was in the kitchen getting supper ready; Martin said something sure smelled good, then wandered into the living room. Freda was there, poring over the fashion section of a magazine. Tall for her age, flaxen-haired and graceful, she was beginning to have beaus, and Martin, as well as checking up on these, teased her unmercifully. Tonight, however, he paced the room.

Johnson and Son. Johnson and Son.

His sister giggled and asked him what he was mumbling about. He denied mumbling. Then, as she went into the kitchen to help with supper, he said it aloud.

"Johnson and Son."

Idly, he leafed through the magazine Freda had left in her chair, when suddenly, with an impact that was almost physical, an article by Jack London met his eyes. It told of a proposed seven-year trip around the world in a forty-four-foot boat.

The story told, in Jack London's own words, of how the ship, though small, was to be the finest of its kind ever built. Only the most carefully selected woods and finest metals were going into its construction, and the most skilled of craftsmen had been employed to do this work. The article went on to say that when finished, this small but perfect ship was to carry Jack London, his wife, Charmian, and a crew of four on a trip without schedule or predetermined route to distant lands far removed from the sea-lanes of regular travel. And then Martin read with astonishment that one of the crew of four was to be someone in the United States still unknown, who had only to write a letter to Jack London sufficiently convincing to win him a place in the crew.

This is it! This is it! something in Martin shouted. *I'm going with them! I'll steer the boat! I'll take pictures! I'll scrub decks!— I'll do anything—*

The flame of excitement dimmed as quickly as it had lit. He was crazy even to think of such a thing. He, a small-town Kansas boy, without the slightest knowledge of navigation or of boats, a total stranger to the famous Jack London—how could he ever hope to share so great an adventure?

Martin got up. The magazine slid to the floor and, without even a thought for his supper, he went out into the street and walked rapidly and without direction until nearly midnight.

His stomach was hollow with a great desire.

Why not write Mr. London? he heard himself arguing. *He can't do any more than say 'no.' He probably won't even answer, but at least you'll have tried.*

Martin ran all the way home. The folks were in bed. His mother had put some milk and sandwiches in his room. He bolted these as he got out his meager supply of writing materials, then sat for hours chewing his pen.

He began writing. He rewrote. He tore up page after page of the most careful writing to which he had ever applied himself. Finally, down to his last two sheets of paper, he cursed himself for not having paid stricter attention to composition when in school. Then, with something of both recklessness and despair, he just wrote what came. Briefly, he told Jack London how he had knocked and fought his way over a small part of the world, what he could do with photography, that he wasn't afraid of work, and, finally, that he was as strong as an ox. And then, so that he wouldn't tear up this final effort, he shoved it in an envelope, addressed it, and pounded the stamp into place with his fist. Dawn was just edging the horizon.

When the westbound train stopped at Independence a few hours later, Martin was waiting for it. He gave his letter into the hand of the mail clerk, watched the train from sight, and then sat down as suddenly as if his knees had had jelly in them instead of bones.

The mail carrier now became the most important person in Martin's life. Each day the shrill whistle up the block brought him tingling to his feet, and each day as it went by it left him sick and cold. When a week had passed, he berated himself for writing in the first place. It just didn't seem possible that he could have been such a fool. He'd simply forget the whole thing, that's all.

Late one afternoon some ten days later, a Western Union boy delivered a telegram at the store. Martin's father signed the book and was about to open it when he saw it was for Martin.

"A telegram for you, Martin," he called to the back room.

"A telegram!"

Martin came to the doorway and gaped. Then he pounced. In his clumsy fingers the envelope seemed made of some indestructible material. Next, he was staring at the message. Altogether, there were just five words: "Can you cook? Jack London."

Jack London. He didn't believe it.

Can you cook? It sounded crazy. Can you cook? The words beat a sort of tattoo in his brain.

Canyoucookcanyoucookcanyoucookcanyoucook . . .

"What's the matter, Martin?" his father asked anxiously.

"He wants to know if I can cook!" Martin shouted.

"Who wants to know?"

"Jack London!"

Martin leaped to the back room and looked at the wall calendar. It was Monday, November 12, 1906. The article had said December 15 was the sailing date.

There wasn't time. Maybe there was! There wasn't time. Maybe there was!

He ran out the back door, down the alley, and into the rear of Milton Cook's White Front Quick Lunch Room.

Jess Utz, the lean, lank chef, was just sticking a fork into a pot roast.

"Listen, Jess," Martin panted. "How long would it take a man to learn to cook?"

Jess deliberated.

"Me," said Jess, finally. "Me, I bin cookin' somepin' like ten years and ain't larned yit."

"I don't mean to be a first-class chef," explained Martin. "How long will it take me to learn to cook enough to keep six people from starving, including me?"

Jess eyed him suspiciously. "Say, what are you up to?"

"Look, Jess," pleaded Martin, shoving the telegram into the cook's hand. "If I can cook, I've got a chance to go with Jack London on a trip around the world. And I can't go with Jack London if I don't learn to cook. Jess, I've just got to!" He was almost incoherent.

"All right! Don't get so excited! Don't you understand that cooks are born, not made? Yer either a good cook or ye ain't— and I don't think ye are."

Jess looked into the oven and shut the door with a bang.

"A'course," he said, "efen ye want to come in here and work, I'll show you what I kin, and Gawd have mercy on the stomicks of them as has to eat your vittles."

Ten minutes later Martin was in the telegraph office composing his answer to London's wire. It read: "Sure, just try me."

Without waiting for London's reply, Martin sat about learning to cook. All day long he hovered around the stove, blistering himself with hot grease and scalding liquids. As Jess initiated him into the secrets of good gravies and tender meats, Martin painstakingly wrote all the formulas in a notebook. At night, Mrs. Cook introduced him to the mysteries of bread, biscuits, and pastry. Whenever he had the opportunity, he questioned his mother about various dishes she had served at the family table, writing the recipes in his book. He bought a cookbook and practically memorized it.

About four days after the receipt of the telegram, Martin received a long and detailed letter from Mr. London to let him know what he was in for. After this, Martin worked all the harder. There were some doubts about his progress, however. Customers coming into the White Front Quick Lunch Room would ask Milton Cook, "Now, are you sure Mart didn't cook any of this food?"

Martin insisted upon preparing the Thanksgiving dinner at home. Whether it was because he was leaving the next week or because the food was unsavory was never quite determined, but the fact remains that only a small portion of the dinner was eaten, and that by Martin, accompanied by much smacking of lips and other like sounds of enjoyment.

When Martin went to thank Jess for his help and instruction, he said, "Jess, I think I know enough about cooking now so I can make good, don't you?"

"I ain't sayin'." Jess was dubious, even glum.

With his old canvas suitcase pressed into service and the latest-type camera (a parting gift from his father) as his only luggage, Martin boarded the California-bound Santa Fe. As he settled himself once more on the plush cushions, he heaved a sigh of relief. But as he listened, the click of the wheels seemed to say: *Can-you-cook . . . can-you-cook . . . can-you-cook . . . ?* He opened his suitcase and fished out his notebook. A glance through its grease-stained pages dispelled all misgivings, and he answered the wheels, saying, *Sure! Try me!*

According to Martin, it was the slowest trip he ever took. The train seemed to stop every five minutes, and each stop seemed of several hours' duration. Most of the time was spent wondering what kind of man London would be. What did he look like? Was he short? tall? dark?

Writing about his first meeting with Jack London, Martin said: "The article in the magazine, which had first drawn my attention to the proposed trip, had given me little knowledge of the man with whom in all probability I was to spend the next seven years of my life. The nearer I came to Oakland, the California city in which the Londons were then living, the more intense grew my curiosity. Worst of all, I was haunted by a fear that if I didn't hustle and get there, Jack London would change his mind and I should be obliged to come back in humiliation to Independence.

"It was about nine o'clock in the evening when I arrived in

Oakland. As soon as I was off the train, I hunted a telephone and called up Jack London. It was London himself who came to the 'phone. When I told him who I was, I heard a pleasant voice say: 'Hello, boy; come right along up;' and then followed instructions as to how to find the house.

"They lived in a splendid section of the town. I had no difficulty in finding them. When I rapped at the door, a neat little woman opened it, and grabbing my hand, almost wrung it off.

" 'Come right in,' cried Mrs. London. 'Jack's waiting for you.'

"At that moment a striking young man of thirty, with very broad shoulders, a mass of wavy auburn hair and a general atmosphere of boyishness, appeared in the doorway and shot a quick, inquisitive look at me from his wide, gray eyes. Inside, I could see all manner of oars, odd assortments of clothing, books, papers, charts, guns, cameras, and folding canoes, piled in great stacks upon the floor.

" 'Hello, Martin,' he said, stretching out his hand.

" 'Hello, Mr. London,' I answered. We gripped.

"And that's how I met Jack London, traveler, novelist and social reformer; and that is how, for the first time, I really ran shoulder to shoulder with Adventure, which I had been pursuing all my days."

The next morning, Martin met the other members of the crew. There was Herbert Stolz, a young man of about twenty-one, recently graduated from Stanford University. He was a lad of terrific strength and abounding energy. Then there was Paul H. Tochigi, a Japanese boy who had been in America about a year. He was to act as cabin boy. And last, but by no means least, was Mrs. London's uncle, Captain Roscoe Eames, who was the designer and superintendent of construction of the boat, and who would be navigator when they got under way. These three, with Mr. and Mrs. Jack London and Martin as cook, comprised the jolly crew of the good ship christened the *Snark*.

To his surprise and disappointment, Martin discovered the *Snark* was far from complete. They had been working on her for several months, but it was apparent that it would be some little time before she put out to sea. They planned to sail October 1, 1906, but she was not finished. Next November 1 was the sailing date, but she was still incomplete. Then she was scheduled to sail on November 15, then December 15, but each date found her still in the process of construction.

During the next three months, nothing went right. Because of the very recent earthquake, it was almost impossible to hire carpenters or workmen of any kind, and London was compelled to pay exorbitant wages to get any at all. The vast amount of material being moved into an Francisco caused such confusion in the railroad freight yards that one car containing oak ribs for the boat was not found for more than a month. On top of this, a big strike closed down all the shipbuilders, cutting off supplies. The *Snark* was originally planned to cost around seven thousand dollars, but by the time she was finished the cost was nearer thirty thousand.

From the time he arrived in Oakland until they sailed, Martin made his home with the Londons. On bright days he would take a camera across the bay to San Francisco and photograph the construction of the new city rising out of the ashes of the old, or record the progress of the *Snark*.

Sometimes it seemed as if the *Snark* were breaking down faster than it could be built up, and about the first of March, Jack declared that they would sail her to Honolulu just as she was and finish her there. But the *Snark* sprang another leak, which had to be repaired before she could be moved. Finally, one bright Saturday in the middle of March, all got aboard at nine o'clock, and at the command of Captain Eames, the *Snark* slid down the ways without a quiver and was towed across the bay to the Oakland estuary to be fitted and rigged.

While the electricians were doing the wiring and the carpenters worked, Bert Stolz and Martin took turns sleeping on deck. Immediately the galley was finished, Martin tried out his ability as a chef. He caught fish and fried, baked, and boiled them with varying degrees of success. He made bread and pastry and fed it to the workmen. Martin insisted that they enjoyed every mouthful, and as none complained of indigestion, he felt quite satisfied. Jack bought him a bread-mixing machine which saved hours of labor.

Martin felt particularly fortunate in being chosen as one of the crew, but he never did find out just what prompted Jack to pick him in preference to the many other applicants. Jack showed Martin a few of the hundreds of letters which continued to pour in right up to the date of sailing. They were from men, and even women, of every class, color, and creed. Many even offered considerable sums toward the expenses in order to be taken along.

On the nights it was his turn to sleep on board, Martin lay in his bunk and wondered if it were all a dream. He wished nightly that they would get under way. His conscience stirred guiltily every now and then as he remembered his brash boast about he could cook.

One night he was awakened by a shuddering crash. He leapt to the deck to discover that the *Snark* was sandwiched between two lumber scows. In the morning it was found that the rail was flattened two inches on one side and bulged two inches on the other, and from then on the *Snark* was lopsided.

Another night when Martin was alone on board, he was awakened at three in the morning by the anchor chain paying out through the hawsepipe; the *Snark* was pitching and rolling in the teeth of a northeast gale. Rushing on deck, he made fast the chains. An hour later he was again awakened, and this time he found that the boat was within a hundred yards of a pile wharf! Martin was in a panic. The wind was blowing a frightening gale. The rain came down in torrents, hurling oblique walls of water against the unsheltered craft. The anchor had slipped. Martin could see that it was but a matter of moments before the *Snark* would be dashed on the piles. The gale lessened for a moment, and Martin ran to lower the kedge anchor. Just as it seemed that all was well, a tempestuous blast of wind swept the bay with diabolical fury, driving the *Snark* still nearer the piling.

The kedge anchor arrested the progress of the ship, but Martin knew it would not hold fast for long. He knew that unless he could do something, the brave craft would be dashed to splinters. He clung to the rail desperately.

But what could he do? All the fine, strong oak, the shining metals, the efficient instruments and engines—were they all to be destroyed with never a chance to fulfill their destinies? He thought of the money, the hours of labor, the anxieties! And— most hideous of all—his dreams, which were being destroyed!

His dreams, his hopes, his half-answered prayers were being blown to certain destruction. And Jack London too—his hopes and dreams of months.

Hardly knowing what he was doing, Martin screamed a defiant curse into the raging storm and dashed below to the engine room. He tried desperately to start the motor, but there was no sign of life in it. Precious minutes went by as he checked the machine. He made a delicate adjustment, and after another heartbreaking struggle, the engine roared.

Running to the cockpit, Martin turned on the propeller and fought his way back into the bay with anchors dragging. There was but little gas in the tank, and as soon as he had put a safe distance between the *Snark* and the pier, he turned off the engine to conserve fuel.

Again the storm carried him into danger and yet again, but each time Martin fought his way to safety with the engine. Hour after hour he battled the wind and water, not knowing when the fuel would give out or the engine become flooded. In either event nothing could save the ship.

As the morning came, the storm subsided and the *Snark* was made fast again. During the night, more than twenty-five vessels, many of them larger than the *Snark,* had been wrecked.

Week followed week of misfortune and delay (the many causes of which I shall not attempt to put down here), until on April 23, 1907, the gallant little *Snark* sailed perkily out of the Golden Gate, leaving behind a group of well-wishers who were certain they would never again set eyes on the crew.

Chapter 5 _____

Martin hadn't the remotest idea of how to provision a ship. He had crates of cabbages, lemons, apples, carrots, and other perishables piled high on deck, most of which had to be tossed over the side before many days had passed. He had enough spices on hand to supply several large restaurants for years.

The size of the galley was negligible. It would have been considered small for a clothes closet. Martin said that here the old saw about having to go outside to turn around was literally true—if he had a dish in his hand.

For the first meal on the trip, he decided to prepare a nice roast with dressing, vegetables—including fried onions, of all things—and pudding. He got out a half peck of onions, and by the time he had them peeled in that wee galley, he decided nothing more was needed for that meal. The onions burned his nose and throat and watered his eyes so badly he could neither talk nor see. That night the crew had to like onions.

The record of the twenty-seven-day sail to Honolulu in the *Snark* is the record of the most wild and chaotic period six human beings ever spent. To quote Martin: "It was hell on the high seas." They had not been out more than a day or so before they became aware of the fact that they had no navigator. Captain Eames was supposed to keep the ship on its course, but his meager knowledge was pitifully inadequate, and before they had reached Honolulu everybody on the boat was navigating, some with astonishing results. Once, after taking their bearings and consulting the chart, Martin amazed everyone by es-

43

tablishing their position somewhere in the Atlantic Ocean. I often wonder how they ever found the Hawaiian Islands.

They had bad weather from the start, mounting to the proportions of heavy storms. The light boat pitched like a cork. It leaked like the proverbial sieve. The sides leaked, the bottom leaked; water poured in, ruining the tools in the engine room and spoiling a good part of three months' provisions. The coal had been delivered in rotten potato sacks and was washing through the scuppers into the sea. The floors of the galley and cabins were ankle-deep in water.

Everyone was tossed about violently. Martin was covered with burns and bruises trying to cook in the tiny kitchen. More often than not, he was on the stove and the food was on the floor. Never for a moment was it possible to let go of one hold unless assured of another. Mrs. London would have been the envy of all acrobats had they witnessed a double handspring she turned one day after missing her hold on the railing. She soared down the companionway and landed on top of a dinner being served by Tochigi.

Of course, all were desperately seasick. Tochigi lay in his bunk most of the time as if paralyzed; Martin made for his at every opportunity.

To top all this, the gasoline seeped out of the nonleakable tanks, filling the cabins with fumes; the flying-jib boom poked its nose into the water and broke off clean; the ship got into a trough and, through some fault in her construction, refused to heave to; the patent sea anchor, warranted not to dive, promptly started for the bottom when made fast; the beautifully and expensively fitted bathroom went out of commission the first day at sea; a particularly violent blast of wind carried away the jib and staysail; and in spite of the intricate electrical system, there were no lights and fans—the engine wouldn't work—nothing worked! No ship ever went to sea with more things wrong with her. And so the unfortunate vessel creaked and groaned its way across the Pacific toward Hawaii, the sport of every wave.

Luckily for Martin, the appetites of the crew were not at their peak, so most of the time preparing food was merely a matter of warming the contents of a can or two. No bride ever relied more on her can-opener than did Martin. At irregular intervals—dictated usually by the size of the waves—Martin baked bread which they say was not bad. But it was next to impossible to do any real cooking. Dishes defied all laws of gravity, and the stove was caked with food that had slopped over.

On Monday, May 20, 1907, the *Snark,* after skirting disaster for twenty-seven days, dropped anchor in Pearl Harbor and furled her sails. It seemed a paradise to those six sea-weary souls. It was so good to be on solid ground again. According to the newspapers, the *Snark* had been given up as lost and reported gone down with all hands on board.

Martin could hardly walk. The land tilted just like the ship, and for days he would find himself spreading his feet apart to keep from falling.

He swam, he fished, he took pictures, he played. He did everything but cook. He put it more graphically than I can when he wrote, "For my part I had plenty of leisure. After an heroic silence of days, the crew finally broke out in protest against my cooking. They simply could stand no more of it. When on the sea, it had been eat it or starve; but now that they were ashore, there was a greater latitude of choices. We all boarded with different folks in the vicinity, and the poor harassed crew forgot its troubles in the delight of eating once more the things that humans eat, cooked as humans would cook them."

For nearly five months the *Snark* remained in the Hawaiian Islands, being completely overhauled from stem to stern. The engine was put into excellent shape; the boat had a full new coat of paint and, with the exception of Mr. and Mrs. London and Martin, a brand-new crew.

For various reasons (Martin suspected it was mainly on account of the cooking, Captain Eames, Bert, and Tochigi all discovered urgent business back in San Francisco and resigned from the cruise. In their stead, the Londons signed on Captain Rosehill. Here was a real navigator! The way he sailed and anchored the *Snark* was marvelous to those landlubbers who had been handling the vessel as a small boy would a tub.

Martin was advanced to engineer and was beside himself with pride. He had learned all the idiosyncrasies of the seventy-horse-power engine and was undoubtedly worthy of the promotion, but I suspect that Jack did it to get a new cook. Martin wrote to Jess Utz, his cooking teacher, "I guess, Jess, my cooking wasn't so much of a success—they've hired someone else."

Wada, who was Japanese, was a very good cook and could speak fluent English. Nakata, also Japanese, was signed as cabin boy and could speak no English. A Dutchman who gave only the name of Herman was a good-natured deep-sea sailor whom they secured to round out the crew. He worked with great goodwill in storm or calm, always singing in one or another of a half-dozen languages.

With these as a crew, the refurbished *Snark* sailed out of Honolulu, stopping at Hilo and the leper island of Molokai, and on October 7, 1907, cast off the shore lines to begin the two-thousand-mile sail across the Pacific. This part of the cruise was not nearly so unfortunate to incident as the first. It would have been a very pleasant journey except for the fact that in fair weather or foul the boat lunged, dipped, tipped, and surged, shifting and twisting with never an instant of quiet. Many times during a heavy blow the rails and deck would be buried in the sea. Sometimes the ship would be lifted high on the crest of a billow and the next moment plunged into a trough to be surrounded by towering waves.

Once a storm was welcome—it saved their lives. During a frightful gale, one of the Japanese boys failed to close the tanks containing the drinking water. In the morning, not a drop remained in any of the storage tanks, and there was left about ten gallons in a small auxiliary tank. Immediately, Jack put each member of the party on an allowance of one quart a day.

It is difficult for anyone who has never experienced a shortage of water to realize just how inadequate a quart a day is for comfort, especially in the tropics, where one perspires copiously. As the days went by, the thirst became maddening. Martin dreamed of the Saline River and of the old mill. He dreamed of carrying precious water to fill his mother's washtubs. And always as he was about to bury his face in it he would awaken with a gasp.

The situation became more and more acute as the small supply of that life-sustaining fluid dwindled. Twelve hundred miles from land, and no fresh drinking water!

At last a storm was blowing up. They spread a large deck awning to catch as much water as possible. The storm swept toward them. They waited with eager anticipation! Then, to their infinite dismay, some prank of the wind stopped the squall within a few hundred yards.

More rainless days went by!

Death seemed a reality. Then they were awakened by the drum of a heavy tropical rain on deck. Again they spread the awnings, and this time they filled the water tanks to over-flowing.

In many, many years no vessel had ever attempted to cross the Pacific by this treacherous and isolated route. Some had tried it but had been blown far off their course. Others had never been heard from again. But the *Snark* and her crew accomplished the impossible, and in sixty-one days out of Hilo, Hawaii, they put safely into Taiohae Bay, in the Marquesas.

For two idyllic weeks the London party basked in the hospitality of the Marquesans. They visited the Typee Valley, made famous by Herman Melville, and Martin took pictures by the score. Everyone felt a deep pang of regret when Jack decided they had better be getting on.

Their next destination was Papeete, Tahiti, in the Society Islands, approximately one thousand miles to the west of the Marquesas. Between the two groups stretch the low coral reefs of the Paumotu Archipelago. For nine days, through seemingly unbearable heat, nasty squalls, and a steadily falling barometer, the *Snark* nosed its way carefully among these lagoons, which are usually avoided by whaling and trading ships. Large merchant ships have had to spend many weeks trying to get through. Little pearl luggers pile up on the white coral by the hundreds every year. And yet here they were, in the middle of the typhoon season, sailing the part of the world most dangerous for storms, navigating by blind guesswork through the treacherous currents and tides of those hidden atolls. Because of the low, black clouds, they had not been able to make proper observations.

They were long behind schedule, and the authorities at Papeete had given them up for lost, so their welcome was an enthusiastic one when eventually they put into port.

From the mail accumulated over a period of two months, Jack London learned that his affairs were in a frightful muddle, and that there was no way to unravel certain difficulties from a distance. So, leaving the *Snark* and its crew, he made a hasty voyage to San Francisco. Martin spent many days learning the language and songs of the Polynesians, which he later taught to me. He took pictures again, overhauled the *Snark*'s engine, swam, fished, and loafed through the lazy, carefree days until Jack's return.

Herman went on a prolonged drunk and was replaced by a French lad named Ernest. They also added Tehei, a huge Tahitian who was to prove invaluable to them. It was he who pointed the way through the maze of coral reefs as they journeyed from Tahiti to the island of Bora Bora.

Within a day of Bora Bora it became necessary to use the engine. It ran like a watch for an hour or so, then started backfiring and knocking. It heated up until the engine room was almost unbearable, and Martin had to give it continual care. He would run it on two cylinders until they were hot, then turn them off and use the other two.

He worked until he lost consciousness from the exhaust fumes and knew nothing until the big gong signaled "stop engines." Martin roused himself enough to throw the switch and crawl on deck. When he came to, several hours later, Mrs. London was bathing his face with cold towels. They said his heart was barely beating. A sound—the clang of a gong—had saved his life.

After ten delightful days at Bora Bora, they set sail for the Samoan group, with the decks knee-deep in fruit, chickens, vegetables, and all sort of delicacies. In fact, the *Snark* was so packed with the result of native hospitality that walking was difficult, and every now and then oranges, bananas, and coconuts would slide into the sea.

The Manua Islands were sighted thirteen days later and soon the *Snark* lay anchored off Tau, the largest of the group, and for several days was entertained by Tui-Manua, the descendant of a long line of the most powerful South Sea island kings. The next stop was Pago Pago, and then Apia, Samoa, the largest of the Polynesian cities and the site of the grave of Robert Louis Stevenson, which, of course, they visited.

From the Samoan islands to the Fiji Islands the distance is nine hundred miles. In the teeth of a hard summer gale, the *Snark* tossed for three days, and then suddenly the squall ceased as quickly as it had formed, leaving them rolling on a glassy-smooth sea completely surrounded by reefs. Around and around they sailed for two days and two nights, looking for an opening. It was like a labyrinth. Eventually Martin discovered a gap of a mere two hundred feet in the reef. How they got into that place without piling up still remains a mystery.

Another week, and the *Snark* was anchored in Suva, Fiji, the most modern city in that part of the world. When they sailed from the harbor a few days later, they had a new captain. Jack took over the navigating and eventually landed at the island of Tanna, in the New Hebrides, where Martin got his first glimpse of real "savages." For a week Jack and he made pictures of the natives and their villages and huts, trading tobacco and cheap jewelry for curios, then continued the cruise.

The Solomon Islands next appeared on the horizon, and the *Snark* dropped anchor in Port Mary at Santa Anna Island.

A note from Martin's diary: "Sunday, June 28, 1908: Hundreds of natives ran down the beaches, and tumbling into canoes, darted after us, all the time screaming at the top of their voices . . . people who in looks and action fully justified my expectations of what South Sea Islanders would be.

"They had big heads of bushy hair. Half of them wore large nose rings of tortoise shell and of wild boar tusks. All of them were adorned with earrings. . . . One had the handle of an old tea cup in his ear. . . . One of the islanders had tin wire sardine can openers in his ears; but the strangest of all was the one who had the shell of an alarm clock depending from the cartilage of his nose.

"Their cheeks were tattooed in monstrous designs; little boys ornamented just as fantastically as were the elders. Their teeth were filed to points and were dead black; their lips, large and negroid, were ruby red.

"These natives are all head hunters. This village and the

one across the bay are continually at war with each other and each tribe collects the heads of the other. . . . I'm very much frightened about my right foot. On the shin a large sore, big as a dollar, has started, and it is eating right into my leg. It seems that no medicine on board will cure it, and there is no doctor within thousands of miles that we know of. Jack, I'm afraid, has one of these eating ulcers, too. If no doctor is on Florida Island, and if we are no better when we get there, I think we'll sail for Sydney, Australia, for treatment, and that without delay."

Making a leisurely cruise of the larger islands, the *Snark* company saw thousands of natives, and while they never actually witnessed a cannibal feast, they saw plenty of evidence of the practice. Nosing in and out of the islands, the crew of the *Snark* formed a complete list of casualties. The sores were caused by poisonous coral by which they had been scratched when swimming and to which white people were very susceptible. Jack and the captain, as well as Martin, were affected. The others were down with island fever.

More from Martin's diary: "In addition to the ulcers and fever, a new trouble has come into the life of the Snark family. Jack's hands have begun to swell, turn very sore and peel skin. The nails are very hard and thick and have to be filed. And it is the same with his feet. . . . The traders and beach-combers could diagnose ulcers and fever, but not this. Both Jack and Mrs. London are considerably alarmed at this strange manifestation."

There are dozens of islands in the Solomon group, the interiors of which have rarely been penetrated by white people. There are others where no white person has ever set foot. Once the *Snark* was caught in the tail end of a hurricane and nearly beached on the shores of an island not marked on their chart, and when the natives saw them you cannot imagine their amazement.

After two months of oceanic cruising, with three white people in a serious state and Jack's mysterious illness growing steadily worse, the *Snark* crew decided to put in at Penduffryn, the largest copra plantation of the Solomon Islands, and it was here that Martin made his first motion-picture exploration. It came about by another of those many accidents that shaped the course of his life.

Pathé Frères of France had sent three French cameramen to Sydney to photograph the reception of the American fleet, then ordered them to the Solomon Islands for pictures of savages. It had been the dream of two traders (a Mr. Harding and a Mr. Darbishire) to organize an expedition to make motion pictures of the cannibals in the interior of Penduffryn, and the arrival of the Frenchmen made this possible.

Martin, entranced with the large professional motion-picture camera, the first he had ever seen, hovered around during the preparations for the trip and asked innumerable questions. He ached to be a member of the party, and, unexpectedly, his opportunity came when the three cameramen, unused to the damp climate, were stricken with island fever. Martin offered his services and, after obtaining permission from Jack, went into the interior up the Mbalisuma River to a village called Charley—named, he was told, after a native of more-than-average bravery. No white had ever before been in this area, and some unique and interesting pictures were obtained.

Jack's strange malady grew worse. The gaping sores with which Martin and the rest suffered forced a decision. Something had to be done, and their only hope seemed to be the doctors of Sydney. So, leaving the two Tahitians and Wada to look after the *Snark,* Jack, Mrs. London, and Martin boarded the *Makambo* and on November 15, 1908, found themselves once more in civilization. Jack and his wife went to the St. Malo Hospital in Ridge Street, North Sydney, and Martin entered the Sydney Homeopathic Hospital, on Cleveland Street.

Martin lay on his hospital cot and reviewed the cruise. It had been uncomfortable (his bunk was inches too short), it had been hard work, it had been dangerous—but it had been glorious. He had seen much, but there was still much more to be seen. He tried to figure out a way to get a motion-picture camera, which he felt he must have to record the rest of the cruise. He planned various things he would do to make the

Snark more comfortable, the appliances he would buy, the ventilators he would—

And then the letter from Jack London. It read in part: "The biggest specialist in Australia in skin diseases has examined me, and his verdict is that not only in his own experiences had he never seen anything like it, but that no line is to be found about it in any of the medical libraries. . . . I must get back to my own climate. . . . I shall have to give up my voyage around the world. . . ."

Martin was dazed. It couldn't be. Why, the *Snark* had been their home for two whole years. It was like deserting an old friend in a far corner of the earth.

Sell the *Snark*!

Abandon the voyage!

It took a long time for Martin to realize that this was really the end of the cruise. Finally he demanded his clothes of the nurse and went to Jack at the hospital.

It was all too true. Jack was a sick man, and the accommodations aboard the *Snark* were not suited to the needs of a sick man. He had to have fresh fruits, fresh vegetables, and fresh meats in place of canned foods and salted meats.

And so Martin, with a pilot, returned to the Solomons and sailed the *Snark* back to Sydney, a journey of more than two months. From then on things moved rapidly. The *Snark* was sold and all business wound up as quickly as possible.

Little was said in parting. Jack tried to express his appreciation to Martin for his loyalty and for standing by, but he gave it up.

They shook hands, promising to meet in America.

Martin left Sydney on March 31, 1909, "heading" home via Tasmania, Ceylon, Aden, the Suez, Naples, Genoa, and, of course, Paris.

One summer evening of 1909 found him at the gates of Luna Park, in Paris. His pockets held just eleven francs; the admission price was ten. It was the fourteenth of July, and a dispassionate and uninformed onlooker might have concluded that the Bastille had fallen only that day. Martin pushed his way through the shrieking merrymakers and wished he had a job. Unexpectedly, one presented itself.

The only carousel in the park was silent and motionless. The owner, a small, bald-headed man with a large stomach, alternately berated the sweating mechanic for his failure to start the merry-go-round and implored the derisive crowd to be patient.

Martin, on the edge of the jeering circle and knowing something of the Latin temperament by now, saw that the grease-smudged operator had lost his head and would completely wreck the machinery unless something were done about it. Without so much as a *s'il vous plaît,* he elbowed his way through the crowd, past the proprietor, and gently but firmly pushed the mechanic aside. A little adjustment of the mechanism, and the gaudily caparisoned wooden steeds sprang into action, the calliope took up its lusty tooting, and the crowds cheered. Gay pennants fluttered from the red-and-white-striped awning, the proprietor's plump wife took her place on a high stool and sold tickets for the next ride, and the proprietor, beaming, shook hands with himself and kissed Martin on both cheeks.

For two months Martin remained as engineer of the Luna Park carousel, but more and more he thought of home, of his mother and father and Tom, and of the money in his pocket, which was just about enough, with careful figuring, to take him back to Independence. At length, shaking hands with the proprietor and his wife, both of whom wept, he patted the wooden horses and caught the boat train for Le Havre.

Chapter 6 _____

Independence awoke one morning to find that a proud duty lay before her: the welcoming home of a distinguished son. A hurried town meeting was called to determine the extent of the welcome, and while a few of those present said that Martin Johnson couldn't be any different from what he'd always been and why all the fuss, the general opinion was that Martin Johnson unquestionably had become a person of note. Wasn't he the first citizen of Independence to circumnavigate the globe? Hadn't he been where no other white man had been? Why, three times the town had mourned when the *Snark* was given up for lost, and three times it had rejoiced when the little craft and all aboard were reported safe. And the *Independence Star* had thought him important enough to print, right on the front page, excerpts from his letters to his family!

Some of Martin's former teachers said—and the principal himself, embarrassed, agreed—that a man who had been accepted for two years, more or less, as the close companion of that bright literary light, Jack London, must have qualities of intellect that, mysteriously, had remained undiscovered by Independence. Further, the principal gave it as his opinion that a general holiday should be declared to celebrate Martin's return. This was put to a vote and carried unanimously.

John Johnson found the whole thing a little terrifying as, on the eventful morning, he was on his way to his jewelry store and saw the flags and bunting usually reserved for the Fourth of July and Election Day blossoming along the main street in honor of his son.

Came train time, and Mr. and Mrs. Johnson and Freda were unable to get anywhere near the incoming express, since practically the whole of Independence was there ahead of them. The town's band had polished up its brass and perfected its liveliest numbers and, as the train came to a stop, blared forth with "Stars and Stripes Forever."

Martin, standing on the platform, complacent only in the possession of some decent luggage, good shoes, and a suit that was not frayed, wondered what was up. Must be a celebrity about to get on the train, he thought. Maybe the governor. He craned his neck to see, and the crowd caught sight of him. A roar went up, and he was astonished to find the whole town of Independence rushing at him, and scores of hands reaching up for him and his baggage.

He stood frozen, his knuckles white as he clutched the iron rail of the train platform. The faces of Jess Utz, Opal White, Hannah Scott, Charlie Kerr, and the rest were turned up to him in a blur of excitement. The whole thing was as fantastic as a jungle-fever dream. Then his eyes searched the howling crowd for his family and, finding them, he grinned for the first time and sent a half-wave, half-salute in their direction.

The crowd, led by the band, marched en masse from the station to the Johnson home, and there on the lawn the band gave an impromptu concert. Notable for volume rather than harmony, it defied speech and deafened the ears of the Johnsons, and by nightfall their faces ached with smiles.

To walk a block in any direction, Martin found, meant being stopped and made the target of endless questions. The presidents of various clubs in the surrounding counties called in person and invited him to talk before their organizations. He refused all of them. There was one invitation which he found great satisfaction in refusing, and that was from the principal of the high school: the very principal, a little grayer and a little wiser, perhaps, who some eight years before had expelled him. The invitation became almost a plea.

"It is your duty, Martin," the worthy principal said almost humbly. "You are a hero to the young people of this town—to all of us, I might say, you have seen places of great interest geographically which they will never see, and in the interests of education, Martin, I ask you to reconsider."

"In the interest of education?"

"Precisely. Also as a model of forthrightness, of enterprise, of perseverance."

"Well, hardly all that."

"Yes. Of sticking to a job, my boy, no matter how hard, and seeing it through. And last but not least, as an example of loyalty: your loyalty to Mr. London."

"Well, why wouldn't I be? What's that got to do with—"

"Character, my boy, it shows character. Through fair weather and foul, you—"

"Well, it's very nice of you, I'm sure, but I never made a speech in my life. . . . I—"

The day of the ordeal arrived. The principal led Martin behind the heavy velvet drapes of the high school auditorium. A long, narrow table bearing a pitcher of water and a glass was flanked by two chairs. Martin sat in one, the principal in the other.

The drapes parted. The auditorium was packed. Martin's eyes darted over the sea of faces, found his mother, father, and Freda, and fastened there.

The principal now arose and went to the center front of the stage, and presently Martin heard himself extolled in a flow of rhetoric and oratory that had him clutching his knees and looking toward the exit. Before escape was possible, however, the principal had finished and was waiting, smilingly, for him to stand on his feet and talk. Martin got up and moved forward automatically, to be met by a blast of applause, which, stopping abruptly, became a blast of waiting silence.

"A trip like I took," he said very loudly and remembering that his talk was supposed to be educational, "sure does learn you a lot."

It didn't take the shout of derisive laughter to tell him of his error. *Teach* was on his tongue—Jack London had put it there in their many months together—but habit and old associations now replaced it with *learn*.

What he said or did after that he never knew; his voice went on and on and on. Then, after a while, he felt the principal's hand on his arm, and there was a pained smile on his face and a rasp in his voice as he said whatever was necessary to bring to a close the unhappy and embarrassing occasion.

*   *   *

Martin next set about sorting the hundreds of photographs he had taken, cataloguing his curios, and organizing himself in general. How he was going to turn this wealth of material to account was a problem, until late one evening he went into Charlie Kerr's drugstore. Charlie was about to lock up.

"How are you, Martin?" inquired the genial druggist. "You came just in time. I'd have been closed in another minute. What can I do for you?"

"Give me another bottle of that paste. The large size," Martin said.

"It's none of my business, but what the heck do you do with all that paste—eat it?" asked Charlie, setting the bottle on the counter.

"I'm just fixing up some scrapbooks and putting labels on those pictures and curios and stuff," Martin explained.

Charlie Kerr wrinkled his forehead and leaned on the showcase.

"What are you going to do with all that stuff, Martin?"

"That's what I've been wondering." Martin put down a quarter and pocketed the paste.

"One of the boys was saying that you've got some moving pictures you took. That right?"

Martin nodded, and told about substituting for the sick cameramen down in Penduffryn, and how he had stopped in Paris on the way home and bought a print of the two-and-a-half reels from the Pathé Frères Company.

Charlie Kerr's eyes widened, and he snapped his fingers as an idea hit him.

"Why don't you make a show out of it? You know—run the moving pictures, have some lantern slides made from those other pictures you took, and give lectures. I'll bet people would come from all over the county."

"I thought of that," said Martin, "but it would take a lot of money. You'd have to fix up a theater, buy a projection machine, get the slides made . . ."

"Yeah, I suppose it would." Charlie moved about, slowly turning off the lights.

"Well, so long," Martin said, going toward the door.

"Wait a minute, and I'll walk over with you," said Charlie.

He closed the front door and gave it a hearty shake to test the spring lock before he spoke again. "Would you, if I put up the money?"

"Would I what?" asked Martin, puzzled.

"Open up a show."

"You know I couldn't give a lecture. Look what happened at the high school," protested Martin.

"Sure you could. All you'd have to do would be write it down, then learn it by heart. You'd be in the dark and no one would see you. They'd just hear you talk about the picture on the screen."

"It would take too much money." Martin shook his head. "Maybe more than you've got."

"I'll sell the drugstore."

"Oh, no, I couldn't let you do that. Anyway, how do you know people would come?"

"I'll take a chance."

And take a chance he did. Charlie Kerr sold his business and rented another store several blocks down the main street. The front of the new store was rebuilt to represent the bow of the *Snark,* and inside, the deck plan of the yacht was outlined in lights on the ceiling. Martin selected a large number of his best pictures, took them to Kansas City, and had vividly colored slides made of them. He spent hours of agony writing and re-writing his lecture and committing it to memory. Seats installed, the big screen hung, the projection machine set up with Dick Hamilton as operator, and the Snark Theater was ready for the opening. If the Snark opening were held today, there would be great searchlights sweeping the sky to attract attention. Radio stations would carry a description of the event into every home. But all the ballyhoo then available in Independence was a phonograph set up in the lobby of the theater grinding out Hawaiian melodies, audible for not more than a block. Still, it was sufficient to fill the little theater to capacity.

When Martin stepped in front of the screen on November 3, 1909, he was greeted with thunderous applause. He grinned sheepishly. His face turned a deep red. The applause died down and the audience waited expectantly. Martin opened and closed his mouth but made no sound. Several people in the back rows shouted "Louder," whereupon he bolted from the stage. Charlie Kerr then did the only thing left to him: the lights dimmed, and the first slide was thrown on the screen abruptly and without benefit of Martin's carefully rehearsed opening speech.

Everything possible went wrong that opening night. Just before the show started, Dick dropped the box of slides, breaking only a few, fortunately, but mixing them up hopelessly. Added to this, he found he could not hear the click of the tin locust which was the signal to change the slides. As a consequence, the pictures on the screen and Martin's lecture seldom met at any point.

After the show, Martin confronted Charlie Kerr.

"I told you I couldn't lecture," he groaned.

"Now, don't you worry about it," soothed Charlie. "You'll be fine tomorrow night—you'll see."

"Tomorrow night?" shouted Martin. "Why, I wouldn't go through that again for a million dollars! You'll have to call everything off, I tell you. I can't do it. I get so weak in the knees, I—it's all I can do to stand up!"

Undaunted, Charlie had a carpenter, a plumber, and a tinner on the stage of the Snark Theater early the next morning. The carpenter built a high desk, the plumber made a railing about two feet square out of water pipe, and the tinner cut sheets of tin a little larger than a letterhead. When the job was finished, Charlie rang Martin to come right over.

Martin, apparently, had spent a sleepless night.

"You've just got to let me out of this thing, Charlie," he said desperately. "You can use my stuff and collect the money, but I just can't get out there again and talk."

Charlie grinned and said nothing; he let his handiwork in the middle of the stage talk for him. There, pasted neatly on the sheets of tin where they could neither blow away nor crumple, were the typed pages of the lecture. The copy of the lecture, Charlie pointed out, would lie on the breast-high table inside the pipe railing. Then, with pride, he explained the function of the railing itself.

"All you got to do is hold onto that iron pipe," he chortled, "and your knees can't give way!"

From this point on, the little enterprise prospered, and soon Charlie and Martin had equipped another store as a motion-picture theater and called it Snark No. 2. Here they ran current films, offered popular illustrated ballads, and found themselves launched in the amusement business. Requests for Martin's lecture began coming in from neighboring towns, and Charlie, who at that time dreamed of a chain of theaters, saw Martin as a sort of advance agent and encouraged him to accept. The whole thing was handled in businesslike fashion. Advance notices were sent out, and a careful itinerary was planned. Included in this itinerary was Chanute.

Martin and Osa in the New Hebrides, now Vanuatu, 1917

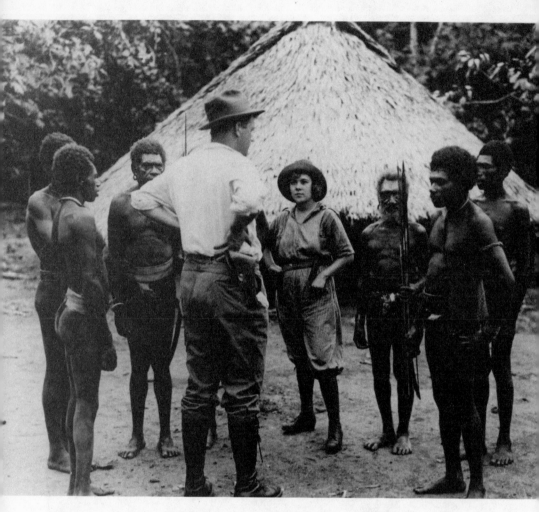

The Johnsons with Tomman Islanders

A happy time on the boat owned by Harold Markham, seen here with the Johnsons and a native employee

Osa poses in high-fashion swimming garb on the beach at Vao.

After the scare of their lives in 1917, the Johnsons returned to the New Hebrides in 1919 still eager to photograph the Big Nambas. Osa stands beside the fearsome Nagapate, chief of the Big Nambas. Her smile seems somewhat forced.

Nagapate stands by the "boo-boos," large slit drums of wood, used in ceremonies.

Dance of Tethlong's men on Vao

Osa found it difficult to understand and communicate with the women of this totally different culture.

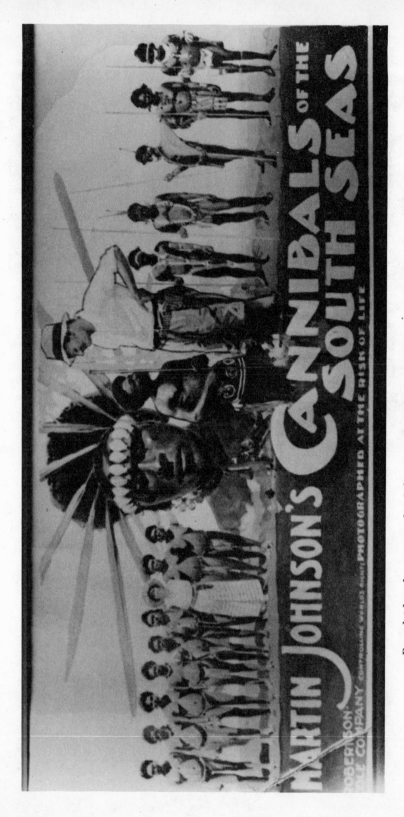

Broadside advertising the Johnsons' first feature film, *Martin Johnson's Cannibals of the South Seas*

*Chapter 7*_____

On a bright Saturday in November 1909—I was just sixteen—
I was one of a giggling group of high school girls that climbed
the stairs to the Roof Garden Theater for the afternoon show.
We were there not because some man from Independence was
giving a talk on his "Trip Through the South Seas with Jack
London" and something about cannibals in the same region,
but because our friend Gail Perigo was singing there.

Gail had been my bosom friend for four years. We had gone
to school together, never had secrets from each other, often
dressed alike, and were determined, when we grew up, to have
our weddings fall on the same day. Not only could Gail sing
but she could dance wonderfully and roller-skate too, and she
had taught me all these things. Recently she had quit school
to sing with colored slides at the Roof Garden, and most Saturday afternoons saw me there with a group of the girls from
school. We were all motion-picture fans, of course, and sighed
and wept with all the persecuted little picture heroines of the
day, but our chief delight was applauding Gail.

As Gail bowed gracefully from the stage on this particular
day, the manager of the theater came forward and introduced
"that intrepid young traveler from Independence, Mr. Martin
Johnson."

A tall, thin young man walked out on the stage, blinked at
the lights, ran his finger around his collar, and began to talk.
Every now and then he clicked something in his hand, and
slides were thrown on the screen showing a boat with some

people on it. This went on for quite a while, and I began to think about ice cream. Then the lecturer said something about cannibals, and on came a reel of film showing people of such horribleness I couldn't look at them.

I sent a whisper along the line that I had had enough, and we left in a body, seven of us.

Gail and I sang in the choir at church, and, as was my custom, I called for her one Sunday morning. Since I had seen her the day before, she told me blithely, she had accepted an offer from Mr. Martin Johnson to go to Independence and sing in his Snark Theater No. 2. And did I remember Dick Hamilton? They'd been sweethearts their first year in high school. Well, he was the operator in Mr. Johnson's theater, and wasn't it all too thrilling?

"If you can go away like that and not care whether you ever see me again, then I can see that our friendship means nothing to you," I said dramatically.

The street we were taking to church on this particular morning ran past the hotel. We were almost there when out of the door walked Mr. Martin Johnson.

"Oh, you must meet him," Gail whispered. "He's wonderful!"

"I never want to meet him as long as I live," I said and, turning, walked straight across the middle of the street and in front of a couple of brisk horses pulling an empty dray. Mr. Martin Johnson shouted his alarm and I leaped clear, then climbed the high curb on the opposite side with what I hoped, passionately, was both dignity and grace.

It was only a week later, on a Saturday; I was up to my elbows in flour with the week's bread baking, and Papa, home from a long freight run, sat at the kitchen table. He was in his shirtsleeves, reading the paper. Mama was at the sink, and Grandma, in a rocker near Papa, was mending one of his hickory shirts.

"Osie," Papa called out, "I see where your friend Gail Perigo just got married down there in Independence."

I left a trail of flour behind me as I ran to the table.

"She couldn't, not without telling me—we promised—she couldn't!"

"Well, it says here in the paper she married that Dick Hamilton boy, and the ceremony was performed right on the stage of some theater—it says the Snark or some such name." He chuckled. "Why, it says here that folks were strung clear up the block trying to get in."

"She couldn't! I don't believe it." I was crying tragically and loudly by now.

"Don't take on so, honey," Mama's arms were around me. "Dick's a right nice boy, and Gail always did like him, you know."

"Sure, sure, don't take on so, Osie," Grandma said. She went right ahead with her mending. "Folks get married. That's right and natural." She was suddenly troubled. "Seems like it would have been more fittin', though, if they'd been married in a church."

"Yes," I wailed, "in a church, a double wedding, the two of us on the same day. It was a promise!"

Papa grinned, "Come on now, Osie. Why, you haven't even got a beau right now. Too peppery and choosy, I reckon, and you wouldn't want Gail to wait—"

Suddenly my anger focused. "In the Snark Theater," I raged. "Everything's his fault, that's what it is. Everything!"

I was inconsolable for days. Then a letter, all dignity and new importance, came from Gail inviting me to visit her in Independence.

Grandma put her foot down on the whole idea. Since she was my self-constituted chaperone from the moment she had witnessed a game of kiss-the-pillow at one of my birthday parties, it looked as though I would have to take her with me. But Mama persuaded her that Gail, now married, was herself a proper chaperone.

This was my first journey alone, and as my father put me on the train he warned me against talking to strangers. Grandma had already admonished me, if spoken to, to give attention to the tips of my gloves, and that the top flounce of my dress, when I was sitting, would be the proper focus for my gaze. She added, a little severely, that my instep was as high as my dress should ever be lifted. Mama, as she hugged me good-bye, said it was always safe to ask directions of men in uniform; she told me to be cautious in all things, certainly, but not to be afraid.

At all events, I arrived without mishap at a theater named Snark No. 1, where the box office looked like the prow of a boat, and I thought this very cute.

The Snark to which Gail's letter directed me, however, was No. 2. I asked directions from a gentleman behind the ticket window, then realized with a shock that not only had I spoken to a man without a uniform but had addressed Mr. Martin Johnson.

He smiled suddenly. "Oh, you're Gail Hamilton's friend from Chanute, aren't you?" he asked.

I looked at my gloved fingertips.

"It's just a couple of blocks up," he said, coming out of the box office, "and as a matter of fact I was just on my way over there myself."

He reached for my portmanteau. Haughtily, I picked it up myself and started along the street.

"I wish you'd let me carry that," he said. I heard his footsteps just behind me. The wind was blowing gustily and presented three problems: to hold my big hat firmly atop my pompadoured hair, to carry my portmanteau, and to keep my long dress from blowing and exposing more than my instep.

By the time I had reached Snark No. 2, I was in something of a temper. Gail lived in the flat over the theater. I pushed open the street door and climbed the stairs. Martin Johnson followed. At the top landing, Gail rushed out to meet me.

"Oh!" She seemed pleased and laughed. "You two have met!"

"No," Mr. Johnson grinned, "though it isn't my fault."

"I never speak to strangers." I was angry and cold at the same time. What did he think he was laughing at? I tried to straighten my hat.

"Well, anyhow," Gail put her arm around me, "Mr. Martin Johnson, this is my best friend, Miss Osa Leighty."

Dick Hamilton, looking very proud and happy, came and shook hands with us, then led the way into their cute little flat.

"Gail's got lunch all ready," he said, then winked, "and I think she kept a piece of our wedding cake for you to sleep on, Osie."

Martin Johnson looked at me when Dick spoke about my sleeping on the wedding cake; it was a long, thoughtful, unsmiling look, and I found myself shivering very pleasantly. He had widely set gray-green eyes, I noticed after a minute, and they were nice and clear.

The next time I visited Gail, he came to the flat.

"Miss Leighty," Martin Johnson said, very formally, a little while later, "I was wondering, would you like to go to Coffeyville for lunch tomorrow? They're opening a new pavilion, and I thought—I wondered—"

"I don't think I can, Mr. Johnson," I answered primly. "Not without my grandmother."

"Your grandmother?" He looked perplexed.

"I almost never go to amusement places without her," I replied.

"Oh, a chaperone. Well, we'll fix that. Gail and Dick here will go along."

We went and in style, in a big touring car hired by Martin for the occasion—one of the first of its kind to appear in the state. It was my first automobile ride, and I was astonished and delighted at the speed and ease with which we moved along, and more particularly with the skill of Mr. Johnson in handling it. I began to see that he was quite a remarkable man, though, of course, I must never let him see I thought anything one way or the other. That would be bold.

We reached Coffeyville in just no time at all, and brought up with a flourish before the new pavilion. First we had lunch on a sort of balcony, but I was too excited to eat. People here and there recognized Martin and pointed him out as the famous young traveler. Then the music started for dancing. Dick and Gail went out on the floor.

I had begun to feel that I was just nobody at all. Martin didn't ask me to dance, and I made up my mind he didn't like me, so I told him I thought his cannibal pictures were horrible and I could see no excuse whatever for showing such ugliness to people. I told him, too, that I walked out on his lecture that day in Chanute. In other words, I let him see I thought him conceited, and that I didn't think he had anything to be conceited about. Gail and Dick came back to the table and were surprised we hadn't danced.

"Let's go see the roller-skating rink," Gail suggested.

"Sure," Martin grinned. "but don't ask me to skate. I'm no good at it." Then, to me, "How about you, brown eyes?"

"Oh, I can stay on my feet," I answered modestly.

The rink was wonderful. Painted a pale green, it was decorated with bunting and colored lights. There were tiers of seats all the way around, and a little solid wooden fence stood between the seats and the skating floor.

Already a hundred or so couples were out on the floor. I led the way to where they had skates for rent. Gail and Dick wanted to go out on the floor too. Martin just picked a seat for himself and looked a little bored. Like a pelican on a rock, I thought, but if he'll just stay right there, I'll show him he isn't the only person around that can do things. He thinks all he has to do is go on a boat, come back with some pictures, and never stir himself the rest of his life.

Gail and Dick were so much in love, just married and all, I didn't blame them for going off the minute they had their skates on. The floor was wonderful, the band was playing a waltz, and pretty soon they had everybody looking at them and thinking how professional they were. Feeling very sad and lonely and without so much as a look in Martin's direction, I just skated off down the hall by myself.

Down at the other end of the rink I came on a group getting ready to do a mixed chariot race. This name is pretty accurately descriptive. Two boys—fast, sure skaters—are harnessed together. They are the "horses." Straps from their harness, like reins, go back to a third skater, a girl, who is the "driver" in the mixed races. Six chariots were to start out, three abreast.

The waltz had ended, the band blew a fanfare, and a man with a loud voice asked that the floor be cleared for the next event. He announced the chariot race and the names of the contestants. Everybody cheered.

As the chariots were moving into position, I saw one of the drivers swerve and bend over her right skate. Then she shook her head; something was wrong.

The band was blowing another fanfare. With a crazy and unaccountable impulse I darted forward and told the girl I'd take her place. She looked startled but gave me the reins. There was a roll of drums, a blank cartridge was fired, and we were off.

I glanced out of the corner of my eye as we swung past Martin and had the satisfaction of seeing him suddenly grip the arms of his seat and lean forward, staring. We hadn't picked up much speed as yet, and I began to be afraid the whole thing was going to be mild and silly. The next forty-five seconds or so told a different story. The floor, being new, was smooth and even; the skates of the boys in harness were ball-bearing and built for speed. I caught just two impressions as I flew like the tail of a comet around that floor—Gail, white as chalk at the side of the rink, and Martin, straining forward in his seat, his eyes bulging.

The reins began to slip through my moist hands. To let them go would mean failure. And with Martin watching me! I would rather have died. Waiting for the straightaway, I skated hard and got enough slack in the straps to wind them around my wrists. Now, I thought with satisfaction, they can't slip.

Twice more around the rink, with the wind sharp on my face. I narrowed my eyes; we were just at the turn where Martin sat. I looked again to see if he were noticing me, and he was—his face drained of every bit of color.

What happened in that moment of inattention I don't know, but I suspect that I must have failed perhaps by no more than a fraction to take the turn. At the speed we were going, that was enough. I felt myself suddenly jerked from my feet, the straps around my wrists held as if riveted there, and I was swung clear from the rink over the fence and into the first row of seats.

There was a confused roar in my ears. Then I saw Martin pushing through the crowd toward me. I was all tangled up in the seats somehow but managed to be on my feet and brushing myself off when he reached me.

"I still think I can do it," I heard myself saying.

"Are you hurt bad?" he croaked.

"Of course not." I was furious at him for asking. With great dignity, I led the way from the skating rink. And then I refused to sit with him in the front seat of the car on the way back to Independence.

For me to fly into a temper, it was only necessary for one of the three to ask me what had happened, whether I was hurt anyplace, if I felt all right, so the subject was dismissed. Martin turned once after a long and awkward silence and said, with honest concern, that maybe I didn't have any bones broken, but he bet I was black and blue from head to foot. In a rage I said I wasn't. I think it was because I hurt so all over that I lost my temper, but anyhow I threw the horse blanket off my lap—I guess I had in mind jumping out of the car—and it went over Martin's head. Since he was driving, this nearly had us in the ditch, but Dick seized the wheel and saved us. From then on and until we arrived in Independence, no one spoke, and I decided to go home that night instead of waiting until the evening of the next day.

Chapter 8 _____

Back in school as usual the following Monday morning, I ached all over, inside and out. The chariot race accounted for the outside ache, but not for the in. Of course, I knew it was love. Always completely happy and carefree until now, all this misery seemed more than I could bear, but I saved up all my crying until after I'd gone to bed, and in that way I kept the whole thing to myself.

I was quite sure, of course, that I'd never see Martin Johnson again. I knew he must think me completely horrid, and I made up my mind calmly and dispassionately that all the rest of my life a brave smile would hide my broken heart.

The postman's whistle up the street meant nothing to me the next Friday morning as I went out the gate on my way to school, but when he waved a letter at me I waited for him.

"A letter for you, Osie," he said.

"Oh! Oh, dear," I said. I was all hot and cold, for in the corner opposite the stamp it said, "The Snark, Independence," and below that in a scrawly hand was the name, "Martin Johnson."

I couldn't read the letter there in front of the postman, and I saw Grandma waving at me from the window, so I ran all the way to school and opened it behind my geography, where I read it all day long at every study period. It said, with sufficient formality to suit even my grandmother: "Dear Miss Leighty, May I call to see you Sunday and meet your folks? Yours truly, Martin Johnson."

77

Sunday. That was the day after tomorrow.

Papa was away on a long freight run, so he couldn't be consulted. Grandma approved the tone of the letter but didn't like the idea that a man who had been to Paris, the South Seas, and a lot of other foreign places should be courting Osa. Mama voiced the single doubt that perhaps he was too old for me.

This lack of enthusiasm was powerless to take one whit from my happiness, and on Saturday I baked four kinds of cake, some gingerbread as well as plain bread, and early Sunday morning I fried chicken and made some ice cream. Mama finished a rose-colored satin shirtwaist she had had in the making for me, and I washed my hair.

I ran all the way home from church, bolted my dinner, washed the dishes, then rushed upstairs to put on my new blouse. All three of the afternoon trains from Independence came and went. I took my hair down and put it up again five times. I tried it with "rats" and without "rats," braided and tied with a ribbon, and loose and in curls. The six o'clock train came and went, and Mama called me to come down for supper. I couldn't swallow even a mouthful. Grandma said she was afraid of this. All foreign-traveled young men trifled with young ladies' affections. Vaughn, my brother, said that what he'd heard, this Johnson fellow had once helped some cannibals eat a missionary. I burst out crying, and Mama led me gently upstairs and put me to bed. She had no sooner put out the light and closed the door than I heard footsteps come up on the front porch and the bell ring.

Martin had come.

With women's clothes as complicated as they were in that day, even with Mama's help, it was nearly half an hour before I could get downstairs. Entering the parlor, I saw that Grandma and Vaughn were making Martin anything but comfortable. They had had the doubtful pleasure of one another's company for some little time; nevertheless, I introduced them very formally, but completely forgot to introduce Mama. She took care of this with her unfailing tact and grace. Martin thrust a two-pound box of candy at me and we all sat down.

"Sure he ate a missionary." Vaughn tossed this blithely into the silence. "He just said so."

Martin winked at me.

"Well, not a whole missionary. Just half of one."

"Missionaries are very nice people and should not be joked about, especially on Sunday," Grandma said firmly.

Mama got out the family album, which I thought was very clever of her, especially when she put it in my lap and Martin had to come and sit beside me. I showed him pictures of Papa and his family, and Mama and Papa just after they were married, and Grandma when she was younger, and of me as a little girl.

Martin said he thought the photography in all of them was terrible. Nettled at this, I said I thought the photography in all of them was wonderful.

"It's all terrible," Martin insisted. Then, suddenly, "Wait a minute—all except this one." Enthusiastically, "This is good."

I was disgusted, and quite sure by now that he was horrid.

"Well, if you like that one, I guess we'll never agree on anything," I said, and shut the album with a bang. The picture was one of Vaughn as a little boy with his hair all tousled.

"Hey, wait a minute. Let me look at that!"

He opened the album with sharpened interest.

"Why, I took this picture! This is my photography!" He laughed as if it were a fine joke. "And he's the little boy," pointing at Vaughn, "and you're the little girl that brought him to my place in Williams' Opera House!"

"Yes," I rejoined hotly, "and you took off his nice white collar and roughed up his hair and made him look like a poor little boy just out of an orphanage!"

"Osie." My mother was gentle but firm. "Mr. Johnson is our guest. You must remember that."

That picture being taken without the collar had always rankled with Grandma too, and she said so.

Martin looked uncomfortable.

"Well," he said, "I didn't like collars when I was a boy, so I thought I'd take it off."

Mama was distressed and suggested that I sing for Mr. Johnson.

As I went to the piano, I saw that Vaughn was making inroads on my box of candy, but I didn't care. I asked Mr. Johnson if there were any particular song that he liked and he said there wasn't. I thought he might at least come over and turn the music for me, but he didn't, so I sang "Glow Little Glow Worm," "After the Ball," "Mighty Lak a Rose," and "Ring Down the Curtain," one right after another, then stopped. There had been no response whatsoever from Mr. Martin Johnson. Even Mama noticed this.

"Don't you care for music, Mr. Johnson?" she inquired.

"Well," he lifted one long leg and crossed it over the other, "I guess I like it all right. The only thing, on account of me being what they call tone-deaf, I—"

"Deaf?" Grandma was startled.

"No, not that way. I mean, I can't carry a tune and I can't hear one either. It's just a lot of noise to me. Some people are color-blind just the same way."

I had spent half an hour singing to him and it had been just a lot of noise.

Mama hurried out and came back with some sandwiches, cake, and milk. We all ate this very rapidly, then sat and looked at one another a little helplessly.

"What kind of work do you do, Mr. Johnson?" Grandma asked abruptly.

"Me?" Martin looked a little baffled. "Why—well, you see, I travel quite a lot. Take pictures." Then, with growing confidence, "And then, of course, I've got a couple of theaters with Charlie Kerr there in Independence."

"That's very nice," Mama said. Her eyes begged Grandma not to ask any more questions.

"And your papa. What does he do?" Grandma wasn't to be stopped until she'd got what she was after.

Martin beamed with pride.

"Oh, Dad, he's a jeweler in Independence. Why, he's one of the biggest jewelers in the whole state of Kansas, I guess."

Grandma relaxed a little. "And you'll go into business with him, of course?"

"Well—" Martin began, but he was on to Grandma now and changed the subject. "You'd like my mother, too, and my sister, Freda. My mother's a wonderful cook."

Mama was distinctly happier with the way things were going,

but Grandma was as persistent as a horsefly.

"Any of your folks fight in the Civil War?" she demanded.

"Oh, yes, sure."

"On what side, young man?"

Martin moved carefully.

"And my mother, she was a Constant, and her great-great-grandfather, or something, came over from France with Lafayette and fought in the Revolutionary War."

This won Grandma completely. It was nine o'clock, and she told Martin it was time for him to go, because what with school tomorrow I had to be in bed early, but she hoped he'd come again soon. The good-byes at the door were somewhat confused, and, indeed, I can't remember saying good-bye at all.

"A very nice young man," Grandma said. She fixed my mother with her eyes. "Don't you think so, Belle?"

"Why—why, yes, only I still think he's a little old for Osie. Nine years between them."

"Fiddlesticks," Grandma declared. "It's just enough difference to give him some sense, which, goodness knows, one of 'em's got to have when they get married."

"Who said anything about getting married?" I screamed. "I'm sure I didn't. I'm sure he didn't—and I hope I never lay eyes on him again."

Martin came again a few weeks later, and except that he brought a bigger box of candy, everything remained exactly as it was. We sat awkwardly, the four of us, and looked at one another, and that's about all there was to it. What I felt or thought about him seemed completely in abeyance; largely, I think, because he neither did, nor liked, any of the things I did or liked. He wasn't interested in dancing, roller-skating, or singing, and what else was there?

And then, all unexpectedly, the following Saturday afternoon I found myself on the train going to Independence. Martin had telephoned my mother to ask if she'd mind if I sang at his Snark No. 2 theater that night. Gail had a sore throat, he said, and he had to have a substitute. Then he added quickly that the whole thing was Gail's idea.

Mama was too bewildered to be able to think clearly. If only my father were home and she could talk to him. Then Martin put his mother on the phone. The moment Mama heard her voice she was sure everything would be all right. Grandma talked with her and, to my complete amazement, thought so too.

Martin's mother and sister, Freda, met me at the train. I went home with them and they helped me dress for the theater. Mr. Johnson came home from the jewelry store, looked at me a minute, then kissed me on the forehead, called me "Pinkie," and decided I was almost as nice as Martin said I was.

I didn't see Martin until I arrived at the theater. He met me just inside the door.

"Oh, hello." He looked at me crossly. "You're late."

"Well, this whole thing wasn't my idea," I retorted, suddenly hot and mad all over. I wondered how it was possible for anybody to make me as mad as this man always did.

He led the way along the side aisle and up the three steps to the back of the stage. Here he pushed a piece of music into my hands.

"It's one of those things you sang that night at your house." He took my arm almost roughly. "You go on here in front of the screen, not in back of it, and don't fall over that cleat."

I had on my prettiest dress and he never even looked at it.

"I'm going to give the signal now for the colored slides." He gave me a shove. "Well, go on, go on," he whispered impatiently. "Don't you know an introduction when you hear one?"

"Yes," I answered as loudly as I could. "Don't you know a lady when you see one?"

I marched out on to the little stage. I suppose I looked as cross as I felt; anyhow, a little boy in the audience laughed. Another yelled, "Get the hook!"

I stepped right up back of the piano, and a light was turned on me. Then I saw that the pianist, a Mrs. Snyder, was nodding anxiously at me to begin. She played part of the introduction again, and then it was I recognized a tune I'd heard on the player piano up the street from our house. So far as I knew, I'd never heard the words. The sheet of music in my hands was no help, since it was "In the Good Old Summer Time."

Well, I could see Martin scowling at me, so I just sang any old words that came in my head, smothering them, sort of, in my mouth and covering them with a lot of sound. At the end of a verse every now and then I rhymed "love" with "above" and "moon" with "spoon," and at the finish of the song I hit a high C and held it till all my breath was gone.

The audience applauded, and I bowed and went off smiling the way I'd seen Gail do a hundred times. Martin pushed me on for an encore, and there was nothing to do but talk to the pianist over the footlights. By this time I was having a lot of fun. Mrs. Snyder and I agreed on "My Hero" as an encore, and we were off. What I lacked in finesse I made up for in volume, and when I climbed finally to that last high note and let it go, the blast astonished even me. I held it, too, until Mrs. Snyder signaled me that for goodness' sake that was enough.

Audiences in that day liked volume and rewarded me with a burst of applause. I bowed as nearly in the manner of Gail as I could and walked off, my head in the clouds. Coming to Independence, I had found my career. I decided I was going to be an actress.

"You did all right," Martin grinned. "For a pint-size you certainly make a lot of noise."

"I'm going to be an actress," I said.

He looked startled. "Fine," he said, then, "Here, I want you to meet my partner, Charlie Kerr."

I shook hands with Mr. Kerr and was very happy.

When Mrs. Johnson tucked me in bed that night with Freda, who was already asleep, I announced my new ambition. She laughed quietly, kissed me, then shook her head.

My father telephoned at noon the next day, Sunday. He was just home from one of his long freight runs and insisted that I return on the five o'clock train. He would be at the station to meet me. I had never heard my father take quite that tone before, so I promised I'd be there.

The trophies which Martin had brought home from his trip with Jack London were all over the house, and I was polite and said I thought they were very nice. As a matter of fact I didn't think so at all; I thought they were horrid, especially a dried-up brown knob of a thing with a hank of straight black hair which he said was a human head. The fact that it might have been, or was, human didn't seem to bother him at all.

About this time a new girlfriend of Freda's came to call.

She was very pretty, with dark hair, and spoke with the cun-
ningest French accent. She thought Martin was wonderful. She
even thought the mummy head was wonderful, and when
Martin began telling her some of the things about his trip, she
followed him around and never took her eyes from his face. He
had picked up a little French on some trip or other to Paris,
and they talked and laughed. Suddenly I found myself completely outside of everything. I also found that I was in a sick
sort of fury which I had never known before, and I was honest
enough to admit to myself that it was jealousy.

"I think I'd better go now," I said suddenly. This was right
after dinner and about two o'clock. Mr. Johnson looked at his
watch.

"But there won't be another train for two hours," he said.

"Well, it looks as if it might storm, and I'd rather wait at
the station."

I kissed Mrs. Johnson and Freda good-bye and shook hands
with Mr. Johnson. I also offered my fingertips to the little French
girl.

"Au revoir," I said, making it sound just the way it's spelled.

Martin picked up my portmanteau and walked glumly at
my side. I was sure he was glum at leaving the little French
girl and quickened my step. After all, I still had my pride.

"What's all the hurry," Martin said testily after a bit, "or do
you like to sit in railroad stations?"

"As long as you have company at home, I don't want to
detain you," I replied in my most formal manner.

He stared at me.

"What company?"

"Your little 'parley vou' friend," I answered crossly.

"Her? with those earrings? Huh!"

I went suddenly weak with relief. I blew my nose so that I
wouldn't cry. We were just passing the Snark No. 1. Martin
put down my portmanteau.

"As long as it's still a couple of hours before your train time,
do you care if we stop here at the Snark for a minute? I ought
to put up the posters announcing tomorrow's show."

I said of course it was all right. It began to sprinkle a little,
so he opened the door for me to go in and sit down. It was

thundering now, and suddenly a heavy rainfall swept the front of the theater. Martin came in and sat down beside me. He had left the door open and we could see the rain. It was like a bright curtain and made a soft, swishing sound. It smelled very cool and sweet.

"Might as well sit here as over at the station," Martin said. "I'll call the livery stable and get a buggy when it's time to go."

"That'll be fine," I replied. My voice squeaked a little.

"Not catching cold, are you?"

"No."

"You're shivering."

"That's nothing. I practically always shiver when it thunders."

"Afraid?"

"No. Just shivering."

"Maybe you're cold," he insisted.

"No."

That was all for a while, then suddenly he spoke again. "Will you marry me?"

I opened my mouth, but no sound came.

"Will you marry me?"

"Yes."

"Right away, I mean."

"Yes."

"Tonight?"

"Yes."

He took my shoulders and turned me toward him. "You won't ever be sorry?"

"No."

Martin went to the telephone and called Mr. Kerr, saying he was going to get married and could he borrow some money against their partnership, and what did he think was the quickest way to get a license?

Apparently he listened to Mr. Kerr for a minute, then he spoke again.

"No. No, not her. Nope. . . . What? . . . Her? . . . I should say not, we were just friends. . . . No, no! This is a little girl from Chanute—you met her yesterday. She sang. Big brown

eyes, taffy hair . . . Yes, that's her. . . . What? Sure, marriage
is a serious thing, I know that. . . . Yes, and I've seen girls all
over the world, too . . . What? . . . Young? Well, maybe so,
but she's got spirit and spunk . . . You say if I call the probate
judge you think he can fix it up about the license even if it is
Sunday? All right, Charlie, and thanks."

Martin came back to where I was sitting. He had turned on
only one dim light in the theater, but he looked very tall and
handsome. I think I was very proud—anyhow, I couldn't speak
for a minute.

"I think I ought to go and see Gail before I go home," I
heard myself saying, "if she's sick and all." I got up.

"What do you mean, 'go home'?" Martin scowled. "Are you
backing out already?"

"N-n-no, but I think I ought to go to Gail's. I—I always tell
her everything."

"Well—all right." Then, after a moment's thought, "I'll get
the license, a minister, some sandwiches and things, and we'll
be married in Gail's flat. That's a good place."

He went back to the telephone and called the livery stable
to send over a horse and buggy right away.

At nine o'clock I was saying yes, I would take Martin for
my lawfully wedded husband. I wore the pretty dress in which
I had sung "My Hero" only the night before. I also wore white
carnations in my hair and at my waist and remembered vaguely
that about five dozen of them had come with the sandwiches.
Martin wore one too.

Gail kissed me and cried when it was all over, and so did
Dick. I think Mr. Kerr was there, and Martin introduced me to
a Mr. John Overfield, Mr. John Callahan, and some more people, and everything seemed very strange. After a little while in
which everybody, except Martin and me, ate sandwiches, Gail
helped me put on my traveling suit again and we all got into
buggies and drove very fast to the railroad station. Then, with
everybody waving good-bye, Martin and I were on the train
going to Kansas City.

"Why are we going to Kansas City?" I asked. "Why aren't
we going home to Chanute?"

Martin grinned. "Well, the fact is—I'm a little worried about this whole thing and figured we'd better be married again in Missouri."

"What?" I asked.

"In Missouri. John Callahan—he's a lawyer, you know—he said that, considering you were quite a lot under age, your father could have our marriage annulled, and that if we wanted to make it permanent, we'd better get into another state as fast as we could and be married again."

Just then I happened to think that I had been married without my father, mother, and grandmother being there; I had been married without even letting them know about it. They had expected me home on the five o'clock train; my father was to be at the station to meet me; and I had forgotten all of these things. I jumped up and looked out the window to see where we were.

"We've got to get off the train at Chanute," I said, beginning to cry. "We've got to."

We argued miserably about this for a long time. Martin said all right, if I didn't love him any more than that I could get off at Chanute, and goodness knows he wouldn't try to stop me. We were still talking about this when the train pulled into Chanute. He picked up my portmanteau and led the way to the door.

"I'll be hanged if I want a wife," he flung this at me over his shoulder, "who bawls after her folks in less than an hour after she's married."

I sat down suddenly, more frightened than grieved. The train pulled out of the Chanute station, and there under a strong light I saw my father, staring bewilderedly after the departing train. And then, once more, my grief was greater than my fright, and I cried loudly all the way into Kansas City.

Chapter 9

After five days in Kansas City, where we were married a second time and spent many long hours every day in a telephone booth trying to straighten things out with both Martin's parents and mine, Martin decided the only thing to do was to face the music—in other words, face my father.

This meeting was difficult for everybody concerned. My father was a much smaller man than Martin. but for a minute, as he walked into the room where Martin stood nervously waiting, I didn't know what might happen. His fists were clenched and his face was first very white and then very red.

"Young fellow," he thundered finally, "I never wanted to punch anybody so bad in all my life. In all my life, do you understand?"

Martin cleared his throat.

"Well, yes, I think I do, and—well, I don't blame you a bit, Mr. Leighty. The only thing is—"

"The only thing is this, Mr. Martin Johnson: You've got her, now see that you take care of her!"

For the next few months I was a completely smug and happy bride. Thanks to Mama, I was a good cook and an efficient housekeeper, and it seemed to me that my little flat up over a row of stores was quite the loveliest place in the world. Each piece of furniture shone with all the polishing I gave it, and, of course, our wedding gifts—which, considering our unannounced marriage, were of an astonishing number and variety—were on constant parade. My pride in my handsome husband certainly would have been unendurable in anyone less young, and as I look back on it now I know that I strutted when we went along the street together. And, of course, all of my conversations, whether in the butcher shop or grocery, or even in my own home when a friendly neighbor chanced to call, were brought back without quibble or delay to "my husband."

There were times when I achingly missed Mama, Papa, and Grandma, but I consoled myself with thinking that as soon as Martin and I had enough money we'd build a house big enough for all of us, with another house for Mother and Father Johnson and Freda, perhaps, right next door. I even began studying house plans and landscaping gardening, and walked up one street and down another looking at empty lots. With no disloyalty at all to Chanute, I had grown to love Independence. I had married here. I would raise my family and live here all the rest of my days.

"Darling!" I flew to meet Martin as he came up the stairs. "I've found two of the dearest little lots over on Poplar Street, and I talked to your father about them and he says he'll help us, and there's no reason at all why we couldn't start building . . ."

I stopped and looked at him, then added lamely, "Is there?"

Martin closed the door and stared at me helplessly.

"We can't do that," he said. "I'm just not like that at all!"

"Not like what?"

"About buying lots and building houses. I can't do it!"

"But—your father says he'll help us, and of course we'll pay him back. I'm a good manager, I am—we'll save—and I mean, we must do it now while we're young, and then the money we spend for rent—"

"Osa, I don't want a house!" Martin said.

"But—we've got to live someplace, and why can't we live in our own house? It'll be much cheaper in the end."

"Because we're going away, that's why, before you have us anchored here!"

"Anchored?"

Martin took me in his arms.

"Having a home—and everything—means so much to you," he said miserably. "I guess your father was right—we should never have married."

"Not married! You mean—you don't like me anymore?"

"Oh, you know it isn't that, but—I'd go crazy if I thought I had to stay here all the rest of my life."

He looked so desperate I couldn't think of anything to say. And besides, things were all mixed up in my head.

"We're going around the world, Osa!" This came out very abruptly.

"Well—all right, dear."

Martin stared at me. "Did you say 'all right'?"

"Yes."

"Oh, darling!"

"I was just wondering, though. What about the Snarks?" I asked.

"Well, I'll just turn them over to Charlie Kerr," he answered. "It's his money that's in them anyhow."

I tried to think. "It costs a lot of money to go around the world, doesn't it?"

"Well, of course, it depends on where you're going. But I thought we could sell our wedding presents and the furniture."

"Yes, Yes, I hadn't thought about that." I swallowed a big lump. "Would that be enough?"

"No, it wouldn't. But what I thought was that I could take my slides and the film, and lecture in different towns until we got enough."

"I think that's a very good idea," I said without enthusiasm.

"Do you really?"

"Sure. When do we start?"

"As soon as we can sell the stuff," Martin said happily.

"Only thing—are we going to those places where they have cannibals?"

"You bet we are. They're—why, they're practically savages down where I went with Jack London, and what I want to do some day is to get a good, honest, complete motion picture of them to show people who've had all the advantages of civilization—in big cities and places like that—so they can get an idea of what they themselves were like, maybe half a million years ago."

Dimly, then, I began to grasp the fact that I was married to not only a very unusual man, but a man with an obsession besides. I grasped the additional fact that we probably never would live the way other people did, and it seemed to me suddenly that under the circumstances I had an excessive amount of pride of the wrong sort. Acquiring a fine home, nice clothes, having a successful husband—all the substantial things—had been very important to me. But now, as I looked at Martin, I began in a fumbling way to shape a different sort of pride.

I began to wonder if I couldn't help increase our revenue by singing at the theaters where Martin lectured. Martin improved on this idea by teaching me some Hawaiian dances and songs, or, at any rate, his version of them. I made a Hawaiian costume out of bright-colored cloth to wear during the performances.

"We're going around the world," I told my friends on the day we sold off our furniture and wedding presents. That night we said good-bye to Father and Mother Johnson and Freda, and the next morning we left for Kansas City.

After our engagement there, we went to Emporia, Kansas. Emporia probably didn't mean to be unfriendly or uninterested in what Martin had to say about his trip on the *Snark* with Jack and Charmian London, but in spite of our personally distributed handbills and announcements in the papers and posters, the attendance at the theater only increased about ten percent during the week that we were there.

"For one thing," the plump manager of the theater was quite jovial about it, "it must be pretty near a year since you got back to Independence from that *Snark* trip. We carried the whole thing in the paper here. I guess folks kind of think it's old stuff now, or maybe that you could've come around this way a mite sooner."

"Yes, I know," Martin said lamely. "It's just that I've been so busy. You know how it is, with my own theaters and everything."

"Oh, sure, I understand, but that doesn't help the box office none." The manager counted out eight dollars.

"Your percentage, son," he said, "and come around again some time when you got something new."

Martin and I went back to the hotel and talked things over.

"If that's the way they feel," Martin said glumly, "I guess we'd better go to some other state where I won't be just a Kansas boy that made good."

"A year ago," I added thoughtfully.

"Like a barrel of apples that's stood too long." He grinned wryly.

"You're no such thing," I said indignantly.

Then his grin faded. "The money we've got won't last long this way. Maybe we'd better go back to Independence. I can always go to work for my dad."

"If you did that, it would be because of me." I found myself suddenly being very firm. "What other state do you think we ought to try?"

"Well, I was wondering about Colorado," Martin said.

"Sure," I agreed. "I bet they like Jack London up there, and I bet they'll like you too."

The next morning we left for Colorado. It was a good idea, Martin said, to try the small towns first. And we did. But our outgo was still more than our income. Neither of us said anything about its being Thanksgiving time. I fried some eggs over a gas jet and the next morning we left Rocky Ford.

"I've got it all figured, this poor-attendance stuff," Martin said glumly. "It's the holiday season. People haven't either the time or the money to go to shows." Then, after some deep thought, "Maybe we'd better go to Denver. People are sort of gayer in big towns when it's holiday time. Yes, I guess that's what we'd better do." This, it seemed to me, was a positive inspiration.

It took nearly everything we had for railroad fare, so when we arrived on Christmas Eve in Denver we pawned Martin's watch for five dollars, then hunted up a rooming house within walking distance of the theaters in the center of town where we hoped we might secure bookings.

"This will be fine, Martin," I said, trying not to look at the torn places in the wallpaper. "You go out and get some eggs and bread or something while I unpack, but don't spend more than fifty cents, because we might not get a booking right away."

"Yes," replied Martin in a kind of croak. "Our first Christmas together, and all I can do is go buy some eggs for my wife to fry over a gas flame."

"Martin!" I ran to him. His face was hot and flushed. "You've got a fever—you're sick!"

"I'm not sick, I'm just mad and disgusted with myself. I had no right to drag you into anything like this!" He was shouting by now. "Look at that wallpaper!" He seized a piece that was loose and ripped it from floor to ceiling. He began to laugh.

I wanted to cry, but instead I scolded and bossed him and got him into bed, then took fifty cents of our five dollars and ran out to get some lemons and quinine.

It was dusk now, and sharply cold. In no time at all the tip of my nose was numb, and my feet felt like stumps in the hard-packed snow. I found a grocery store in the next block and bought some lemons. The nearest drugstore, I was told, was three blocks down and one block over.

Somehow I lost my way, I don't know how, and still strong upon me was my mother's warning not to speak to strangers. I doubled back; I turned corner after corner in streets that were dark and alien. The tears ran unchecked from my eyes and nose, and with no sobs to dramatize them. My handkerchief was now a frozen ball that scratched my face.

I turned another corner and there, suddenly and miraculously, was a window edged in frosty lace like a valentine and holding in its frame the great, round crystal globes of green, blue, and red liquid that said here was a drugstore. All terror dropped from the night as I stared at them, limpid clear, glowing, warm. Here I would find the medicine I needed for Martin. Tomorrow was Christmas—I'd nurse him out of his cold and, with care, our four dollars and fifty cents would see us through until he was better. Why, the very size of the city, which had been so frightening when I felt myself lost, assured me that somewhere there would be a theater that would want to put on Martin's fine lecture. It began to snow big, feathery, gentle flakes.

It was warm in the drugstore and bright, with a clean, bitterish smell. I bought the quinine and had twenty-five cents left. The druggist, a kindly gentleman in a very white apron, directed me back to the shabby street where our rooming house stood, and I set out on the run. Martin would be worried. Perhaps he would also be hungry. Most certainly I was.

I caught sight of a hand-lettered card in the window of a lunch room. "Christmas dinner now being served," it said. "Twenty-five cents."

Wonderful, I thought, and went in. The proprietor was a stout, energetic little woman who bounced as she walked. She listened sympathetically when I told her my husband was sick, and piled up a tray with some beef hash over which she poured a dark gravy. "Genuine turkey flavor," she said. Some mashed potatoes, pickled beets—"exactly the color of cranberries"—two thick slices of bread, a sad-looking piece of apple pie, and a cup of coffee completed the "Christmas dinner."

The tray was heavy, and the snow now drove straight into my face. My footing on the ice-rutted sidewalk was precarious at best, and to see it at all I now lifted the tray to the top of my head. Added to my worries, of course, was the fear of breaking the dishes and having to pay for them out of our little bit of money.

Panting but relieved, I reached our rooming house with nothing spilled except the coffee. Hurrying up the stairs to our room on the second floor, I pushed the door open.

Cutting cleanly through the stale odors of cabbage, dust, and grease was the fresh, spicy smell of carnations. Then I saw them in the water pitcher, a great bouquet—all white, as I loved them best.

"Martin—the flowers—who—here in Denver? Who sent them to us? How did they find us?"

My husband lay shivering, the bedclothes pulled up around his head, his feet uncovered, out at the bottom. I set the tray down and fixed this, then, shaking the snow from my coat, put it over him. The bed quilts were thin and filled with wadded cotton. I looked around for something else and wished passionately for some of Grandma's good lamb's-wool quilts. Martin's big overcoat. That would help. I picked it up from the chair over which he had thrown it and found it damp to my hand. And there on the shoulder I saw some flakes of only partly melted snow. I looked at the dressing table then where the four dollars and fifty cents had been. It was gone.

*   *   *

Martin wrote home for help, which came promptly. I wrote home that we were living on the fat of the land. Martin was soon over his cold—he was thinner, and so was I, after the experience—and we set about securing bookings. The holiday season, we were told—and already knew too well—was bad in the theater. Things wouldn't pick up until around early spring, maybe. At any rate, we made enough to move into a slightly better rooming house, and this, we felt, was distinctly a step ahead. Looking at the whole thing squarely, however, we couldn't see that we were any closer to going around the world than we'd been on the day we left home.

"Tell you what," Martin said one night late in March after a close study of an item in the newspaper, "we're going to pick up and go to Black Hawk."

"Go where?" I asked.

"Black Hawk. It's right here in the state of Colorado. A gold-mining town, and there's a strike on. Now, I figure those fellows will have a lot of time to kill, and as well as giving them the *Snark* stuff and the cannibal pictures, I'll tell them about Jack's gold-mining experiences in the Klondike."

"Why, that's wonderful," I said.

Black Hawk proved even more than wonderful. There were two nickel theaters on the wide dirt street. We made a deal with the one that offered the best percentage, and, in spite of rain and mud, ankle deep, and the boosted price of ten cents, the theater was packed from nine in the morning until two the next morning. Martin's lecture went over in a fine way. The men liked him for his simple, direct manner, and they liked, too, what he told them about Jack up in the Klondike. I sang what passed for some Hawaiian songs.

We remained in Black Hawk until every man in the place had paid his ten cents' admission to the theater. The living problem was somewhat complicated. The shack-like hotel was packed, with four and five men to a room, we were told. There were no sleeping quarters to be had anyplace in town at any price. Had Martin been alone, of course, he could have managed. Some nights we tried fixing up a place at the theater after the crowds were gone, but it was so stuffy, with bad ventilation, that we couldn't stand it. On fine nights we sometimes

slept on the benches at the railroad station, but found ourselves early in the morning the objects of too much curiosity.
On our third week in town, Martin, completely desperate, went
to the owner of the hotel to see if something couldn't be done
in the way of a bed for me at least.

From that night on and until we packed up and left, the
pool room was ours. What Martin had to pay for this I never
knew. Of course, we had to wait until nearly daylight before
the men cleared out. It smelled of stale tobacco smoke and
other smells too numerous to mention, but we opened the windows, and I was astonished that a pool table, spread with our
coats and a blanket borrowed from the hotel, could seem so
luxurious. It was somewhere along in here that I discovered
for myself the meaning of relative values, and I was pleased to
think that I was becoming quite profound.

And, of course, I was intensely proud of Martin. Coming to
Black Hawk had been his idea; we had nearly five hundred
good hard silver dollars saved up; and it seemed to me we could
start going around the world practically any minute.

"Five hundred dollars is a good beginning, of course," Martin said, "but it will take more than that to buy even a secondhand motion-picture camera." Our future was assured, though.
I knew it, and so did he. It was just a matter of a little more
time.

Optimism is a fine thing to hang onto, I found, and carries
one blithely over the bad places. Sometimes its promise, like a
pretty balloon, explodes, but usually it serves its purpose gaily
and well.

There were no more Black Hawks on our self-selected itinerary, and little by little our five hundred silver dollars dwindled. The whole trouble, of course, was the five- and ten-cent
admission price. Only under exceptional conditions, such as
were afforded by the miners' strike in Black Hawk, could enough
business be done to net us an even adequate income.

In May, our first wedding anniversary found us in western
Canada, in the town of Calgary. Martin had heard that admis-
sions up there were generally higher than in the States.

We seldom spoke of the trip around the world now; we just
did the best we could with each day as it came. Largely because of Martin's dogged insistence that I should always have

the best that he could afford, our brave five hundred dollars dropped to around three hundred, and I think our only expressed goal by this time was to build the sum back to five hundred.

We had selected a nice, clean little room in a small but charming hotel just a block from the theater where Martin had secured the promise of a booking. He was there now, closing it, I fervently hoped. The view between the clean white scrim curtains was of a green, lush countryside, with pretty cottages and gardens.

There was a sudden sharp hunger in me for a place I could call home, and for security and permanence. I thought of the furniture and wedding presents I had given up, and the nice Hoover kitchen cabinet which had been Martin's wedding gift, and I began to cry. Purposely I had refrained from reminding Martin that it was our anniversary. To keep him from spending money foolishly on me was my most difficult task.

Suddenly I heard him come whistling along the hall. Blowing my nose, I ran to let him in and found him carrying a box which he had to turn on end to get in the door.

He said, and his eyes were shining, "This is your reward for marrying me one year ago today, Mrs. Martin Johnson."

"Oh, Martin, you shouldn't.!"

I was trembling all over as I untied the string and removed the lid and then the lovely white tissue paper. It was a hat. The biggest, most beautiful hat I had ever seen, and on it a mauve willow ostrich plume that swept clear to my shoulder.

I held my breath as I contemplated its beauty. I held it a second time when I thought of its probable price. I looked at Martin, and he read my question in my face.

"Well, only thirty-seven fifty," he admitted guiltily, "but it looked just like you and I—well, I couldn't help buying it."

"No, of course not," I said, though my heart sank, "and it's wonderful, and cheap as anything at the price."

I had put the hat on, and Martin was staring at me.

"You know," he said, "it's funny what a good-looking hat will do for a girl, but the way you carry your head and all, that hat gives you the look of—well, of a great lady!"

Nothing would do then but that I must keep the hat on. Martin ordered our anniversary dinner sent up, and to the

amazement of the nice stout little waiter, I sat grandly all evening eating roast beef and Yorkshire pudding and feeling almost as wonderful as Martin said I looked.

"I've got it! I've got it!" Martin yelled suddenly.

"What?"

"A great idea!"

The next day the sedate little city of Calgary looked both
startled and impressed when a small but lively brass band made
its way through the quiet streets, followed by a livery-stable
phaeton in which a tall young man bowed affably right and
left, and a young woman, a little scared and very erect in an
immense plumed hat, also bowed right and left.

The purpose of the parade was made known with utmost
restraint. Indeed, it was not disclosed until after the parade had
passed, and then it was told very modestly on a white oblong
card fastened to the back of the phaeton. Here, it said in neat
black letters, were the two world-famous travelers and lectur-
ers, Mr. and Mrs. Martin Johnson, and that night and for only
a brief period thereafter, they would appear in person at the
city's most popular theater.

I felt a little bad about the whole thing because I was neither a world traveler nor a lecturer, but a sudden drenching
thunderstorm put everything else out of my head, and my lovely
hat was a ruin.

Western Canada was very kind to us indeed. Our five
hundred dollars was once more intact, and Martin decided we
should head toward Chicago. The bigger the theaters the better the earnings, he said. Chicago was only moderately interested in us, however, so Martin next decided on New York. He
thought that there he might be able to get some between-times
jobs, that we couldn't go on forever fooling around and letting
five hundred dollars—whether we had it or didn't have it—be
so all-important. We'd never get anywhere that way. In other
words, the way we were going, we had lost our real goal.

New York it was, then, a New York that, for longer than I
care to remember, was indifferent to whether we lived or died,
and certainly was emphatic about not liking my type of singing. Twenty-five dollars a week, and that not regularly, was all
Martin could get out of his lectures.

Another Christmas was drawing near, and I had a serious talk with Martin about it. Presents were out of the question, I insisted, and if any money at all was to be spent, it must go to buy shoes for him and some rubbers.

"Those thin shoes—your feet are wet every night when you come home. It just won't do." Then it occurred to me that I was scolding him a lot lately, but I had to take care of him. For good measure, I reminded him how sick he had been that time in Denver.

"All right," he grinned. "You're the boss."

On Christmas Eve I heard him come whistling to the door. This time he brought me an ermine neckpiece and muff. What it cost him I don't know, but since we were able to pawn it for twenty-five dollars, it must have been a lot.

Finally, feeling myself completely useless, I decided to take in roomers. What we had to pay for single, dingy rooms gave me the idea. So I rented a flat with seven rooms, two of which, a small bedroom and kitchen, I kept for ourselves.

Martin was in a fury with me over this, and when I started serving breakfasts I began to be afraid I had gone too far.

"We're going back to Independence," he shouted. "If you think I'll let you turn into a scrubwoman, you'd better think again!"

"And if you think that because you married me you can't do the things you did before you married me, you'd better think again too!" Martin had worked things out simply enough without me, I knew that. It was having me that made everything difficult.

I went on. "You keep talking about the big theaters and that they pay bigger money, and yet all you do is fool around with the little ones. That big vaudeville theater over on Seventh Avenue near Forty-fifth—I bet you've never even been near it!"

"But that's the Palace! I'd look nice, wouldn't I, going in the Palace with my old scratched film and those slides. You haven't seen those slides lately!"

"Well, you can get some more, can't you, off the negatives?"

Martin left without kissing me. I made five beds and cried

into all of them. Then, I don't know how many hours later, I heard him coming to the door—whistling.

I ran to let him in. He took me in his arms and held me and held me, and when one of his tears went down the back of my neck I knew he was crying in that silent way men have, and then I cried too.

"I saw Martin Beck," he said after a bit.

I tried to think who Martin Beck was.

"Well, if he's somebody from Independence," I said, "for goodness' sake don't tell him about things—being the way they are, I mean. The folks would get to know, and that would be just awful."

At this my husband held me tighter than ever and laughed and laughed, and then he told me what it was all about. Mr. Beck, he said, was the big man of the Orpheum vaudeville circuit, and he had given Martin a contract on that very afternoon.

My blank stare was an exact reflection of my state of mind.

"The Orpheum circuit, Osa! Big theaters—and good money, do you hear me, good money!"

I sat down suddenly. "Good money!"

"Yes, and we're getting out of this dump today. We're going to the Waldorf!"

Now I asserted myself. "Oh, no we're not," I said.

"Oh yes we are. If you think I'm going to let my wife be a boarding-house keeper—if you think—"

"If you have half the brains I give you credit for," I said severely, "I think you'll save that money and buy a motion-picture camera and go around the world the way you always said you would." I was full of scorn. "The Waldorf!"

"Yes, I know, but—you—like this—"

"And besides," I went on, "you don't want to go on talking about the *Snark* all the rest of your life, do you?" I eyed him curiously. "Or do you?"

Martin fairly exploded at this. "Good God, no!" he said.

And back west we went. The Orpheum circuit took us back to Michigan, to Iowa, Indiana, and on to the West Coast. And finally I met Jack London and his wife, when they came to the theater in Seattle, Washington.

Completely secondary to Martin, though not to me, was the fact that the critics, nearly everywhere we went, spoke favorably of Martin and his lecture, some even saying he was the "best thing on the bill."

With the accumulation of money in the bank, we now dared to talk about our dream and the plan to make it come true. I say "our" because it had become just as important to me as it had always been to Martin. Even the talk of going down to the South Seas among the cannibals now seemed a perfectly normal and right objective.

"What clothes do you think you'll need?" Martin asked one Sunday morning in the early fall. We had, just the day before, put our thousandth dollar in the bank.

"I don't know," I said doubtfully. "I suppose some high boots and things like that." Snakes were a secret terror to me, even more so than cannibals who ate people and then dried their victims' heads into hard brown knobs with the hair still on.

"Yes, boots." Martin put that down. "Two pairs."

Chic Sale and his wife were on the same bill with us, and the four of us became great friends. We were all relatively unknown and struggling. Marie Sale and I used to get together and make our own hats. We got the cost down to seventy-five cents apiece, which we thought was very good.

"And some denim overalls and huck shirts," Martin said, following me into the kitchen.

"For me?" I asked.

"For both of us," he replied.

I tried to picture myself dressed that way and wondered whether I ought to cut my hair. Martin was against this so emphatically, however, that I decided to wear it long and heavy as it was.

"We can do it for an even four thousand dollars," Martin announced in triumph at length. And he asked our friends if they would chip in and form a syndicate to finance our expedition.

Chic Sale grinned. "I've only listened to you tell about that trip a couple of hundred times," he said, "and I'll give you a thousand dollars to change your routine."

As the circuit took us toward Oakland, Martin talked of little except Jack and Charmian London, and especially of Char-

mian and what a fine wife she was to Jack. It was all arranged
that we were to visit the Londons for a few days at their ranch
near Glen Ellen.

"You'll have to go some to beat her," Martin said, grinning
at me.

"Well, for goodness sake," I said, "it's too bad she hasn't got
a sister!"

In all my life I've never been as nervous as when we walked
up the steps of Jack and Charmian's home. I had made up my
mind that they wouldn't like me at all, and I was miserable.
And I continued to be miserable until the day we left. I was on
probation, and I knew it.

Then, on the last day, just as we were saying good-bye,
they kissed me warmly. I must have looked completely bewildered.

"You see, Osa," Jack said, laughing, "Charmian and I had
just about adopted Martin, and when he wrote us that he was
marrying—well, we were sort of worried."

"Oh, Jack, you brute!" Charmian was laughing, but she tried
to stop him. "That isn't fair."

Jack went right on. " 'A fine career arrested,' we said. 'Poor
fellow.' "

I couldn't think of anything to say, so I just waited for the
rest of the verdict.

"It was just because you looked so young," Charmian
put in.

"But now we've gotten to know you," Jack finally added,
"we can see that everything's all right."

Charmian hugged me. "It's better than all right, and we'll
never feel sorry for Martin again."

Then Jack dubbed me "Snarkette" and I've never felt so
proud; nor have I ever seen Martin as proud as when Jack gave
him his best gun.

My scrapbooks of reviews were growing. Los Angeles, Salt
Lake City, Denver, Kansas City, Louisville, and then, London.
Martin was booked at the Victoria Palace in London. And when
we returned, we were scheduled at the Criterion in New York
City. We had truly arrived.

The next few years passed quickly, and with the help of our friends we had our four thousand dollars and were on our way, first to Chanute, and then to Independence, for farewells which we knew would be painful.

I find it difficult to look back on them even today. Mama, always gentle and thoughtful of other people, nevertheless looked tearfully at Martin and asked him how he could do such a thing—take her baby down into those heathenish lands among a lot of cannibals.

Papa, fists once more doubled, asked Martin if this, then, was the way he proposed to take care of me. Grandma, always practical and a bit of a philosopher, bustled in with two lovely new patchwork quilts for the trip.

"You, Belle," she looked at Mama's tears, "I'm ashamed of you." Then, to Papa, "And you too!"

From the day she had first doubted Martin and then was won over to him, her admiration had been unqualified. She kissed us both, then hustled us on our way. Prolonged farewells were a nuisance, she said.

Vaughn met us at the gate and told Martin he ought to take him instead of me. "Girls are no good for things like that," he said.

In Independence, the concern expressed for my safety was even greater than it had been in Chanute.

"Martin," Mrs. Johnson was almost angry, "I don't see how you dare take that child down where all those heathens are. Why, young and pretty as she is, there's no telling—there's just no telling!"

Martin winked at me. "Well, she's good enough to eat, I'll say that for her."

And for perhaps the first time in all of Martin's comings and goings, Mr. Johnson expressed the gravity he felt.

"It's all right for you, son, to go risk your neck, but I don't think you've any right to risk hers."

Martin grew a little irritated, finally.

"Why does everybody have to act as if I was going to take Osa down there and dish her up on a platter to a lot of cannibals or something? Gosh, I guess she means more to me than to anybody else, doesn't she?"

Then he swung on me. "Or maybe you don't want to go?" he said fiercely.

Whereupon I burst into tears. "After the way I've pushed you into going, that's a nice thing for you to say!"

Freda gave me three lovely lace-edged handkerchiefs and a bottle of perfume, and finally, with everybody feeling very hot and miserable, we were on our way.

A lot of people were at the station to see us off. We got on the train with flowers, several boxes of candy, a watermelon, and a basket of Martin's favorite fruit, cantaloupes. Just as the train started to move, I saw Gail and Dick, radiantly proud of their first-born son, rushing to say good-bye. Dick lifted the baby to the open window and I kissed his cool, sweet cheek.

We were on our way!

Chapter 10 _____

We were at last aboard the freighter *Sonoma* in San Francisco harbor, and I was practically beside myself.

Martin grinned. "Happy?"

"Oh, yes, my goodness!" That's all I could think of to say.

I had looked forward to getting on the boat and heading for the South Seas as the fulfillment of long-deferred hopes for Martin. That it would hold all this excitement for me was astonishing. Everything about it—the dock, the smell of the sea, the lapping of the green, dirty water against the black hull of the ship, the moment when we finally went up the gangplank—all of these sights, sounds, smells, filled me to bursting. For no reason at all I thought of the time when, as a little girl, I had experimented with pulling in a big breath and seeing how long I could hold it. Perhaps I was holding my breath now.

The trip from Kansas to San Francisco had been uneventful, although I knew Martin was dreading our visit to Glen Ellen. It would be the first time we had seen Charmian London since Jack's death. But it had been all right, and Charmian had come to the dock to see us off.

Even the tiny stateroom delighted me, with its two narrow, white berths, one above the other, and its round portholes—it was ours. I hung my hat on a hook and then, as quickly as possible, started to unpack, while Martin went to see that our trunks were safety aboard. And well he might, for in them were all our earthly goods, not to speak of our hopes for the future.

In the light of subsequent expeditions, our equipment was

meager to the point of not being equipment at all. It consisted of one hand-cranked Universal motion-picture camera, one 5-x-7 Graflex, one 4-x-5 Graflex, plates for the still cameras, Jack London's original Marlin rifle, two automatic revolvers, and, an inadequacy which I look back on today with amazement, only a few thousand feet of motion-picture film. But it was all we could afford. A wool tailored suit, a cotton dress, some high boots, a few hickory shirts, and overalls completed my personal outfit. At the last moment, before our trunk was picked up, Martin found the lid hard to close and discovered that I had rammed in a tin of baking powder and a small sack of flour!

I was so happy that I started to sing as, with great preciseness, I hung our things on the hooks along the wall of the stateroom.

"Hey, little fussy." Martin was laughing at me from the doorway. "That unpacking can wait till we're out of the harbor." He took my hand and hustled me up on deck, and there, leaning on the rail, we watched the cargo, cradled in huge nets, being swung from dock to deck. This and the score of activities that went with readying the ship for her long voyage had me once more holding my breath. I glanced at Martin. He was lazily relaxed against the railing.

"Well, aren't you excited?" I demanded.

"Fit to pop," he said.

"You don't look it," I said accusingly. "Why, I think everything is wonderful."

"Wait till you've embarked as often as I have," he grinned. "You're always excited, but you don't exactly break out in a rash."

"And you said this ship would be a little tub or something. Why, I think it's marvelous, and big, too."

"This is 'peanuts.' "

I looked at him in proper awe. Because he had traveled so much, this was "peanuts." Actually, for the first time since we were married, I think, I realized that my husband was a much-traveled man. "Peanuts" to him, but stupendous to me. I'd never be able to catch up with him, of that I was sure.

Suddenly the rowdy noise of the donkey engine and winches

stopped, and a blast from the ship's whistle shook the world.

"Golly!" I said, breathing hard.

The thick ropes that had held the boat to the dock plopped into the water and the boat shuddered all over; then, suddenly, I knew we were moving. We were under way!

"Golly!" Not knowing what else to do, I squeezed Martin's hand. "It's wonderful!" I said.

Martin grinned. "I hope you'll remember that if it gets rough and you're hanging over the rail."

"Over the rail?"

"Yes. You know, seasick?"

"Oh, seasick."

"Yep. If you get seasick you'll probably wish yourself dead, but everybody does."

"You mean everybody gets seasick?"

"Well, practically."

"You mean—you too? Worse than when we went to London?"

"Lord, yes!" Martin laughed. "A big hard roll of the ship and I'm on my back."

This was a sobering thought. "My goodness," I said.

Captain Trask was a big man with a seamed, weathered face, a fine big nose, and an air of awe-inspiring authority. I admired him very much and was prouder than ever of my husband when I saw how much the captain liked him. They talked a lot, of places and people that I knew nothing about, so I decided the best thing for me would be to listen and learn—and all the more so because it was apparent that the captain had put me down as little, soft, and generally useless. He had known Jack and Charmian London, and very pointedly every now and then—squinting at me under his heavy brows—he spoke of Charmian.

"There's a woman for you," he'd say. "She had the soft ways of a kitten and the heart of a lioness, and her beat never lived and never will."

"You're right there." Martin was thoughtful. "She was perfect for Jack. Never a squawk out of her; the best wife a man ever had."

"Aye," the captain nodded with another look at me. "A

woman that's too soft and sweet is like tapioca pudding—fine for them as likes it." Then he said something about the barometer falling, but I wasn't interested, and when I climbed into my berth that night I thought about snakes and cannibals and dried human heads and wondered miserably if the day would ever come when I would fail Martin. I fell into a troubled sleep and woke up in the act of pitching from my berth and landing on my shoulder. I tried to get to my feet and found that the floor had taken the angle of our cellar door back in Chanute. Just as I had figured this out, the up part was down and the down part was up. Then I heard a groan. It was Martin.

"I wish I could die," he said.

I did everything I could for the rest of the night to help Martin be a little less miserable. Then, when I saw it was morning, I scrambled into some clothes and went up on deck. It was wonderful, though I had to hang on like mad. It didn't seem possible there could be waves of such size. They piled up and piled up, until there was one that curled and broke right where I stood. It hit me with the force of a sack of sand, and the next instant I found myself in a swirl of green water and foam, and being swept to the other side of the deck.

Stunned and limp as a half-drowned kitten, I felt myself being picked up by the back of my jacket, then heard myself roughly ordered below. It was Captain Trask, and he was in a fury that I would show myself above deck on such a day.

"Why aren't you sick?" he thundered. "Sick and in your bunk and out of the way like other decent folk!"

"I don't want to be sick," I replied crossly as he pushed me ahead of him down the companionway. "And I don't like my bunk, and just because you're a captain of a ship I suppose you think you can order everybody around, but I don't like being ordered around—"

We had reached the bottom of the swaying companionway. The captain was still scowling.

"Well, I'm ordering you right now to stay off that deck until the ropes are strung, understand? Whether you're washed overboard or not doesn't interest me. Whether I have to put back to pick you up does interest me. I can't afford the time. Now you get into your bunk and stay there!"

"Then what do I do about breakfast? Martin doesn't want any, but I'm starved, and if you think I'm going back to bed without any breakfast—"

Captain Trask squinted at me. "How about some hot cakes," he said, "and a lot of butter and syrup, maybe some pig sausages and fried potatoes and a couple of cups of coffee?"

"Wonderful!"

The captain grinned. "All right, sailor," he said. "Get into some dry clothes and you shall have breakfast with me." When I found that everybody aboard was sick except the captain and me—and, I suppose, some of the crew—everything brightened, especially when it became apparent that the captain now regarded me as a right and good companion for Martin. Nothing more than this could I ask of either heaven or earth, and cannibals and snakes became mere trifles to take in my stride. At least, so I thought.

All the way across the Pacific to Honolulu, to Samoa, to Pago Pago, and finally to Sydney, Australia, my confidence grew. The captain became jollier by the minute and even played deck games with us, and when, on parting at Sydney, he told Martin I was "all right," it seemed to me I ought to burst, I was so proud. It took a few cockroaches to lay me low.

It was several days later. We were on our way from Sydney to the Solomon Islands aboard a tramp steamer, and while I longed for the departed comforts and cleanliness of Captain Trask's ship, I did what I was sure Charmian London would have done under the circumstances. I wore a smile. The captain, crew, and ship were filthy and the cockroaches everywhere, some no less than two inches long. The mess swarmed with them, and I saw Martin every now and then jounce them off his shoes and go right on eating. Doggedly, I did the same and derived a glum satisfaction out of telling myself that from matters such as these, one probably acquired that easy, well-traveled look.

It's one thing to be brave when you're awake; it's another when you're asleep. Something crossing my cheek that night startled me into instant wakefulness, and in the dim light I saw a roach scurry across my pillow, then heard it drop to the floor. I clenched my teeth against a scream, then suddenly was aware of a curious activity at the tips of my fingers. My hands lay at my sides on the sheet which was my only cover, and I found, on inspection, that roaches were nibbling at my fingernails. My screams must have been heard from stem to stern of the ship.

Martin, laughing, took me in his arms. "That's nothing," he said. "Wait till you get down to the Solomons. Those coconut crabs down there aren't polite enough just to give you a manicure; they take your fingers right off!"

The next few months were disappointing and anxious ones. In whalers, luggers, and merchants we sailed from island to island of the Solomon group and found many primitive people. We even found some that were said to be cannibals, but always Martin shook his head and pushed on. Often I found this difficult to understand. It was incredible to me that anywhere in the world there could be wilder, more vicious-looking people than we had already seen. Because our funds were so limited I knew we couldn't cruise about indefinitely, and Martin insisted that because our film was so limited we could use it only when he was satisfied that he had found natives that were completely untouched by civilization. Then he pointed out that all of those we had seen so far had been under the firm control of British government authorities. They were subdued, tamed. Nothing I could say would persuade him to the contrary. His mouth, tender and fine, could become very stubborn, and his eyes, usually gay and carefree, would take on a look of pure, hard steel.

There were those aboard the different boats we took, traders and the like, who couldn't understand Martin's not herding some of the savage-looking natives together, giving them trade stuff, and "staging" some scenes. It had been done, they said, but then, as always, Martin was a patient, persistent artist who would never be satisfied with anything but the truth. It seems to me that everywhere he went he asked hundreds of questions. He made hundreds of notes, and finally his decision was made. Malekula, the second-largest island of the New Hebrides group, was, he learned, the subject of disputed ownership between the French and British, and this meant a lack of the usual patrolling and discipline. If man in his savage and original state existed anyplace in the world, he existed here. Further investigation revealed that there were parts of Malekula that had never been explored by white men, and it was rumored that cannibalism and head-hunting were common practices.

We returned to Sydney, where Martin searched out the captain of a small ship that was leaving in a few days for the upper part of the Hebrides group. Once aboard, and our destination and purpose made known, a storm of protest and warning broke around us. The captain himself came to us, bringing a copy of the *Pacific Island Pilot*.

"Now, you listen to me, young fellow," he said. "I don't want to scare the little lady, but it says right here in the *Pilot* that the natives of Malekula are a wild and savage race, that they're treacherous, and it's a known fact that they still practice cannibalism!"

Martin smiled. He was happier than he'd been in months.

"I've had some experience with such natives," he said, "and with plenty of tobacco and trade stuff, we'll be safe enough."

A recruiter of blacks, heavy, scarred, and rough, broke into the conversation.

"The captain's right, sir," he said to Martin. "Why, I wouldn't go onto that island for a thousand pounds; at least, not without a gunboat at my back."

"I'm afraid we don't happen to have a gunboat in our equipment," Martin grinned.

"If you go through with this, you'll find it's no joking matter," the captain growled.

"But why should the natives hurt us?" I said, putting in my bit. "My husband is only going to take their pictures."

"Take their pictures!" the captain snorted. "When you two get close enough to them for that, you can tell each other good-bye!" He drank noisily from a flask, then continued: "Pictures of them cannibals! Why, they're ugly as the devil's own brats— and that's what they are, devils! Savage, cruel, murderous black devils!" His voice thundered. "And what's more, I'll not go off my course to set you down on Malekula, understand? Not with a woman along! It would be murder, that's what, woman murder, and I'll not be guilty of it!"

I couldn't even look in Martin's direction, for it was I—my coming with him—that hampered all his plans. Already we were in sight of Malekula. In length it was seventy-five miles or more, the recruiter told us, shaped like an hourglass and about thirty miles across at its widest part.

"There's around forty thousand natives on that island," he continued. "Strong fellows too, especially among the Big Nambas, but much as I'm needing blacks, I'll get 'em someplace else."

Forty thousand natives on one island. I was staggered.

Martin's interest sharpened. "Strong fellows, you say, the Big Nambas?"

"The most powerful tribe on the island, and they've got a chief, Nagapate, that's a holy terror."

Martin prodded the recruiter with more questions and learned that the Big Nambas, who derived their name from wearing a huge pandanus fiber, occupied the greater portion of the north end of the island, and that by sufferance another tribe, known as the Small Nambas, was permitted to occupy a minor portion. The latter, he said, wore merely a bit of twisted leaf.

I could see from the way Martin looked off toward the blue-gray mass that was Malekula that somehow he would contrive to get there. A smaller shape, separated from the big island, now appeared, and quickly Martin asked about it.

"That's the island of Vao," the recruiter said. "About a mile and a half across and maybe four hundred natives." He paused, with a look at me. A couple of tears had dripped off the end of my nose. "You know," he said, "I think Vao would be the very ticket for you and the little lady here. Four hundred wild men would be about as many as you could get in that camera of yours anyhow, and from all reports, even though the British patrol boat circles the island every so often and could rake it from end to end with fire, I hear that those fellows on Vao still bury their old people alive and eat long pig."

"And how far did you say Vao was from Malekula?" Martin asked cautiously.

"About a mile," the recruiter answered, "and there's a French mission there, too, run by Father Prin."

Martin seized his hand: "A great idea," he shouted. "Great!"

The captain eyed us suspiciously as we debarked at Vao; he knew that we could get to Malekula from there with very little trouble. Then he shrugged. If we were reckless enough to risk being served up as "long pig," that was our lookout, not his.

Father Prin gave us a hearty, if puzzled, welcome. This dear soul, who had worked among these people on the small island for nearly thirty years, was a volume in himself, and all the more so when one considered that the only discernible result of his labor was a mere seventeen converts. I marveled at his patience and loved him for his faith.

The little mud-and-grass church, with its quiet images and dim altar, seemed strange and beautiful on this distant island. The priest's small, three-room home adjoining it was a sanctuary of cleanliness and repose. It was here we rested and made our plans.

Father Prin gravely shook his head and confirmed the stories we had already heard of the cruelties practiced even on Vao. How much worse it must be on Malekula, where even the most hardened recruiters feared to land, should, he said, be perfectly apparent to us. I could see reproach in his eyes as he looked at Martin, and, worse, I could see that Martin himself was beginning to fear for me. Always me!

With evening the boo-boos (native drums) began to sound back in the bush of Vao, and suddenly Father Prin pointed from the window of his hut. Martin and I looked, and there at the edge of the clearing we saw peering at us men whose black faces were so seamed and hideous that it was hard to believe they were men at all.

"Th-that thing through their noses," I heard myself asking in a squeaky whisper. "What's that?"

"Bone," Father Prin replied. "Human bone."

Martin drew me away from the window. "I don't know, darling," he said, "but I'm afraid I can't risk taking you to Malekula. You'll be safe here with Father Prin. Please, Osa, for my sake."

Suddenly I was in a rage, with every bit of fear burned out of me.

"If you go, I'm going with you, Martin Johnson. That's what I came for and that's how it's going to be—the whole way. The whole way!" I repeated.

Seeing that I would not be swerved, the good priest gave us every help in his power, and a twenty-eight-foot whaleboat together with a crew of five trustworthy Vao men was put at our disposal. Before sun-up the following morning we were stowing our cameras, film, and trade goods in the boat. Then, hoisting a small jib and a miniature mainsail, we pushed off for Malekula, with Father Prin giving us his blessings from the shore.

Following the good father's advice, we first landed at a small saltwater village on the Vao side of Malekula, where the natives, because of their accessibility, had learned to respect the British gunboats and to recognize authority beyond their own, and where we added three more to our crew. Their being Malekulans would help us, Father Prin felt, to contact the bush people of the island. We then set sail for Tanemarou Bay, in the Big Nambas' territory.

The trip along the rocky shore was not very reassuring so far as the aims of our little expedition were concerned, for only now and then did we catch a glimpse of the natives, and they vanished as we rapidly approached. This apparent timidity eased our fears for our own personal safety, however, and when we reached the beach at Tanemarou, a strip of dazzling yellow sand separating the sea from the thick bush, we found it deserted, and stepped boldly out of the whale boat.

"How does this look to you, kitten?" Martin asked. His eyes were dancing with excitement.

"Why—all right, I guess," I answered doubtfully. Then, trying to be funny, "But I thought somebody said something about forty thousand natives on Malekula."

"Don't worry. They're back there in the bush, plenty of them."

He pantomimed to the men to take the trade stuff out of the boat. Our one precious motion-picture camera he handled himself.

"Looks like a kind of trail into the bush over there," I said. Then I stopped short. "Oh!" I said.

A lone native had appeared out of the jungle. Our men, seeing him, moved back toward the boat—and with good reason. He was the most horrible-looking creature I had ever laid eyes on. Coal black and incredibly filthy, his shock of greasy hair and heavy wool beard were probably the nesting place of every sort of vermin.

A gorget of pig's teeth hung around his neck, he wore a bone through his nose, and he was entirely naked except for a large breechclout of dried pandanus fiber. As he came nearer, I saw that his deeply creviced face was horribly distorted. It made me think of a grotesque mask—one I had seen on a theater program in New York, I think—representing "Tragedie." I moved closer to Martin.

The black spoke in a gutteral Bêche-de-Mer that astonished me with its scattering of English words.

"My word! Master! Belly belong, me walk about too much!" He pressed his hands dramatically to his stomach.

I looked at Martin incredulously. We had come to Malekula warned and forewarned of natives who dealt swift and savage death to intruders, to be met by a native with a stomachache!

We rocked with laughter—which doubtless was part relief—then I opened our kit and poured out a small handful of cascara tablets. Martin explained carefully to the gaping native that he was to take part of them when the sun went down and the other part when the sun came up. The native listened with apparent intentness to the end of the instructions, then opened his slobbery mouth and downed all the tablets at one gulp.

During this little comedy, several more men had slipped quietly out of the bush—I think I counted ten in all—each as horrible in appearance as their advance man with the stomachache, and each apparently as harmless. Martin lost no time in setting up his camera—which they dismissed after a casual inspection—and exposed perhaps a hundred and fifty feet of film. I could see he was measuring it carefully.

The natives were carrying on what to me was an unintelligible jabber. Our carriers began to show signs of nervousness and to edge toward the boat. Martin understood a little Bêche-de-Mer and, with an air of complete casualness as he busied himself with the camera, told me what was up.

"They're saying that their chief is back there in the bush. He's been watching our boat as we came around to the bay—"

"You mean—the big chief—the Big Nambas' chief, Nag—"

Martin stopped me with a sharp gesture. "Don't speak his name," he cautioned. "Play dumb."

"But—if we could get him in the camera! Oh, Martin—if we could!"

"It would be worth the whole trip."

I saw how terribly he wanted to plunge into the bush with his camera but that he was afraid because of me.

"I'll take some trade stuff and go ahead," I said as casually as I could. "I'm not afraid of these old natives and their stomachaches." I began gathering up some tobacco and calico. "Just a lot of big bluffs." I started toward the trail.

"Wait, Osa! I can't risk it. Not with you. I'll come back tomorrow."

I kept right on going.

"All right then, wait," he shouted after me. "I'll get one of these men to lead the way."

Organized at length, with one of the Big Namba men acting as guide and our three carriers bringing up the rear with tripods, film, still cameras, and the bulk of the trade stuff, we plunged into the jungle.

After the glare of the beach I seemed suddenly blind, and slid and stumbled along a dark trail that was treacherous with hidden, muddy streams and wet creepers. The heavy, steaming breath of the swamps pressed down on us with the weight of something dead, and in it was the ominous smell of rot and slime. Then we started to climb. Suddenly we were in the hot glare of the sun once more, and the slope was sharp and covered with brush and tough cane. We climbed for what seemed hours. A pulse beat hard in the roof of my mouth, my breath was like a knife in my chest, and perspiration dripped from my hands.

"Tough going, Osa," Martin said several times. He was just behind me, and I could hear him breathing hard.

I nodded but didn't speak; I didn't know what my voice would sound like. Then, abruptly, we came on a clearing, a sort of plateau, where our guide stopped us as if waiting for something.

I began to look about me. Far below—we must have climbed at least a thousand feet—I saw the yellow strip of beach and our whaleboat, a mere dot at the edge of the water.

Off across a sort of chasm I saw thin columns of smoke. Martin had drawn close and put his arm about me.

"You're a grand little sport," he said. "That climb was tough."

I couldn't say anything, I was so proud. Martin followed the direction of my gaze.

"Making stews of their enemies over there, what?" he said jokingly.

Just then there was a shuffling sound and we turned. A score of natives carrying guns had moved in behind us. I saw Martin's face tighten.

"Don't let them see you're afraid, Osa," he said quietly but firmly. "Leave the trade stuff on the ground and ease down the trail. I'll attract their attention with the camera, and that'll give you a good start."

I turned to obey, but the trail was cut off. By now, there must have been a hundred armed natives in the clearing. From somewhere off in the bush came the low pulsing beat of the boo-boos. I glanced at our three carriers. They had stooped to pick up our goods and were fixed in attitudes of terror. There was neither movement nor sound until a swift-flying parrot—a raucous blade of color and noise—slashed across the clearing.

Then all heads turned, and there on the edge of the bush stood a figure so frightful as to be magnificent. His face, like those of the rest of the natives, was framed in a mass of greasy black hair and beard. A bone was thrust through the cartilage of his nose. He wore the large pandanus fiber clout, but there was a difference in his bearing—the difference of a man of conscious power. There was power in his height, in the muscles that rippled under his glossy black skin, in his great shoulders, in the line of the jaw. Two furrows, amazingly deep, lay between his brows, and his eyes showed intelligence, strong will, and cunning. Here was a chief by every right of physical and mental superiority. Here, I knew, was Nagapate.

He stared at us speculatively and moved slowly toward us. His men drew back slightly as he advanced. To my astonishment, at this moment, I heard the purr of the camera-crank. Martin was photographing the chief's entrance.

"Remember, darling," his voice was low and quiet, "show no fear—smile—open up the trade stuff."

I shaped my face into what I hoped would pass for a friendly smile. Nagapate was coming straight toward me—was now within three feet.

"Hello, Mr. Nagapate," I said, and held some tobacco out to him. He barely glanced at it.

"Try some calico," Martin said. "Keep it up, sweet, you're doing fine. If we win the chief over, everything will be all right. The others will take their cue from him."

"Yes. Yes, I know," I said. "I'll try. I'll do my best."

I saw four rings on Nagapate's hands, one a signet ring with a distinct crest. I felt a shudder creeping up my spine and wondered whether he removed the rings from the fingers of his victims before or after he cooked them.

"Try that piece of red calico," Martin urged, and I clung to the sound of his voice as to the one sane thing left in a world gone grotesquely mad.

"This is a very nice piece of calico," I said loudly and distinctly, holding out the bright cloth to Nagapate. "A very nice color. You would be very handsome in it. It would make a very nice shirt, I think."

Nagapate reached out, but instead of the calico he took my arm. His great hand felt like dry leather,

Martin's quiet voice cut through my terror. "Don't be afraid, Osa. He's just curious, that's all."

Curious! Apparently the whiteness of my skin puzzled the big black man. With gutteral grunts he first tried rubbing it off with his finger. This failing, he picked up a bit of rough cane and scraped my skin with it and was astonished, apparently, when it turned pink. Shaking his head, he then took off my hat and looked at my hair. It was yellow, and I suppose this puzzled him. He parted it and peered down at my scalp, then he pulled it hard. Finally he turned me around, tilted my head forward, and looked at the back of my neck.

"Try to get him interested in the trade stuff, darling. Put it in his hands." Martin's voice shook a little. I looked at him. The film continued to purr through the camera. He was turning the crank automatically.

I got some tobacco and pushed it into Nagapate's hands. He looked at it, then dropped it. I saw Martin rapidly remove the camera from the tripod.

"He won't take it, Martin! What shall I do?"

"Keep cool, darling—and whatever you do, keep smiling."

My husband then stepped between Nagapate and me, and, forcing a grin, clasped the chief's hand and gave it a hearty shake. This puzzled the black czar. Apparently the gesture was new to him. He didn't like it, and scowled.

Returning look for look with the regal chief, Martin spoke casually to me. "Get on down that trail with the carriers, Osa. I'll follow. Do as I tell you, and hurry."

Nagapate was not to be diverted, however, and caught me as I turned away. He took my hand and shook it just as Martin had shaken his. My relief was so great at what seemingly had turned into a friendly leave-taking that I laughed and heartily returned the shake. This may have been a mistake. At any rate, when I tried to withdraw my hand, he closed his fist hard upon it, and then began experimentally to pinch and prod my body. I choked back a scream and looked wildly toward Martin. His face was bloodless, and fixed in a wooden smile.

Then, unexpectedly, I was released. Nagapate grunted an order and his men retreated into the bush. Apparently we had won. Martin sharply ordered the carriers to shoulder the apparatus and we dashed for the trail. Whether Nagapate then changed his mind, or whether releasing us and then recapturing us was a sort of cat-and-mouse game with him, I never knew, but suddenly there was a sharper accent in the beat of the boo-boos, our carriers with the apparatus fled at top speed down the trail, and I found myself seized from behind. This time I abandoned all pretense at bravery and screamed my terror. On almost the same instant I heard Martin's voice shouting at me desperately to remember the pistol in my pocket, and then shouting at the natives to release him. I saw that he also had been seized.

"Martin!" I cried. A native raked his back with a thornbush branch. I turned sick and faint and knew vaguely that I was being dragged backward toward the bush. I screamed again and again. I am no clearer on what happened next than a per-

son is clear on the seeming happenings of a nightmare. I only
know that the natives were suddenly quiet and staring down
toward the bay. The boo-boos were still, and Nagapate stepped
once more into the clearing. I followed the direction of his
scowling gaze and saw what had silenced them. A British patrol boat was steaming into the bay.

Martin tore from his captors and faced Nagapate.

"Man-o'-war—man-o'-war—man-o'-war!" he shouted, threat-
eningly, and his gestures indicated that the patrol boat had come
on our behalf.

Nagapate scowled at Martin, only half believing him, but
my husband held his ground, and reluctantly Nagapate grunted
an order for our release. Then he withdrew with his men into
the bush.

With a sob of relief I started on a run toward the trail, but
Martin caught me and held me to a quiet walk until we were
well out of sight of that fringe of bush where we knew Nagapate and his men were. Then began our race down the steep
path.

Cane-grass chopped at our faces. We fell and scrambled up
again more times than I could count. In places there were sheer
drops to the jungle below of hundreds of feet, but we never
slackened for an instant. We both knew, without even speaking of it, that should the gunboat leave the bay, our recapture
was certain. To reach our whaleboat before that could happen
was our only hope.

After what seemed hours, we came to a clearing above the
bay and there saw the patrol boat slowly turning and steaming
away! Then once more came the sound of the boo-boos. Nagapate and his men up on the plateau were also witnessing the
departure of the gunboat, and without a doubt the boo-boos
were the signal for our recapture.

Neither Martin nor I spoke. Dense jungle still lay between
us and the beach. We plunged on, the increasingly rapid beat
of the boo-boos driving us recklessly over the slimy, treacherous trail. Brush tore at our clothing and flesh, but we felt nothing, stopped for nothing. Other than my terror I was aware of
but one thing, and that an intolerable thirst. Once I fell in the
mud and slime of a morass, but more serious than this was the

fact that we had lost our way. Martin pulled me out and held
me close, slime and all.

My fall probably saved us, for instead of plunging farther
from the trail in our panic, we stood a moment where we were
and, looking around us, discovered the trail only a few feet off.
We plunged into it, and I led the way this time because my
eyes were sharper than Martin's.

Added to the terrifying sound of the boo-boos now were the
shouts of our pursuers. They couldn't have been more than a
quarter of a mile behind us. Neither of us spoke. We just ran,
with branches and vines like enemy hands clutching at us, but
at last the jungle thinned. A few more steps and we were at
the beach. They were now so close behind us that we could
hear the slap of heavy, sodden leaves on their bare flesh.

The glare of the sun was almost a physical impact after the
deep gloom of the jungle, and the thick sand clogged our feet.
Martin took my arm, and I felt his hand shake. Then our carriers ran forward to help us. Soon we felt hard-packed sand
under our feet, then shallow water, and next, with the hands
of our Vao crew reaching out to us, we were dragged across
the gunwales of the whaleboat. I raised my head and looked
back. Nagapate's men were just emerging from the bush. I
collapsed in the bottom of the boat, and one of our men
put water to my mouth which I scarcely had the strength to
drink. How long Martin and I lay there I don't know, but we
were safely out at sea when again we lifted our heads. It was
night.

The tropical storm through which we then fought is another story. It is enough to say that when the hard, cool rain
first swept down on us, I raised my face and hands to it and
let it wash off the jungle slime, while Martin, whose exhaus-
tion was no less than mine—for he had had to carry the heavy
camera and film during our headlong flight—got to his feet
and went to work, glad of the skill he had acquired in handling
the *Snark*. My usefulness in what was doubtless a hazardous
trip began and ended in bailing our small open boat and protecting our camera and film as best I could. Reaching Vao,
finally, we were gratified to find that we—including our carriers—had clung doggedly to every piece of apparatus and even

most of the trade goods, and that the camera and film were
unharmed by water.

We had been back at Vao only a few days when the British
patrol boat, the *Euphrosyne*, put in with a letter for Martin from
the resident commissioner for the New Hebrides. It read:

Matanovot, 10th November, 1917

Dear Sir:

I have been endeavoring to find you with a view to warning
you against carrying out what I understand to be your intentions. I am told that you have decided to penetrate into
the interior of this island with a view to coming in contact
with the people known as the "Big Nambas." Such a pro-
ceeding cannot but be attended with great risk to yourself
and all those who accompany you. The whole interior of
this island of Malekula is, and has been for a considerable
time, in a very disturbed condition, and it has been necessary in consequence to make two armed demonstrations in
the "Big Namba" country in the last three years. For these
reasons, on the part of the Joint Administration of this group,
I request that you will not proceed further with this idea,
and hereby formally warn you against such persistence, for
the consequences of which the Administration cannot hold
itself responsible.

Yours faithfully,
(signed) M. King
H.B.M. Resident Commissioner
for the New Hebrides.
In any case I trust you will not take your wife into the danger zone with you.

M.K.

At no time since Martin and I started on our adventures
together can I remember anything to exceed the anxiety we
felt over our exposed film. Those round, flat tins of a thousand
feet each held our future. While Martin was a fine camera artist, this was his first real attempt at professional motion-picture

photography. Our camera and film both had been subjected to heat and humidity far beyond normal conditions. Light in the tropics offered problems not found in the temperate zones, and what we had—or didn't have—we couldn't possibly know. To wait until we were back in the States would have prolonged the agony, and whether the gelatin had been affected by the excessive moisture and heat was something else that had to be determined as quickly as possible.

It was our good luck, on arriving at Sydney, to hear of Ernie Higgins. He had an excellent laboratory, we were told, and knew film developing. More than this, he proved to be a charming person and a careful workman. Martin had done better than he knew in photographing the natives of Malekula, and in a few short months Nagapate's scowling face was looking from the movie screen on Broadway, and within a year had sent shudders around the civilized world.

We leased the film to Robertson-Cole, and to S. L. Rothafel, one of Broadway's great showmen, familiarly known as Roxy, who gave it an opening in his Rivoli Theater. Reminiscent of those days before we embarked for the South Seas was Martin lecturing once more. Our old friends, Chic and Marie Sale, came to the Rivoli, and Chic said dryly that he too was glad Martin had something new to spout about. Mama and Papa and Grandma as well as Mr. and Mrs. Johnson and Freda, came on from Kansas, and Martin and I told each other more than once that it was indeed good to be alive!

Martin insisted that I was just as important to these pictures as he was, and more so, since I appeared in most of them with Nagapate. So there was nothing for it but that I must be up on the stage with him. I wore a pink dress and a garden hat and carried a rare parrot given me when we left Sydney.

The distribution of pictures in those days was not as quickly or efficiently accomplished as now, with the result that money was slow coming in. But we enjoyed ourselves immensely. Robertson-Cole held a dinner for us before we left New York, with Houdini acting as master of ceremonies. Then there were visits to our families in Kansas, and finally we arrived in Los Angeles where we were met by our old friends Mr. and Mrs. Bray, along with reporters. Our time in California was spent—

how else but?—seeing how movies were made. Charlie Chaplin showed us his studio, and we spent the afternoon with Douglas Fairbanks. And we showed our film twice at Grauman's Theatre.

Then we proceeded to San Francisco, where we appeared at theaters, visited with Charmian London, and, finally, on April 8, 1919, set sail again for the South Seas. This time we were better prepared—our equipment even included a laboratory, for Martin's plan was to make a complete record of Nagapate and his tribe. And for our own safety, when the natives of Malekula saw us again, it would be with armed men at our backs.

A gun may seem unsuited to Osa's light summer dress, but that obviously did not affect her aim.

In this low-roofed *gobong*, Osa ascends the Kinabatangan River in North Borneo.

Osa's solution to Martin's back problems, a comfortable, homelike houseboat

Her ability to pick up languages and her genuine interest in people won Osa friends wherever she and Martin went. She is seen with Tenggerese people.

Above: Sharing a joke with a cigar-smoking woman. Left: Watching a blow gun demonstration

Osa drinks from a Borean liana, sometimes referred to as a water vine.

Visiting a longhouse, North Borneo

Osa and friends

Right: Bessie, an orangutan
Below: Sun-bear cub

Juvenile pig-tailed macaques

Kalowatt, a gray gibbon
youngster

Martin and Osa on shipboard, en route to America, leaving Malaya, Ceylon, India, Africa, and England in their wake

Chapter 11 _____

Martin was a man of dreams, and of the will and vision to make his dreams come true. When next we debarked at Sydney, we had equipment with us that made our hearts proud. Sixty-five trunks, crates, and boxes, to be exact, as against the few trunks and suitcases that had accompanied us on our first trip.

Ernie Higgins met us at the boat and insisted that we be his guests while we waited for the S.S. *Pacifique,* the island streamer on which we were to return to the New Hebrides. We had a wait of several weeks, during which Martin and Ernie checked our camera equipment and I ransacked secondhand stores for coats, vests, and hats to present to the natives. Trousers, I was told, were a useless garment in their eyes.

Very important to our plan of making a complete film record of the Big Nambas was projecting the pictures we had taken of them on our previous trip. We wanted to observe their reaction to motion pictures, and we were certain this would also inspire their respect and awe.

Finally, on the eighteenth of June, we were aboard the *Pacifique,* a small craft of less than two hundred tons, and on our way. We grew very fond of this ship. She had comfortable beds instead of the usual hard bunks, and the coffee was excellent.

We put in at Nouméa, on the island of New Caledonia, for a week and then proceeded to Vila. Vila is a typical South Seas town and, as the capital of the New Hebrides, is the metropolis for the white people of the thirty islands of this group.

I was more than pleased to run across Father Prin. Thinner

and frailer than ever, he had finally resigned his difficult post
at Vao and come to Vila to spend the rest of his too-few days.
When we told him we were going back to Malekula, he shook
his head and again warned us. "Big Nambas plenty bad," he
said in Bêche-de-Mer.

We bought nearly a thousand dollars' worth of food supplies
and trade goods here but could get neither a schooner nor a
native craft to take us on our voyage to Malekula. There was
nothing to do but go on to the island of Espíritu Santo, two
hundred miles to the north.

The ship stopped at the little port of Epi to leave mail and
supplies and to take on copra. Leaning on the rail, we were
watching the activity in the harbor when Martin straightened
suddenly. His face was drawn and tense. I followed the direction of his gaze, but all I saw was a small, dirty recruiting ship,
swarming with greasy blacks. The paint had once been white
under all that filth, and her lines were beautiful. Suddenly my
breath caught in my throat.

"Not the *Snark*!" I said.

She was a pitiable sight. They could not alter her trim lines,
but her metal, her paint, her rigging had been shamefully neglected and ill-treated. Frowzy and unbelievably dirty, she reminded me somehow of an aristocrat fallen upon evil days. I
looked up at Martin. He shook his head.

"I'm glad Jack and Charmian never saw her that way," he
said, swallowing hard.

Off southeastern Santo we met with good fortune—we were
able to make arrangements for three schooners to accompany
us to Malekula. Mr. Thomas, of Hog Island, and Mr. Perrole,
an experienced French recruiter, each agreed to send a schooner
to Vao within a week. A third schooner was chartered from a
young Frenchman, Paul Mazouyer, one of the most picturesque, happy-go-lucky daredevils I've ever met. He was like
something out of a novel. Huge and powerful, he was the match
of three ordinary men and took chances no other recruiter would
dream of.

The captain of the *Pacifique* graciously sailed fifty miles out
of his course and landed us on the beach of Vao. While we
knew our three schooners would be along in a few days, I was

as lonely and desolate at that moment as I've ever been in my life, and so was Martin.

The coming of the *Pacifique* had attracted scores of jabbering, naked natives, and when the ship sailed away, there we were—just Martin and I—sitting alone in the midst of our trunks, crates, and boxes, the only white people, and surrounding us in ever-increasing numbers a horde of the fantastic Vao black men with bones through their noses. We admitted to each other that everything had a different look with Father Prin gone.

"Well," Martin said, "even if I'm not in a cage, I'll always know how a monkey feels."

"How do you suppose we could get them to quit staring and lift this stuff off the beach?" I asked.

"The good old tobacco." Martin grinned a little tiredly. I could see he was worrying again at having brought me along.

The tobacco worked. Not only did the natives carry all our trunks and boxes up off the beach, but, under Martin's direction, they repaired the little mud house abandoned by Father Prin. In an amazingly short time we had everything safe from the weather in a shipshape, three-room dwelling. I had learned a lot from our first trip and had included many comforts and some luxuries in our equipment.

We had air cushions and mattresses, and, with an eye to giving Martin some good, wholesome food, I had brought a clear-flamed Primus stove. Bacon, hams, cheeses and other good things filled our chop boxes, and I settled down to make my home in what is considered one of the wildest lands of the world.

Vao is not more than two miles in diameter and is inhabited by about four hundred natives, most of them refugees from Malekula that were vanquished in battle. Not long after our arrival, twenty of the Small Namba men, headed by a powerful savage named Tethlong, arrived from Malekula. The rest of his tribe had been killed, and the women and children taken captive. Tethlong and his men were welcomed by the natives of Vao as an addition to their fighting force. This wily heathen decided to set himself up as headman on Vao, so he sent his men to neighboring islands to buy up pigs and chickens and invited the entire population to a grand feast. It turned out to be a celebration never before equaled on the island. They sang, they danced, they beat on their boo-boos until exhausted, and seven hundred and twenty pigs were consumed. This went on for five days.

I could see that Martin was afraid of the consequences of this orgy, afraid on my behalf. I told him that I thought the time he was spending watching for our schooners to come might better be spent winning Tethlong's confidence—bribing it, rather, with trade stuff—and getting some pictures of the feast. Tethlong proved entirely agreeable to being bribed. Martin secured some fine pictures, and the next few days proved this tactical move to have been a wise one, for Tethlong was made chief of the Vao natives.

There was a lull following this feast. Still there was no sign of our schooners. Martin worked feverishly, installing his laboratory in one of our three rooms, while I set about finding a native whom I could train as a servant among the dozen or so hanging around begging tobacco. Among these was one who claimed to be convert of Father Prin. His name, he said, was Atree. I had worked hard at learning Bêche-de-Mer, the accepted language of the South Seas. Atree spoke it quite well, but my efforts at training this young man had their ludicrous as well as maddening moments.

I asked him on one occasion to heat an iron for me, and, after waiting for the greater part of the morning, I found he had put it in a pot and was gravely watching it boil. Again, I cured a sore on his leg with a little ointment. A few days later he brought me the medical kit and, pointing to his left eye, which was swollen nearly shut, said, "Me gotem sore leg along eye-eye!"

There is something fascinating about this queer, garbled English, so much so that Martin and I often spoke it even when no natives were around. I discovered, too, that it was habit-forming, for I found myself actually thinking in this peculiar patois of the tropics.

Martin put his new laboratory to the test by developing the still pictures he had taken of Tethlong's feast, and it was a distinct success. I planted a vegetable garden, made Saturday my baking day and Monday my wash day, cooked bigger meals than either of us could eat—and watched for our schooners. Martin, trying to reassure me, said that nothing kept a schedule in this part of the world, but I could see his anxiety also growing. From the day that Tethlong took command of the Vao natives there had been an increasing friendliness with the bushmen of Malekula. Every night the Vao canoes crossed to the larger island and returned with fifteen or twenty Malekulans in each load, and every night we heard the persistent beat of the boo-boos. This, together with the changeless minor note of the natives' monotonous chant, became almost unendurable.

After dinner one hot evening, Martin and I went down to the beach. It was one of the most beautiful nights I had ever known. The reflections of a full moon were on the water, the stars of the Southern Cross were bright in a velvety sky, and the sea purred heavily as it stretched itself along the beach. The air had a bloom-like softness. We were idly watching the luminous trail of phosphorus marking the course of a shark when we heard the soft swish of canoe paddles. Martin drew me into the shadows of a cluster of palm. The canoe beached at the pathway leading to the village, and we saw the natives lift from it a long, heavy object wrapped in leaves. It took some six of them to carry it. Instead of the usual chatter, they were silent, and moved quickly and stealthily from view. Whether or not they saw us there on the beach we didn't know, but obviously they wanted to keep secret whatever it was they were doing.

We crept back to the house, where Martin handed me an automatic. Already the boo-boos were beating their horrible cadence, the natives beginning their weird chant. Martin sat with a rifle across his knees. The tropical night had lost its beauty and was filled with a grisly menace. We did not sleep that night nor until the boo-boos stopped, near morning. When we awoke, much later than our usual hour, we saw Paul Mazouyer's schooner anchored not a hundred feet away. I can't think when Martin and I had ever been happier.

While the men were loading our apparatus aboard, I questioned Atree, and blandly and with relish he confirmed our suspicions. The long bundle had been a man, and the noises those of a cannibalistic orgy.

Once aboard Paul's sturdy schooner with his eight well-dis-

ciplined and well-armed men, and with our fine equipment all
ready for use, I looked at Martin and drew a deep, long sigh of
relief. Both tide and wind were with us. Soon we were sailing
into Tanemarou Bay, and there, to our complete delight, we
were met by our other two schooners.

Before us lay the same broad, sandy beach across which we
had dashed into the surf, tattered, bleeding, and exhausted, to
escape Nagapate's natives. Martin stared off toward it and
pressed my hand. He too was living that scene of terror again.
After a minute he turned his head and winked.

"We've got a couple of surprises up our sleeve for the old
boy this time, haven't we?" he said.

This time we were landing under entirely different circumstances. Three white men—Mr. Perrole, Mr. Thomas, and
Martin—a local named Stephens, twenty-six trustworthy and
experienced natives, and I formed our party.

Paul was impatient to get ashore, so Martin and I stepped
into his boat and we rowed to the beach, followed by the small
boats from the other schooners. To our astonishment, some
twenty of the Big Namba natives emerged from the bush and
came down to the beach to meet us. At their head was none
other than Nagapate.

Oddly enough, Nagapate was now a screen personality to
me rather than a native, and somehow I had lost my terror of
him. Martin told me afterwards that he felt exactly as I did,
and we both dashed forward to shake his hand. The cannibal
chief seemed puzzled at first, but he could see we held no
grudge for his apparent culinary intentions on our first visit
and became almost genial.

Paul, wise in the ways of natives, and knowing Nagapate's
reputation for savagery, was amazed at his good nature, and
thought it wise to bide our time and encourage it. He had been
doubtful whether Martin would ever succeed in his ambition
to secure a complete motion-picture record of the tribe, but he
was now as eager and hopeful as we were that this could be
accomplished.

After a little, Nagapate came and stood beside me on the
beach and pointed toward our schooners. He went through this
motion several times, patting his chest and pointing. I made

out finally that he actually wanted to go aboard. And on my invitation the black chief stepped quickly with two of his men into our rowboat. It was an astonishing thing for Nagapate to do, inasmuch as he had reason to believe the white men fully as cruel as we thought him, Nagapate, to be, and yet he had put himself completely in our power.

Aboard ship, I fed him and his two men some hardtack and trade salmon. While they had never tasted either, they accepted it very casually. They were casual about everything. Martin said this was a studied attitude and, with a grin, got some photographs he had made of the big chief. When Nagapate saw himself, he started incredulously and showed it to his two men. Then all three let out blood-curdling yells. Martin next spread before the black king a life-size colored poster of himself. Nagapate and his men were awed into a silence that lasted for fully an hour in which they'd alternately touch the picture and then settle back on their heels to stare at it.

Their eyes apparently grew tired with all this staring. After a while they began to blink and look away. Martin now brought my ukulele.

"Let's try a little Hawaiian music on the old softie," he said.

He brushed my cheek with a kiss, and I saw how happy he was. In all our long months of earning enough money and getting our equipment together for this expedition, we had always thought of Nagapate—the "holy terror"—as the greatest obstacle to our success. We had brought armed men, and here, on the deck of our schooner, within three feet of us, blinking and content sat Nagapate, with no more violence in him apparently than might be found in an old, fat toad.

The kiss Martin had put on my cheek proved rather mystifying to the cannibal king. He grunted and wagged his head from side to side, then jabbered to his two men about it.

Martin and I hid our smiles. I strummed the ukulele a minute, tuning it, then began to sing "Aloha."

Nagapate gaped at me, his head first on one side, then on the other. His men did the same. This became a rhythmic motion. Then, to my astonishment, Nagapate's mouth opened and out came a tribal chant timed perfectly to the song I was singing. His men, always cuing themselves to him, took it up. Out the corner of my eye I caught a glimpse of Paul, his eyes literally popping.

Still playing the ukulele, I stopped my song, the better to hear Nagapate's. His face was alight, his eyes closed, and he swayed from side to side. Suddenly he became aware of his own voice and stopped singing in embarrassment. Arranging his features quickly in the dignified scowl now familiar to people the world over, he indicated abruptly that he wished to leave. We piled his arms with tobacco, calico, knives, and a top hat—all of which he accepted with scarcely a glance at it, then allowed himself and his men to be rowed back to shore.

Plainly the cannibal king was applying some self-administered kicks for having momentarily lost his dignity.

Early the next morning a score of natives appeared on the beach, yelling and waving their arms. Paul and Martin went ashore. When they returned to the ship they said my presence was required. Nagapate had sent yams, coconuts, and wild fruit, not to Martin or the men but to me. It was unbelievable. Here, as is the case with nearly all primitive people, a woman does not count in the scheme of things except as a slave, to do the work of the village and bear the children, and this with kicks and abuse for reward.

Paul was plainly confounded by the whole thing, and I was doubtful until Nagapate's men laid the offerings of their chief at my feet.

"I suppose he figured it out," Paul said, "that because we all treat you with respect, that's how it is with white people—that our women hold some sort of position black people don't know about."

Martin laughed. "No, it's simpler than that. The old boy can see that Osa's the boss of the expedition, and that is his way of opening diplomatic relations."

Paul, Perrole, and Stephens agreed with Martin and me that the sooner we could show Nagapate and his people the motion pictures we had taken of them on our first trip, the quicker we would have them awed into an acquiescent mood that would permit us to move on up into the village and really settle down to the purpose of our expedition. To attract as many of them to the beach as possible, we spread out our trade stuff. Martin set up his cameras, and we began to take pictures. By dusk it seemed to me that we must have had the larger part of the male population on the beach. Nagapate himself didn't come until almost last. Apparently, after that slip in which he yielded to the temptation to sing with me, he had felt the need of re-trieving his diginity.

Rapidly, now, Martin worked to set up the screen and pro-jection machine. Nagapate and his men seemed to think that with night coming they might as well get back to their village. To hold them became a problem. I played the ukulele, distrib-uted more trade stuff, jabbered to Nagapate in my poor Bêche-de-Mer.

"For goodness' sake, Martin," I cried out finally. "It's dark enough, isn't it? Why don't you start the picture?"

"Because I can't!" he shouted back. "The damned genera-tor won't work!"

He was sick with disappointment, and so was I. The gen-erator of necessity was run by manpower, with two of our men on each side turning the handles. For what seemed hours Mar-tin drove them frantically in relays without the faintest glow from the lights.

The natives showed not the slightest curiosity about the machinery or the screen. Nagapate grew suspicious of my ob-vious efforts at detaining him on the beach. The men contin-ued to grind the generator. It was no use. Martin wiped his forehead, shook his head, and signaled them to stop turning. Misunderstanding the gesture, the men doubled their efforts, the generator spun, and the miracle happened! The lights flashed on!

The bright beam of light shot through the darkness with such suddenness and sharpness that the natives grunted and drew back.

With no means of knowing how these people would react when the pictures appeared, Paul had placed armed guards around the projector, and because of this it now became a problem to get the natives to face the screen. Plainly they didn't want the guards and the machine that shot light at their backs.

There seemed only one thing to do. I took Nagapate by the arm and, with as imperious a manner as I could summon, sat

on the ground facing the screen and indicated that I expected
him to do likewise. Clearly he didn't like being pushed around
by a woman, but he sat down beside me, apparently to think it
over. The rest of the natives, trained to do whatever their chief
did, followed suit. At last we were ready for the show to begin.

Through the titles the natives divided their attention between the screen and the shafts of light over their heads. They
looked from one to the other, chattering like mad, until my
picture faded in on the screen. Their chatter stopped short.
They were literally struck dumb. Here I was on the beach, sitting beside Nagapate—and there I was on the screen, as big
as a giant. Then the picture of me winked at them. This threw
them into a furor. They shrieked with laughter. They howled
and screamed.

They were silent again as they saw Martin and me leaving
the Waldorf-Astoria, and the silence deepened when they saw
the mad throngs of New York on Armistice Day; glimpses of the
great metropolitan centers of the world; flashes of steamers,
racing automobiles and airplanes. Where we expected excitement, there was an uncomprehending silence.

Only once did Nagapate stir, and that was during the pictures of Armistice Day. This troubled him, and he said afterwards he didn't know there were so many white people in the
world. He added that we must live on a pretty large island.

Martin wanted to get a picture of the natives as they saw
themselves on the screen. So he showed Paul how to crank the
projector, and Perrole and Stephens the flares. Then he focused his camera on our strange audience.

After a hundred feet of titles, Nagapate's face loomed before
the natives. Again a great roar went up. Over and over they
yelled, "Nagapate—Nagapate—Nagapate." Martin gave the
signal for the radium flares. They went off, a bomb of light,
and I caught a glimpse of Martin's elated grin as he cranked
the camera and recorded the mingled fear and amazement on
the faces of the people.

Some two thirds of the natives, terrified by the flares,
scrambled for the bush. I touched Nagapate's arm and gave
him my most reassuring and nonchalant smile. This sort of
business, I indicated, was an everyday occurence in the lives

of white people. Nagapate wavered for an instant, then sat back on his haunches again, setting the example for his people.

The flares lasted only about two minutes, and, after we had gradually coaxed the runaways back to their places, we started the reel all over again.

Practically every native shown in the picture was in the audience. As each man appeared on the screen, the audience shrieked his name and roared with laughter. They had not changed a bit except perhaps to add another layer of dirt. Suddenly the roar became a hushed murmur as the figure of a man who had been dead for a year was shown. The natives were awe-struck. Martin's "magic" had brought a dead man from his grave.

After this we felt a definite change in the attitude of the Big Namba people toward us. No longer was there a feeling of treachery or defiance. Instead, they gathered around quietly and respectfully. It was apparent, however, that they were waiting for something else to happen. Inquiry revealed they wanted tobacco as pay for looking at the pictures. As I handed out the sticks, each one grunted the same phrase. I tried to learn what it was, but I never did.

At last everything was packed. We were ready to return to the schooner and about to leave when a native came running down the beach waving his arms and yelling at us. He had come back with a message which said: "Nagapate, he big fellow master belong Big Namba. He, he wantem you, you two fellow, you lookem Mary belong him. He makem big fellow sing-sing. More good you, you two fellow come. He no makem bad, he makem good altogether."

All of which was meant as an invitation from Nagapate to visit his village, and the assurance that we would not be used as the main dish of a savage feast.

Martin hid his elation and said, "We'd love to come."

Chapter 12 _____

Early the next morning we were once more on our way into the Big Namba territory. Martin pressed my hand. We were both thinking of that other time. Today there were thirty-one of us. Four white men, twenty-six trustworthy natives, and myself, all armed with repeating rifles and automatic pistols. We anticipated no trouble, although our natives were skeptical of the worth of our optimism and plainly frightened by these notorious cannibals. Our carriers held back when we reached the beach. They feared ambush in the jungle.

We finally persuaded them to continue, and, equipped with photographic apparatus, trade stuffs, and food for seven or eight days, we plunged up the trail.

At noon we reached a clearing, high up on the island. From here we could see miles of jungle valleys and grass-covered plateaus. Far below in the bay were three small dots—our boats.

As we rested we heard a shout, and out of the jungle came some twenty men sent by the "big fellow master belong Big Namba." They took our equipment, and about a mile farther on we came to a village—nothing more than a few roughly thatched shelters around a clearing. In the center sat some thirty well-armed natives. We greeted them, but they merely grunted.

After a short rest we pushed on, and in fifteen minutes or so came upon another clearing, much larger and with many more huts. Here again were natives—more than two hundred, all armed. They squatted and eyed us in scowling silence. In the center were the boo-boos, the upright hollow log used to send messages and to furnish the rhythm for dances. One was lying on its side, and we whites sat on it for all the world like five schoolchildren.

One native beat on a particularly loud boo-boo, maintaining an irregular cadence that was undoubtedly a code. Were they summoning the natives for a feast? I moved closed to Martin, who patted my knee reassuringly.

The boo-boo stopped abruptly. There was a hush, and from the far side of the clearing stepped the huge figure of Naga-pate.

He stood for a moment looking over his audience, then he moved slowly to the center of the clearing. No Hollywood director ever staged a more dramatic entrance. He roared an order. A native rushed a block of wood as a throne. The chief sat down facing us. We shook hands with him. Having become familiar with this form of greeting he responded graciously, then grunted another command. In response, a native came forward with a large bamboo water bottle. Nagapate gulped down a great swallow, and then the black offered it to me, tilting it at a drinking angle.

I hesitated. The very thought of putting my mouth to the same vessel made me almost ill. It was obvious that this community water bottle was a sort of South Seas "pipe-of-peace."

Concealing my distaste, I took a sip. The others did the same.

With a great flourish, Martin then presented Nagapate with the usual trade goods and distributed two sticks of tobacco to each native. They greedily smoked or ate it at once.

The formalities seemed to be over, so Martin set up his cameras and for three hours took pictures.

I could see he wanted something he wasn't getting.

"You're doing fine, Martin," I called out to him. "What are you frowning about?"

"I'd like to get some action in this thing," he said. "Can't you do something about it?"

"Absolutely," I answered promptly. "How about a man coming out of a house?"

"Fine!" he agreed heartily.

The openings to the huts were so small the occupants could only get in and out on hands and knees. I finally persuaded one man to enter his house and come out again. Nagapate laughed and the other natives took it up, jeering the fellow out of giving us any more action. The rest were too self-concious by now to give us any.

"I'll go in and out for you, Martin," I said. "We'll let them laugh at me for a while."

I took this opportunity to study the houses. They consisted, I found, of merely a few poles covered with leaves and grass. Inside there was nothing but the ashes of fires.

I had been puzzled all along at the complete absence of women and children. It seemed to be wholly a man's world. It wasn't until after we'd been in the village for hours that I saw first one and then another woman peering at us from the edge of the clearing. They were the most miserable creatures I have ever seen. Their clothing consisted of the oddest arrangement imaginable. It was made entirely of grasses. Over the entire head was a sort of widow's veil, solid except for a little peep-hole, and a long train that hung down the back almost to the ground. The dress was a bushy, purple-dyed skirt that reached from the waist to the knees. It was heavy, cumbersome, and unsanitary, and as the women moved about, it gave them the look of animated haystacks.

In addition these strange dresses were matted with dirt, and the wretched creatures themselves were unspeakably filthy. It wasn't their fault, however; bathing for women was taboo. No woman took a bath from the time she was born until she died.

They cowered as we approached, and if we chanced to catch one looking at us, she would squat down and hide her face in her headdress of grass. I tried offering a string of beads and a jar of cheap candy, but the poor, tormented creatures would neither touch our gifts nor look at them. I'm sure that no human creatures were ever so wretched as these daughters of Eve.

Nagapate was said to have a hundred wives, but we saw only ten, and these were fully as wretched as those of lesser station. The scrawny children of the village were as shy as their mothers. The moment we came into sight they scurried off into the bush like frightened rabbits. Most of them were covered with sores, and their bellies ballooned from malnutrition.

For four days we accomplished exactly nothing. The women and children kept under cover, and the men sat around on their haunches and just stared. Nothing we could do aroused either their curiosity or their interest. Once it did look as if there might be a fight between Nagapate's men and a neighboring tribe, but except for a few shots fired in the air nothing came of it.

This minor crisis introduced us, however, to one of Nagapate's important men, a sort of "minister of war" named Rambi. Here was a born exhibitionist if ever I saw one. Shedding every vestige of dignity, he capered, grimaced, and clowned before the camera, almost as if he knew the exact function of that complicated instrument. Soon the other natives forgot their embarrassment and did likewise. I could see that at last Martin felt he was getting something.

It seemed to me that the six or seven days spent in Nagapate's "kingdom" had yielded some fine and authentic scenes of native life, but Martin was far from satisfied. Added to this was the fact that the natives, much like children in temperament, soon tired of the novelty of having us about and seemed distinctly bored with our cameras. They simply would not cooperate, and at times even seemed a little ugly. Another complication was Nagapate's attentions to me. Every morning he laid gifts of wild fruit, coconuts, and yams at the doorway of the hut which Martin and I had made our temporary quarters. He followed me about as I taught games to the small children, and I grew increasingly uneasy. Paul and Martin agreed with me that we'd better start packing up.

Late on the afternoon of the day we came to this decision, Martin and I walked a little way from the village talking over the best method of taking leave of our strange host. We strayed farther than we realized, and came upon a much-traveled path leading to the tiny doorway of an unusually large hut. Always curious, Martin got down on his hands and knees, peered in, and entered. I followed. As my eyes gradually became adjusted to the dim light, I saw what looked like baskets of black grapefruit. I picked one up to examine it more closely and dropped it in horror.

It was a dried human head!

There were dozens piled in baskets. Most grinned at us from the eaves in a macabre frieze. Pendants of skulls dangled from the rafters. Untidy heaps of human bones lay in the corners. I loosed a shuddery groan. Martin clapped his hand over my mouth and dragged me as quickly as possible through the doorway into the open, and here, after one quick look about, he took my arm and hurried me back to the path leading to the village. Whether or not we had been seen entering or leaving the sacred headhouse we couldn't know. If we had—and there might be one or a dozen men and women of the village moving like shadows through the dark bush—our lives and that of every member of our party would pay for it. Paul, Perrole, and Stephens agreed that we must pack up and be off by dawn in the morning. Martin always regretted not being able to get a picture of the headhouse.

"The best pictures," he remarked with a sigh, "like the biggest fish, are the ones you don't get."

Up at dawn the next day, we packed in record time and sent for Nagapate to bid him good-bye. He paraded slowly across the clearing in his usual dramatic fashion. As an excuse for our abrupt departure we made an elaborate explanation of the fact that we had exhausted our provisions and supplies and were forced to return to our boats. What we didn't tell him was that we were afraid one of the poor, timid women or one of their children might have seen us, and that we wanted to get out before they got up the courage enough to speak.

We were surprised when the black chief not only agreed to our departure but volunteered to escort us to the beach. On our arrival he again indicated his wish to go aboard our ship and, once there, squatted down and waited to be fed some hardtack and salmon. When bedtime came, he was still with us and made clear that he wanted to sleep on board. Martin promptly led our royal guest and his bodyguard of two to the engine room. Nagapate seemed to think this was fine. We peeped in on them at midnight, and there they were, stretched out on the oily floor, sound asleep—the greatest compliment, certainly, that the savage chief could have paid us.

Paul sailed us back to Vao, and the other two schooners went their separate ways.

Martin had much to do on our arrival, for he had exposed more than a hundred and fifty plates and nearly two hundred Kodak films. The heat and humidity made it necessary to develop these still photographs at once. A method devised by him before we left New York made it possible to seal the exposed motion-picture negative and keep it safe without developing for several months. Without this, we would have had to return the thousand or so miles to Sydney before our work in this strange part of the world was complete.

I was helping Martin in his hot little darkroom the day after our return from Malekula. He was very thoughtful as he worked.

"What I think we ought to do before we leave here," he said, "is to circle Malekula and put in at different ports and get pictures of the different tribes if we can."

"But you'd need a boat bigger than that whaleboat. Too bad you didn't think of it sooner, and get Paul or Mr. Thomas or maybe Mr. Stephens to take us."

"I did think of it and I asked them, but they all make more money at trading than I can pay them."

I reviewed our procedure to date with considerable regret. "If we'd known Nagapate was going to be so friendly," I said, "we needn't have hired three schooners and spent all that money in a bunch. One schooner and maybe ten armed men would have been enough."

"Yes," Martin said, "and maybe he was friendly because we did have the schooners. Maybe he was impressed."

"But I still don't see how. We're practically marooned here until the British gunboat or something comes along."

"Well, that's what I meant. The *Euphrosyne* will be along sooner or later, and instead of packing everything up and going back to Vila for connections to Sydney right away, I'd like to take only our cameras and trade goods."

"And leave the rest of our stuff here—come back?"

"Yes, keep Vao as our headquarters." Then, hastily, "That is, unless you'd rather not.

"Why, no. No. That's fine."

"We'll be able to make a dicker with some trading boat or other."

I went for a walk to think this over and to rid myself of a touch of homesickness. Every now and then I wanted "home" so terribly. I even found myself longing for a nice, tall, foamy ice-cream soda. The tide was low and I probably went farther along the beach than usual. I was astonished to see a very old man sitting outside his wretched hut just above the tidewater line. Apparently he lived quite alone. Sightless and obviously starving, he was a pitiable object.

Hurrying back to my well-stocked kitchen, I packed some stuff which I felt the old savage could eat in his weakened condition and sent our native boy, Atree, with it. Martin was surprised when I told him of the old man. Old people, as we had been told, and from observation knew, were not permitted to live. The next day, as soon as the tide was low enough, Martin went with me. He wanted a picture of this rare specimen of savagery. I took some foodstuff. Arrived at the miserable hut, we found a freshly dug grave and several natives about.

"He stop along ground," they explained.

We had drawn attention to the old man, unfortunately, and the chiefs, deciding with relentless logic that he had outlived his usefulness, buried him alive, as was their custom. He had been permitted life this long, Atree cheerfully informed us, because he once had been an important chief.

With his laboratory work complete, and the equipment in order, so that we could leave at a moment's notice when a boat did put in at Vao, Martin grew daily more restless.

"Why not take some pictures of the Vao natives while we wait?" I suggested one day.

Martin shrugged. "I can't get up much interest in them— not after the Malekulans. Too tame."

My husband agreed, finally, that perhaps something interesting would develop. Next morning, with Atree as guide, we went into the interior of the little island. There we took pictures of the villages, the huts, the boo-boos. The natives paid very little attention to us. Obviously they resented our presence on their island, but only mildly. We ran across a minor feast, the birth of a boy. Because every event of birth, marriage, or death is celebrated with a feast, pigs play an extremely important part in the lives of these natives. Pigs are wealth with which a man may buy a wife. The number of pigs he has killed on the hunt is the measure of his prowess, and pigs' tusks are the

New Hebrides money. Most natives keep them in a "bokus be-long bell," a European-made box obtained from the traders, in which a bell rings when the lid is raised. The idea must have originated not out of necessity but with some smart trader, for, as Martin loved to tell our friends and business associates back in the States, "these people are uncivilized, therefore they do not steal."

We had started back to our camp "home" when we heard, perhaps a quarter of a mile away, a woman's piercing screams. Pushing as quickly as we could through the thick under-growth, we came upon a scene which for sheer horror I have never seen duplicated.

A young native girl lay writhing on the ground in an agony of pain. Two great holes had been burned in the fleshy parts of her right leg, just above and below the knee.

"One fellow man, him name belong Nowdi, he ketchum plenty coconuts, he ketchum plenty pigs, he ketchum plenty Mary [woman]," Atree explained, completely unmoved.

It seemed that Nowdi had paid a top price of twenty pigs for this girl, but she would not live with him, and four times had run away. Each time she was caught and brought back. The last time she eluded her captor for nearly six months but was caught hiding in the jungle. The chiefs of the village then had passed sentence, and what we had come upon was the result. Four men had held the girl, Atree said, while a fifth placed a white-hot stone in the hollow of her knee, then drew her leg back until the heel touched the thigh. It had been bound there for an hour.

That was the custom, Atree concluded pleasantly, and I re-membered one or more women in every native village we had visited whose leg had been drawn and crippled just as this girl's would be when it was healed.

Only a few moments before, the thong had been cut and the blackened stone, carrying some of the girl's flesh with it, had rolled perhaps a foot away and lay there, still smoking. Jeering, the men jerked the girl to her feet and told her to run away—if she could.

I must have fainted, for I found myself being carried in Martin's arms. Atree was carrying the camera, and we were beyond reach of the tortured girl's screams.

*Chapter 13*_____

It must have been all of a month after our return to Vao. Each day we had waited with steadily decreasing patience for a boat, any boat, to put in there. I was giving Martin his supper when right before my eyes I saw a large schooner steaming into the little harbor.

"Martin! Look!" That's all I could think of to say.

We ran down to the beach, got into our little canoe, and paddled straight out to what we agreed was the queerest but most welcome vessel we had ever seen. Nearly as wide in the beam as she was long, she reminded us both of a very fat woman as she moved to what she decided was a satisfactory spot for anchorage. As we paddled up under her bow we found she bore the astonishing name of *Amour*. And, to our delight, we learned that her commander and owner was none other than Captain Charles Moran, whom we had met more than a year before in the Solomon Islands.

Fortunately for us, the captain had no particular destination. He was merely sailing about, picking up copra wherever he could find it, and we were overjoyed when he agreed to rent his schooner to us. Together with his brother, who was the engineer, he probably knew as much about the islands and natives of the South Seas as any living white man. This was indeed luck.

While the crew was cutting fuel for the *Amour*, for she was a "wood-burner," Martin and I loaded our supplies. At dawn the next day we were off.

152

With perfect weather to help us, we reached Lambuma Bay on the morning of the third day. This was on the isthmus connecting northern and southern Malekula.

We had heard many conflicting tales of this section. Some said it was uninhabited; others told of nomadic tribes. We wanted to find out. So, leaving the *Amour* in charge of a couple of men, we started out with Captain Moran, his brother, and most of the crew as an escort, in search of natives. The moment we landed we knew the territory was populated because of the well-beaten trails leading to the interior. It was beautiful country, gay with tropical birds, and orchids hung from nearly every tree. I carried armfuls of them and felt grander than any lady going to the opera.

For two days we saw no natives, but on the third morning Martin turned a sharp bend in the trail, around a big banyan-like tree, and almost collided with one. To his astonishment, the man literally melted into the jungle, and the rest of us, right on Martin's heels, neither saw nor heard him. Again and again we caught fleeting glimpses of these elusive people, but we began to despair of ever getting close enough to photograph them.

The seeds of these banyan-type trees take root in a palm or other tree and send rope-like tendrils to the ground. Each of these then takes root and gradually thickens into a trunk, often twenty feet in diameter. The trunk grows branches which in turn drop their tendrils, and so on indefinitely, until each tree becomes an individual forest crowned with heart-shaped leaves. It was Martin's interest in studying the curious construction of these trees that led to the solution of what had been a baffling mystery: the unique talent of the natives for just plain vanishing. It was all very simple, Martin discovered. A ladder made of the tough tendrils had been hung in the center of most of the large clusters. By means of these ladders, plus their natural agility, the natives were able to disappear almost instantaneously into the overhead.

The more difficult a task, the more stubborn Martin became. He was determined not to go back to the boat until he had secured some pictures of these tree-climbing natives, and his persistence was rewarded. We were having breakfast on the beach one morning when a native, small of stature, finely muscled, and highly intelligent, marched boldly down to us and demanded in bad but vigorous Bêche-de-Mer what we wanted, who we were, where we came from, and what right did we think we had to chase him and his people all over the treetops. In short, they were growing very tired of the whole business.

Martin, answering in Bêche-de-Mer, started to assure the indignant man that we meant no harm, but he got no further. That, in effect, said our interviewer impatiently, was apparent. He and his people had studied us for days from the branches of the trees. He himself had once been "blackbirded" off to Queensland and hence knew white men and their methods, but what we were up to neither he nor his people could decide, and they were very tired of being worried by us.

We put a clay pipe, a box of matches, and some tobacco into the man's lean, strong hands. We talked and he talked. Naturally, it was impossible to convey anything to him about our camera or what we wanted to do with it. He studied us all closely. Captain Moran and his brother held doubtful attention for some minutes, but something about Martin himself apparently assured the man, for abruptly he agreed to lead us to the headquarters of his people.

The trail along which we were led was one we had already explored, but suddenly our guide turned off into another trail, the entrance to which was masked by cane-grass. We followed this for perhaps a mile and then were brought peremptorily to a halt by our native friend. A born leader if ever there was one, he commanded us to remain where we were, then vanished into the depths of the trees, and it seemed to us, watching him closely, that not so much as a leaf moved. When he reappeared, he was accompanied by three young natives and an old man.

I stared open-mouthed at this aged native. His bright, shoe-button eyes glinted out from a mass of woolly hair. A set of beautiful white, perfect teeth was visible each time he opened his enormous mouth. His movement were quick, nervous, and sure. His feet were almost ape-like. He could grasp a branch with his great flat feet almost as easily as I could with my hand. Martin's attempt at a handshake alarmed him, but our presents of trade goods, together with the endorsement of their "envoy," reassured him.

We were extremely curious about these unusual people, but all attempts to extract information from them met with utter failure. They talked a great deal, but only among themselves, and they completely ignored our Bêche-de-Mer. Their appearance, while grotesque, was peaceful, and when they rubbed my skin to see if the color would come off, examined my hair to see if it was really yellow and straight, and fingered my boots admiringly, I felt no apprehension whatever.

Some wore the clout of pandanus fiber of the Big Nambas, and others were scantily draped with leaves after the fashion of the Small Nambas. They had no villages, built no huts, cultivated no land, raised no livestock. On the contrary, they kept continually on the move and, like monkeys, made the treetops their homes.

Little by little, after much probing, Martin pieced together the history of these natives and found that what lay behind their nomadic existence on this small and savage island was the history of the larger world repeating itself. In the northern and southern ends of Malekula lived powerful tribes who for generations had preyed upon the lesser tribes of the isthmus, killing their men and carrying off their women and children. The gardens and villages of these peace-loving and industrious people were the centers of attack, and one by one they were abandoned. Without weapons, these people lived in the almost impenetrable jungles of the lower lands and fought simply to exist. Generations later, when we found them, their number had increased to several thousands, and they had learned to elude their invaders by hiding in the dense tops of the trees. Their food consisted almost entirely of whatever wild fruit and nuts they could find, together with an occasional fish caught along the shore of the bay. Refugees from the Big Nambas in the north and Small Nambas in the south accounted for the variations in their dress.

We spent only five days among these intelligent and interesting people, but with the help of the man who first accosted us and then acted as our guide, Martin secured some extremely fine pictures.

Back on the boat we sailed at once, and at midnight we were anchored in what is known as the Southwest Bay of Malekula. Early the next morning we launched one of the *Amour*'s small boats and explored a narrow and sluggish river. The water moved so slowly that a green scum along the banks was left undisturbed, and the fetid smell of rotting vegetation hung heavy in the warm, moist air. Some two miles farther, a bend in the river brought us to our destination, the village of a tribe of longheaded black people.

We went ashore, taking with us our usual trade stuff and cameras, but these strange natives showed little interest either in us or in our gifts. There were possibly thirty men, women, and children about the small village when we landed, and they stared at us, but without either fear or curiosity. In most people the instinct to live is strong, but these people appeared to be wholly without even this impulse. Their apathy showed in the flabbiness of their bodies, the decay of four or five huts, the disintegration of their idols. These last apparently had fallen to the ground. Very little effort would have restored them to their upright positions, but they were allowed to remain where they were, crumbling into the earth. There were no signs anywhere of either ceremonies or celebration. Mental and physical decay lay heavy here, and, saddened, I drew close to Martin. His sensitive mouth showed that he was affected exactly as I was by the hopeless lives of these people.

Apparently the only custom kept alive was that of elongating their heads. This was done by binding soft, oiled coconut fiber around the skulls of infants shortly after birth and leaving it there for something over a year. The narrower and longer the head when the basket contrivance was removed, the greater the pride of the mother. That her baby had cried almost without ceasing during this period of distortion was of no concern whatsoever. Martin and I wondered whether this one surviving custom, this one evidence of pride, wasn't perhaps the very thing that had brought about the decadence of a once alert and virile tribe of natives. Certainly the ancient human heads hanging from the rafters and center poles of the huts, blackened and dried with the smoke of perhaps a hundred years, suggested that these once had been an active and aggressive people.

On our return to the *Amour* that evening, Captain Moran's native men told us excitedly of seeing scores of other natives along the shore of the island, all painted in war colors and armed with guns. This promised to be interesting. Martin whistled happily that night as he polished his camera lenses and loaded our film.

At daybreak the next morning, Captain Moran and his brother and the five men of the crew, all well armed, took us in the *Amour*'s sturdy whaleboat on a cruise of the shore.

We ran along the rocky island coast for perhaps five miles without seeing a trace of the natives. The spiral of smoke from a recent camp on a smooth stretch of beach drew our hopeful attention. We turned the nose of the boat into the shore, but just as we were beaching, our men paddled frantically out again.

Some twenty of the most ferocious-looking men I had ever seen were marching down to the beach from the jungle. Each carried a gun and all wore paint—nothing else. From the edges of their hair to the soles of their feet, their coal-black bodies had been painted in dizzying designs, with stripes, dots, and circles in yellow, white, blue, and red running a fearful riot. Their bushy hair stood straight out from their heads and bristled with harshly brilliant feathers.

Peremptorily, these warrior natives signaled to us to land. Martin was beside himself with eagerness. Here was material made to order for the camera, but our native crew, with eyes popping, stubbornly held the boat out beyond the surf, and there was nothing that Captain Moran, either with threats or offers of money, could do about it.

Martin solved the problem finally by swimming ashore. Our crew moaned dolefully as they watched him and rolled their heads from side to side; they expected momentarily to witness a murder. My face was fixed in what I hoped passed for a confident smile. Then we saw my husband simply walk out of the water straight into the midst of the natives, and next we saw them stacking their guns. Promises of tobacco, Martin said afterward, brought about this miracle.

Our crew, though still reluctant, now rowed us into shore. As we beached our boat the natives pushed close around us, demanding their tobacco. Our men clutched their guns in panic, assuming this was an attack, but Martin quickly handed out the coveted weed and some clay pipes, and all panic subsided.

More than solving our immediate problem, Martin's swimming into shore had won the painted natives completely. They
knew they were a fierce-looking people, and to them his bravery was something stupendous. They invited him—then included us—to attend a feast in a village some three miles inland.
Martin accepted, after examining their guns and finding that
only two contained cartridges and that the rest were broken or
too rusty to shoot.

"All front, these men," my husband said, grinning at me.

After a walk of perhaps half an hour over a good trail, we
began to hear the throbbing of jungle drums, and again, as
always, the nerve-shattering boom sent a wave of instinctive
panic through me. We were now at the foot of a sharp hill, and
our escort of twenty painted black men told us that they were
permitted to go no farther until summoned, that we must go
on alone. We did so, with Captain Moran prodding his reluctant men from the rear and with each difficult step of the climb
taking us closer to the boo-boos, which now took on a wilder
cadence. The pulses in my throat began to beat chokingly in
the same rhythm.

A short, hard climb brought us to the top of the hill and
there, spread before us on a sort of plateau around their huge
boo-boos and idols, were more natives than I had ever seen
gathered in one place—easily a thousand of them—all naked
except for their paint and head feathers. The effect from their
viewpoint must have been satisfactorily impressive and frightening. To me it was terrifying, and I saw Martin's face tighten.

Abruptly the thud of the boo-boos stopped. Every eye was
upon us. There was a moment of tense silence. Then out of
the center of the painted throng stepped an old man smeared
from head to foot with yellow ocher. We were pushed forward
into his immediate presence, and he glared at us in apparent
rage. In Bêche-de-Mer he demanded to know what we wanted,
and how we dared intrude here. His eyes darted from one to
another of us, and I put on my set smile of confidence.

"We walk about, no more," Martin explained humbly. "We
bringem presents for big fellow master belong village."

The old fellow's eyes narrowed shrewdly, then, grandly and
with much chest-thumping, he announced that he was the most

important chief of all chiefs, and that therefore he must receive the most presents. Then he pointed out that there were many other lesser chiefs and that we must make presents to all of them. There was no show of either courtesy or diplomacy. He had said "must," and he meant it. Martin and I exchanged quick looks, hoping we'd have enough stuff to satisfy this greedy chief, and then set about distributing our trade goods. Never before had we given out so much, and never had I known such chaos. The barbarians milled about us, pushing angrily, shouting orders until we were deafened, and there was something in the voices of these natives that chilled me to the marrow. Our men huddled back to back, fingering the triggers of their rifles.

Some experiences can't be measured in actual time. This was one of them. I had turned to thrust our last stick of tobacco into the hand of a clutching native when, to my utter amazement, I saw Martin setting up his camera. That I should be so frightened, and he should be so cool and have such presence of mind in the face of what might turn out disastrously, held me, staring blankly. Then I saw his hand shaking as he turned the camera crank, and next I saw him grinning with relief: The entire mob had started running for cover. (He afterwards admitted to me that he had set up the camera to divert the minds of the barbarians from the fast-emptying sacks of trade stuff, for in their frenzy they were capable of thinking of but one thing at a time.)

Old Yellow Ocher, of all his people, remained where he was. Quite apparently he was frightened by the camera, but he had courage enough to stand and demand pompously to know what it was all about. Martin opened the camera and showed him the little wheels and the ribbon of film. The old bluff nodded and pretended to understand everything, then ordered his people out of hiding and made them stand while he made a show of explaining the little wheels and ribbon of film. They were all much impressed—not with the camera, but with their chief.

Everything was now on a more friendly footing. Martin and old Yellow Ocher grew quite chummy over the camera and its mechanism, and the rhythm of the native festivity was once more resumed to the accompaniment of the inevitable boo-boos. I don't know just when the dancing started, but it grew out of that pulsating, compelling beat of the drums, and soon there were two hundred or more natives chanting and dancing in the clearing. Dancing doesn't seem the word for it. It was more of a hop-and-skip grand march around and around the idols and boo-boos, punctuated now and again by leaps and blood-curdling yells. As some dropped out, exhausted, others joined in.

Martin, beside himself, was grinding out film of the magnificent native spectacle. The beat of the jungle drums quickened. More and more of the painted men leaped into the gyrating circle, and apparently our presence was forgotten in the orgy that followed. Chanting, leaping, screaming, their eyes rolling back and foam from their mouths spattering their gaudy, naked bodies, they might have been out of a scene of mass torture in some inferno. I had felt, and now I was certain, that a sort of madness takes possession of some primitive people under the hypnotic beat of their drums.

I dug my nails into my palms: "Martin!" I screamed. "I can't stand any more of it. I can't!"

My husband gave me one look of quick concern and started to take down his camera. He was packing his equipment with the help of Captain Moran when he discovered some two hundred sticks of tobacco which had been overlooked. And then he made a mistake. He dumped it on the ground and motioned Yellow Ocher that he could have it. Some eight or ten young men pounced on it, and in less than five seconds several hundred natives were fighting for it. They howled and scratched like a pack of hyenas. Their painted bodies churned in a dizzying, kaleidoscopic mass, and soon the bright circles, stripes, and dots decorating their black skins were stained with a darker color. I waited for no more and took to my heels down the steep incline.

Hours later, and safely aboard the *Amour* under a clear, windless tropical night, I stood close beside Martin on the deck and tried to explain that even though I still shook a little, it wasn't because I had been frightened; it was rather an instinctive reaction to what we had witnessed. Faintly in the distance then, as we stood there, we heard the boo-boos once more. Apparently the battle over the sticks of tobacco was at an end, and the dance had been resumed.

We continued our journey after a day's rest and put in occasionally along the shore. Martin was no longer interested, however, in just the average native at an average task; we had thousands of feet of film of these. At length, Captain Moran asked if he would be interested in taking some pictures of a tribe that made it a practice to smoke the heads of both relatives and enemies over open campfires. Martin thought this would be fine. I remembered the little brown mummified head, a relic of the *Snark* trip, which had given me the shivers, as we set sail for the little island of Tomman about half a mile off the southernmost tip of Malekula.

Captain Moran had traded at Tomman and said that the natives there were well disciplined by the British government. He added that it would be perfectly safe to take me ashore.

We arrived in the little island bay too late in the day to go ashore, but we took the trail into the interior early the following morning. It was a pleasant island, and, if outward appearances could be believed, the natives lived peaceably enough. A peculiar characteristic was their strangely shaped heads, which were almost twice as long as the normal head and sloped to a point at the crown. The married women, we observed, had no front teeth; their husbands had knocked them out, as part of the marriage ceremony.

Following a well-beaten trail, we came to a clearing in which were eight or nine crude huts. In the center of the clearing, before a devil-devil, an old man carried on a solemn solo dance. Nothing more uncomplicated could be imagined. He simply lifted one foot very slowly and put it down again, and then lifted the other foot, also very slowly, and put it down again. A hoarse, chanting whisper was his only accompaniment. After four days he was still at it, but no one could tell us why. Unquestionably, however, it had to do with the eerie scene on the far side of the clearing, where a group of old men squatted beside a smoldering fire and gave earnest and undeviating attention to a human head impaled on a stick and held over the smoke by a very ancient member of their group. I counted five other heads impaled on sticks nearby, doubtless in various stages of "seasoning."

Martin set up his camera and photographed the scene, and

neither comment nor protest was made. After a little my husband went and squatted beside the old head-curer, and found that he understood Bêche-de-Mer. He drew him on to talk of his strange "art." I tiptoed in and listened.

The head, freshly cut from the body, the old man said, was first soaked in a chemical concoction of certain fermented herbs, which both hardened the skin and in a measure "fireproofed" it. Next it was held over a fire and turned in the smoke until all the fat was rendered out and the tissue dried. Then it was smeared with clay and baked. All of this took some weeks of constant work. Lastly, it was hung in a basket of pandanus fiber, and time put its finishing touches to the job. Naturally, the old patriarch added, only the heads of friends and relatives were given this amount of care and time. The heads of enemies, merely smeared with clay, took their chances of either drying or cooking in the hot ashes.

Proud of his craft, and apparently expert at it, the old man told us that in his time he had done many chiefs. These he dried "whole," which must have been a job indeed, involving, it seemed to Martin and me, certain awkard mechanical complications.

The people of Tomman liked Martin—and me too, I think—and when we left, we had photographs of the interiors of their headhouse. Even the mummified bodies of their chiefs were brought out for us to see and photograph.

Grateful to Captain Moran for having suggested Tomman, we chugged happily away and cruised around the southern end of Malekula, then put in at Port Sandwich, where we bade a reluctant farewell to the captain, his brother, and the fat, sturdy little schooner so romantically named *Amour*. Luckily, we found the British gunboat *Euphrosyne* in the harbor. Commissioner King was aboard and made us most welcome, and we sailed with him back to Epi. Here, through the kindness of the commissioner, we were guests on one of the largest coconut plantations in the South Seas. Our thoughtful host, Mr. Mitchell, the British manager of the plantation, wore white tie and tails every evening for dinner, even when alone. I felt both silly and uncomfortable in my hickory shirt and overalls, and these none too clean.

It was another three weeks before we were able to make boat connections back to Vao. A hearty welcome awaited us. Fully a hundred natives were on the beach yelling and cheering, and they let us know at once that they had missed our tobacco. Nothing could have been simpler than for them to break into our stores and help themselves, but however many their vices, stealing was not among them.

We were nearly ten days sealing our motion-picture film and developing the hundreds of exposed "still" pictures, and as we worked we thought of home. I had even begun to pack my personal things when a small cutter owned by a Tangan trader named Powler dropped anchor in the bay.

I looked at Martin. He had that eager glint in his eye that meant just one thing: another trip.

"We are going home now, aren't we, Martin?" I asked.

"Huh? Sure. What?" he replied.

In less than an hour we were abroad Powler's boat bound for Espíritu Santo, an island some forty miles to the north.

Powler was a good-natured giant. We had heard of him in our wanderings about the islands, and he had an enviable reputation for honesty and fair trading unusual among white men in these parts. Also, he was familiar with all the languages of the island tribes. He had heard of Martin and had stopped at Vao on the chance that his knowledge of the different islands and their natives would be of value to us. The trip to Espíritu Santo was his suggestion, and one for which we were to be most grateful.

Landing with us, Powler took three of his best men, all armed, then gathered up fifteen natives. With these we set out for the interior. After a three-hour tramp over well-beaten trails, we came upon a tribe of little men. Though at first they were frightened, Martin's friendly manner and smile soon won their confidence, and he secured some fine pictures. These little people might also be classified as dwarfs. I persuaded them to walk under Martin's outstretched arm, and there was a clearance of a full inch even above their bushy mops of hair. Their weapons were bows and arrows.

My husband urged the little men to talk about themselves, and they confided at length that they were ruled by a madman who occasionally ran amok and killed a number of his subjects. They never knew when this might happen and therefore lived in constant terror of their irrational chief.

"He bad," they explained earnestly. "He takem plenty pigs; he takem plenty women; he killem plenty men."

Suddenly one of them was inspired with the idea that Martin was the very person to rid them of their mad ruler. The others took it up and enthusiastically suggested hanging as a good method of killing him. Martin regretfully declined the task of executioner and shouldered camera to leave, whereupon the little men were thrown into a state of great dejection and eyed him with sadness and reproach.

We had gone a little distance from the clearing when Powler struck off through a thick screen of brush that hid a well-packed trail. Following this, we were able to make good time and presently, off in the distance, we saw smoke and caught the beat of the inevitable boo-boos. Powler quickened his stride; apparently he knew of something here of which he had not spoken.

Another half mile, and the jungle drums were loud on our ears. We also caught a faintly sweet smell of roasting flesh.

Advancing cautiously, we stopped behind a thin screen of bush, and Martin set up his camera for a long-range shot of the native celebration which was in full swing. There was nothing unusual about the celebration. The natives, small and graceful, were much less ferocious in appearance than many we had seen. The dance was the usual circular shuffle around the devil-devils in the center of the clearing. Yet, somehow, I had a sick, uneasy feeling that may have been part instinct or may have been wholly the result of Powler's quiet, meaningful smile as he looked at Martin. I looked sharply toward the fire, and then I knew. Those pieces of meat spitted on long sticks were not the usual pork—they were parts of the body of a human being.

My husband, always watchful of me, put his arm around me and pulled me close for a moment.

It was growing dark when Martin, after a whispered consultation with Powler, gave a radium flare to one of our men and instructed him to move into the clearing and mingle with the celebrants for a few minutes, and then to throw the flare on the fire.

This was done. The explosive suddenness of the white glare sent the natives yelling in terror for the brush. Some headed in our direction; then, seeing us for the first time, their terror was doubled, and they leaped off in the opposite direction. Several with pure animal instinct snatched the meat from the fire as they ran, and I heard my husband groan with disappointment. He had hoped for a picture of it.

Martin and Powler, with me at their heels, dashed into the clearing and made straight for the fire. Looking over Martin's shoulder, I felt the blood drain from my face, for there lay something which the fleeing natives had failed to retrieve. In the red embers lay a charred human head, with rolled leaves plugging the eye-sockets. (Powler's humor sometimes took a grisly turn, for he told me afterwards and with relish that the leaves used for this purpose were always selected carefully from the bush of a spicy herb!)

With the aid of flares, Martin secured some excellent pictures of the roasting human head. These were considered important for the reason that they rounded out his film record of South Sea Island natives and proved conclusively that cannibalism there is still practiced. I did not linger, however, to watch him taking these pictures, and I didn't know until we were once more putting out to sea that he had wrapped the head in leaves and carried it all the way back to the boat; that the round bundle tied up in a piece of bright-red trade calico and lying beside the camera and cases of film actually was it.

"There's proof nobody can get around!" Martin said.

I protested that it was enough proof to have the film—are we now going to carry that gruesome thing with us everywhere we went? Martin said that anyhow it was double proof. At best my protest was a feeble one, and suddenly I was sick. Sick at sea, though I insisted then, and do now, that I was not seasick.

I don't know when I've ever been so happy at the thought of going home. Eight months among dirt-encrusted man-eating strangers had brought on a homesickness that was almost beyond my bearing. I was hungry for dear, familiar things—for my own people, and most of all, and for the places where I had spent my simple and uncomplicated girlhood. Equally intense, if in a different fashion, was my longing for just plain hot water and soap. Plenty of it. And these were not my feelings alone. They were also Martin's; he wanted home and his people and civilized living every bit as much as I did.

Osa and Father Johnson pose by the Johnsons' new Ford wagon in Nairobi, 1921.

"Oh Martin, it's Paradise," and so the lake was named. Note the wide game trail leading to the lake.

Buildings and fences at Lake Paradise, their home in Kenya's Northern Frontier District

Boculy, the Johnsons' guide, and Osa examine an elephant track.

The Johnsons enjoy a picnic with the Duke and Duchess of York, later to become King George VI and Queen Elizabeth, in the Northern Frontier District, 1935.

In camp. Left to right: Blayney Percival, Mary Jobe Akeley, Carl Akeley, Dr. Aubrey Stewart, Martin and Osa Johnson, and George Eastman

George Eastman and Osa baking bread

On a trip up the Nile with the Johnsons, George Eastman photographs Shilluks at Kodok in the Sudan. Mr. Eastman was understandably intrigued with the name.

Three boy scouts arrive to take a six-week safari with the Johnsons. Left to right with their hosts: Doug Oliver, David Martin, and Dick Douglas

The boy scouts examine a weapon carried by Masai *moran*.

Osa shops for supper.

When Rattray of Isiolo was attacked by a leopard, he killed it with his bare hands, but not without injury to him and his dog. Martin took this photograph shortly thereafter.

Martin and Osa with Samburu

Chapter 14 _____

"Well," Martin said, "want to buy a house?"

"A house?"

"Yes. Settle down in Chanute. Or in Independence. Well, what I mean," Martin went on—eyeing me pretty closely, I thought—"is that with what we'll be getting out of the pictures, we could settle down and have a little home—if you want to."

I didn't answer right away. I just looked straight back at him.

"If you want to," he repeated. I saw an anxious line appear between his eyes.

"Why, my goodness," I said finally. "Where'd you get such a crazy idea?"

"Good!" he shouted, and hugged the breath out of me. "Then we're going to Borneo!"

"Borneo?" I said blankly. The name always had had an unpleasant sound to me.

"Yes. I've talked it over with the Robertson-Cole people, and that's where they want me to go this time—to get pictures of the natives there. The headhunters." He eyed me closely again. "Would you like that?"

"Why—"

I was really very tired of headhunters and cannibals.

"Why, sure. That's fine," I said.

The beauty of Sandakan, capital and principal port of British North Borneo, held us in a spell of sheer delight as we steamed into the bay. Stretching along the shore for two miles and back into the deep valley for another mile, it is the home of some ten thousand strangely assorted people. A range of moderate mountains forms a picturesque backdrop against an intensely blue sky.

We found the streets almost deserted during the day, but at sundown Chinese lanterns were hung in front of the low houses and shops, and the streets were soon thronging with people of a dozen nationalities: Chinese women in bright silks; Japanese in quaint kimonos; Filipino belles in long-fringed mantillas; Malays in intricately designed batik sarongs; Europeans in their familiar tailored things; and would-be native dandies in amusing combinations of their own and European dress.

All the sound seemed high-pitched after the low tones of boo-boos and cannibal chantings. Here the voices were shrill and mingled with the shriller music from the Chinese and Malay theaters. Even the colors and smells were in a higher key. Martin and I never wearied of strolling through the narrow streets. Often we saw the procession of a funeral or a wedding, both of which were identical except that the bride was carried in a sedan chair, while in the funeral the body, enclosed in a coffin of rough boards, was slung on ropes and borne by coolies. It was an exasperation to Martin that the picturesque activity of this beautiful town should only come alive in the cool of the evening, and that for this reason, with light gone, it would always elude his camera.

We put up at the surprisingly bad hotel only long enough to look around and find a place which, however briefly, we could call home. I doubt that ever a woman lived who had a stronger instinct for homemaking than I, or a man with greater need for a home than Martin. Fortunately, we learned of a missionary on the point of taking a leave of absence, and his hilltop dwelling of two houses just outside of town, together with cook, waterboy, and houseboy, became ours for four months. These houses, like most of those owned by Europeans there, were built carefully of wood with high, pointed grass roofs. Lizards in large numbers shared our new quarters. Their favorite diet of huge, fat spiders, and scorpions up to five inches in length was well supplied here, and, plump and saucy, they seemed to know themselves to be more than welcome. I had supposed we had become insect-hardened down in the New Hebrides, but here, it seemed to me, we were forced to pay blood-tribute to an even greater variety of Mother Nature's hungry insect hordes.

My husband's patience, where small annoyances were concerned, was a source of never-ending wonder to me, and an example of which I was much in need. A man of unerring singleness of purpose, he used his energies for the things that really counted. While I fussed about the house—quite as if we were settling down for at least a year—cleaning it, reorganizing it, routing the deadly scorpions out of the corners, teaching the cook some of the dishes which I knew were good for Martin, and between times prowling around the garden with my .22 and polishing off the somewhat too numerous snakes, Martin was going quietly about arranging for our first trip into the interior and learning Malay. I joined him in this in the evening, with a saucer of kerosene oil and a swab of cotton at my elbow for the mosquitoes. The wetter I made my face and arms with the smelly stuff, the less mosquitoes liked me, I found, so I took my choice of the two evils.

During his inquiries into the best methods of going into the interior on our animal quest, Martin learned that here, as in the New Hebrides, distinct dangers lay ahead. He said little to me about these, but even after all our plans were made he lingered in Sandakan. Then one morning, some three weeks later, I saw him shaving with more than usual care.

"You can come along if you want to." He grinned. "Better put on something besides those overalls, though—a skirt, I mean."

"Well, my goodness," I replied, but hurried to do as he suggested. "Must be important," I added as I got out a fresh white shirtwaist.

It was. Less than an hour later we were ushered into the presence of Sir West Ridgeway, who had arrived at Sandakan just the night before. The president of the British North Borneo Company and virtual ruler of British North Borneo itself, he was a tall, erect, keen-eyed old gentlemen of seventy-five who appeared less than sixty. He had spent most of his life in the service of the British colonial government, serving with Kitchener in Egypt and as governor and commander-in-chief of Ceylon from 1896 to 1903.

I liked the old gentleman instantly, even though he was a little truculent toward Martin and his plan to go into the interior and take me with him.

"She ought to be at home with her mother or in school," he said impatiently, fixing me with a scowling, contemplative look. "Women weren't made for such hardships."

"Yes, I know, but my wife—" Martin began.

"An expedition such as you contemplate would be dangerous even for experienced, hardened men. I tell you, Mr. Johnson, death in a hundred forms awaits any white man who ventures into the interior. Poisonous insects, fevers, snakes, animals—headhunters, sir, as vicious as any on earth!"

"I know," Martin said. "I've heard of the pirates of Borneo. Hafees, I think they're called. They use blowpipes, don't they, and poisoned darts?"

"Exactly, and yet you would take a woman, young and soft— your wife, sir—into such dangers! Why, you must be a madman!"

Martin smiled. "I know that's how Osa looks, Sir West, soft and weak, but when you consider that she's the only woman who ever dared to cross Malaita down in the Solomons, and that she's even been where white men haven't dared to go among the natives of the New Hebrides, then you'll realize that there's more to her than you'd first imagine."

"Bless my soul!" said Sir West.

A few days later we received word to present ourselves at the offices of the British North Borneo Company, where we were graciously received by Sir West and informed that the government was very much interested in our plan to make a motion-picture record of Borneo's wildlife; that it would be pleased to accept Martin's offer of a print for its permanent files; and that certainly the safeguarding of our lives during this project would be its first concern. To which Sir West added that he, personally, would not sanction Martin's taking me on the expedition—irrespective of earlier hazards braved and survived—unless every precaution possible were observed.

How carefully our needs were considered may be gathered from the fact that the government furnished us with an escort of native policemen, an interpreter, four coolies as carriers, and a government launch. The salaries and food allowances for the men assigned to us were to be paid by the government, and our party as it continued its journey was to be put up at government outstations that lay along our route.

Before venturing on our long trip into the interior, Martin felt we should make a trial excursion or two to test our equipment and familiarize ourselves with the country. Less than a week later we were off across the bay in the government's fine, sturdy launch. We went up one of the many rivers that empty into the ocean there. It was alive with crocodiles. Soon the nipa-thatched native huts gave way to a jungle so dense with giant trees, vines, and parasitic roots that it appeared impenetrable fifty feet back from the shores, and monkeys, literally thousands, jabbered at our intrusion.

Martin, beside himself with delight, set up his camera, but he encountered a curious difficulty. Monkeys the color of mud remained on the dark earth at the foot of the nipa palms, monkeys the color of rust remained among leaves of a reddish hue, and leaping about in the high branches were big-nosed monkeys with long snouts, little black monkeys that were all tall, and large brown monkeys with practically no tails whatever—all blending exasperatingly with the grays, greens, browns, and reds of their background, or else losing themselves in the thick shadows. It was clear even on this first experimental trip that the photographic problem was going to be a serious one.

We chose another river out of the bay for our second trip and, at the suggestion of one of our native guides, anchored the launch about thirty miles upstream and went ashore. The jungle thinned a little here, and we were able to penetrate for perhaps a quarter of a mile where, in a clearing, we came on a herd of forty water buffaloes. The light was good, so Martin set up his camera. It was a moment of great excitement for us as he ground out his first hundred feet of wild-animal film.

Suddenly a grizzled, wise-looking old buffalo decided to resent our intrusion and, snorting, lowered his head for a charge. The rest followed suit, and the herd came at us. Martin caught me and swung me behind him with one hand and kept on grinding with the other. The natives had already scrambled for cover.

Both angry and frightened at what seemed the certain destruction of our one and only motion-picture camera, and with it the end of our entire expedition (that our lives might be in danger didn't occur to me at the moment), I let out a scream that for noise and shrillness must have been startling indeed, for the lead buffalo threw up his head and swerved off, the rest of the herd following him. Martin kept right on grinding, with the result that we returned to Sandakan shortly, much pleased with the result of our second experimental trip.

I shall never forget my introduction to some of the more noisome inhabitants of the Borneo jungle—for one thing, snakes in amazing numbers, king cobras among them. Fortunately, most of those reptiles, with all their deadliness, are inclined to flee rather than attack. Death in the jungle would be certain were it otherwise. We were on our way back to the launch, triumphant after securing our shot of the buffaloes. It was frightfully hot and steamy, and I paused to push my hair more securely under my hat when my hand encountered something clammy and soft on the back of my neck. I screamed and pulled it off. It was a yellow tree leech, some two inches long. And then I found five more of various colors attached to my arms, to my back under my shirt, and one on my leg just above my high boot. Many more had attached themselves to Martin. All were fast swelling with our blood. Our native carriers immediately took us in hand and singed them off. To pull them off meant to leave a bad sore, they said. The one I had already pulled from the back of my neck soon proved this to be only too true. We found these pests everywhere in the jungle, hidden on the underside of leaves of their own color and waiting to drop on man or beast below. They had the look of thin worms before their meal. Equipped with a most efficient sucker at each end, they swelled with the blood of their victims to many times their original size and, when full, dropped off. An ugly red mark remained for many months. The ability of these leeches to accomplish all this without the knowledge of their victims will always be a mystery to me.

Between our different experimental trips, Martin made his plans for our major expedition. After much conflicting advice, he decided upon the Kinabatangan River, the largest waterway in North Borneo, as our quickest route deep into the interior. Some one hundred and forty miles inland, at the village of La-mag, we learned there was a government station. The resident commissioner there, Mr. Holmes, informed of our plans by the British North Borneo Company, came to Sandakan to give us his help and advice. We can never be grateful enough to this charming Englishman, who not only supplied us with provisions and native boatmen and coolies but, in addition, accompanied us on our difficult and often dangerous trip.

At length we were ready, and by daybreak we had crossed the twenty miles of the Sandakan Bay and were at the broad mouth of the Kinabatangan River. There were five of us: Mr. Holmes, Martin and I, an interpreter, and a government man to take us in the launch as far as Lamag. There we were to pick up our native men and coolies, together with the larger portion of our provisions, and continue our journey up the narrowing river in native canoes, or gobongs.

The deeper we went inland, along the always-narrowing river, the more excited we became over what lay ahead, for there were increasing evidences in the thick, green jungle on both banks that here indeed was wild-animal country. We were a little over three days in reaching Lamag, where we were glad to leave the comfortable but close confines of the launch.

Here at the government station we were met by an army of four privates and a corporal who were drawn up at salute to greet us. Six dogs and a pet monkey gave Mr. Holmes a rousing welcome, and fifty more monkeys, on a raid of the sweet-potato patch, chattering wildly, raced back into the jungle.

We spent two days as Mr. Homes's guests. The official residence, the barracks, and a slightly larger house were built of wood on piles some ten feet from the ground and were thatched with nipa palm. These and a few native huts, all hard-pressed by the thick jungle, made up the government station.

It did not take Mr. Holmes long to organize our excursion, and we made quite an imposing gobong fleet (a gobong, or native canoe, is sometimes hollowed from a tree trunk and sometimes made of boards). In the first canoe were three well-armed police boys. Next came Mr. Holmes's personal deluxe gobong, which was thirty-five feet long and completely enclosed with nipa leaf, and required eight boatmen to paddle it. It carried as passengers Mr. Holmes, Martin, me, and a native hunter, together with our film and camera equipment, which were seldom separated from Martin by much more than the length of his arm. Following in a smaller canoe were an interpreter and the native Martin had selected as his personal camera assistant. Then came ten canoes loaded with provisions and general equipment.

I observed that the native police in the canoe ahead kept their guns always ready at hand, and that they watched closely the jungle walls on either bank for the slight breaks that indicated the mouth of brooks. These waterways, dark and narrow, cut through hundreds of miles of jungle and empty into the larger streams. I learned after much probing that they are the hiding places for island pirates, descendants of the Malay pirates that once were the terror of the South Seas. We were told by Mr. Holmes that the very nature of these water labyrinths makes it extremely difficult for the government to bring the hafees under control, and that hence they are a constant menace to river traffic.

Our destination was the Tenggara village at the headwaters, the farthest navigable point on the river. En route we stopped at Pintasin, the native capital of the Kinabatangan District and the home of Hadji Mohammed Nur, chief of all the tribes in a territory covering hundreds of square miles.

The chief himself, an elderly, intelligent-looking man with clear, parchment-like skin and a firm mouth, met us at the log wharf accompanied by two dignitaries. All were attired in colorful native garb and turbans. They wore shoes in our honor and escorted us to the chief's house where, with much ceremony, we sat down to dinner. The entire village and thirty dogs looked on, and we in turn supplied a dinner for countless hungry fleas and sand flies.

We spent three days at Pintasin. As we were about to leave, Chief Hadji offered to accompany us in his own elaborate gobong. Martin and Mr. Holmes were delighted, for his presence insured the fullest cooperation of the natives wherever we might choose to go in the Kinabatangan territory. One happy circumstance in this connection was the renewal of our crews. Few natives will travel far from their villages, so we were obliged daily to arrange for a fresh group of paddlers. The good Hadji solved this problem for us by taking from his boat a brass gong and a stick of native hard rubber and beating a tattoo. There was the sound of answering drums in the distance, and we awoke in the morning to find a crew of the needed number awaiting us.

Another bit of magic which I have always attributed to the Hadji was the appearance every so often of natives along the river banks carying freshly gathered wild lemons, guavas, and bananas. A few ounces of salt, we found, would buy all the fruit we needed from day to day. Martin, in his careful inquiries regarding the interior, had learned that salt was prized even above money and had had the foresight to bring a plentiful supply.

The more deeply we penetrated into the interior along the narrow waterway, the hotter it became. My head ached, I ached all over, I was a mass of mosquito bites, and the pain in my back from the crouching position I was forced to maintain in the canoe under the low nipa canopy was excruciating. Every now and then we stopped at springs and plunged our hands and faces into the cool water, but this did little good.

I often think a more patient or more considerate man than my husband never lived. He must have been far more uncomfortable than I, if for no other reason than his height. Taller than average, there was so much of him to fold up in the limited space. Too, he felt that he must be constantly alert with the cameras, and yet I never heard him complain. On the contrary, all of his concern was for me. Often he insisted that I stretch out and try to sleep, even though my doing so crowded him that much more. His concern also extended to Mr. Holmes, to Chief Hadji, and on down to our crew.

During all this I said little, but I made up my mind that on the trip back at least I was somehow going to have things better for him. When we had stopped and made camp on a sandbar, I consulted Mr. Holmes.

"I've simply got to do something about Martin," I said as I hurried about preparing supper. I laid nipa leaves on the sand for a tablecloth. Our twelve gobongs were safely beached and the crew—nearly fifty, I think—were cooking their rice and dried fish over little campfires.

"What are you going to do about me?" Martin grinned, coming up. He had been directing our hunters as they drove small trees into the sand of the riverbed to keep the crocodiles away from our camp. This also gave us a place where we could bathe safely.

"Look at you," I said. "You can't even straighten up. You'll grow that way!"

"Oh, I could straighten up all right if I wanted to," he said, "only if I stay this way I fit the gobong better when I get back in."

"Gobong disease, that's what it is." I was indignant. "And I'm sick of it!"

We all laughed and let it go at that for the time being.

My plan, as I confided to Mr. Holmes, was to arrange at the nearest village this side of the rapids to have the natives build a sort of little houseboat, with regular sleeping bunks and chairs and a table, a nipa roof high enough so that Martin could get up and walk around under it, and a kind of porch where he could set up his camera and take pictures in decent comfort as he moved back down the river.

"And we must stop early evening and make a suitable camp, for Martin's simply got to have properly cooked meals to keep him well."

Mr. Holmes smiled and said he saw no reason at all why it couldn't be done.

"We'll move in on our way back from the rapids," I concluded, happy just thinking about it. "And it will navigate easily because we'll be going with the stream."

A terrified squealing just back of us in the jungle seemed to freeze me where I stood. This stopped and was followed by a horrible crunching sound. Martin, Mr. Holmes, and our hunters ran to investigate. Hurrying back for the camera and flares, they said a python had captured an enormous wild pig and was devouring it. Measuring the snake where it lay asleep the next morning, we found it was twenty-seven-and-a-half feet long. The pig with which it bulged was estimated to weigh about two hundred pounds. Chief Hadji said the snake would lie asleep for six months digesting it. I had no appetite for dinner that night.

I often wondered how we managed to keep healthy on this trip. Night brought relief from the heat of the day, but regularly for about four hours it rained. Usually we pitched camp in the vicinity of the villages. Occasionally we tried sleeping in the huts, but while we were drenched wherever we slept, we found ourselves splashed with mud in the huts and went back to our gobongs.

Martin, I knew, was growing a little discouraged. We had traveled all of two hundred and fifty miles from Sandakan. The jungles on either side of the river were teeming with wildlife, but how to photograph it was the problem. The growth was so thick that the men had literally to cut an opening in it before we could advance even a foot. By the time we had advanced a hundred feet, all the animals in the vicinity had scattered beyond our view. The Hadji, who was most sympathetic with our problem, assured us through our interpreter that at the headwaters we would be on higher ground where the nature of the growth would be different—thinner, he said, and less difficult to penetrate.

Nature seems full of strange tricks in this fantastic country, tricks designed to make miserable anyone entering it. The nanti-dulu ("wait-a-minute") thorn, so called by the natives, grows in thousands on a bush with long, flexible, vine-like branches and has the shape of a fishhook, which snags you as you pass. Martin swore they even reached out after us. In some instances, however, nature is kind. One case in point is the water-vine, a blessing to man and animals alike. Its stems, the thickness of a man's arm, give out clear, cold, pure water when cut, and as much as a pint can be had from a piece less than two feet long.

At length we reached the village of Sungei Iyau, where, it seemed to Mr. Holmes, we would be wise to have the houseboat built. Chief Hadji was taken into our confidence, and the careful instructions given to the natives by that gentleman (and he was a gentleman by any standard) gave us every assurance that upon our return from the headwaters, a little floating home would be ready for our use on the long trip down to Lamag.

I had kept this entire plan from Martin because I was afraid he would think it an unnecessary expense. But to see him get up morning after morning as early as three o'clock and work until sunrise in the cramping quarters of the canoe, changing motion-picture film and sealing negatives as well as developing plates, was more than I could endure. It is true that our funds were low, and yet to make my husband as comfortable as conditions would allow for the difficult work he had to do—and this also meant safeguarding his health—seemed distinctly to be my part of the whole undertaking. Fortunately, he was so intent upon securing motion pictures of the natives in the village that he never once suspected our conspiracy.

It was at the edge of the village, outside the door of a wretched hut, that we came upon Kalowatt. A baby gibbon ape, she was on a chain—a pathetic little ball of silver-gray fluff. Martin and I stood and stared at her and clutched at each other's hands, and then Martin picked her up and cuddled her against his cheek. From that moment we knew we must have her. We rapped at the door, and two women, fully as wretched as their hut, came outside and stared at us. One was probably Eurasian, the other Malay.

The baby ape seemed to belong to the Malay woman, and so it was with her that we bargained. Apparently she loved the little thing and didn't want to part with her, and it wasn't until we offered a stiff price—six dollars Malay, or three dollars U.S.— that she would consent to let us have her.

At parting, the poor woman, whose ribs showed on her torso like bars and whose back ran in raw welts, wept bitterly. It seemed cruel to take Kalowatt away from her, and yet crueler not to, for from the looks of the frail little creature she could not have lived long without better care than the Malay woman was giving her.

As it was, with a little box about the size of a shoebox for her bed, and with the good, nourishing food she could eat, we soon had her filling out, and in no time at all she became the most important member of our expedition. As a matter of fact, she never left us from that moment on until her tragic death in Nairobi, British East Africa (now Kenya) many years later.

Our next stop was at Penangah—the last native settlement, apparently, to have contact with the outside world, and that only rarely, for few of the people had ever seen a white man, and none had ever seen a white woman.

These were handsome people, both the men and the women, with lean, erect bodies and well-combed straight hair. Their features were quite fine, with occasionally a definite Chinese look. They smoked long pipes, and all the men carried a parang—a wicked knife used throughout North Borneo for making trails through the jungle and skinning and cutting up animals, and as weapons for personal combat. These people also carried blowguns and a bamboo quiver of poisoned darts. Martin took many pictures of these people, whom he found much more interesting than those on the lower parts of the river, and I'm afraid our friends of the faraway New Hebrides suffered considerably by comparison.

Next we came to the rapids, and I doubt that any but our native crew could have got us and all our equipment safely over them. At last we were at the headwaters where lay the Tenggara village.

Chapter 15

From Tenggara we planned to continue perhaps a mile farther up the river and then to travel afoot into the higher and somewhat thinner jungle, where we hoped to secure pictures of at least some of the monkey and ape species. The presence of the Hadji in our party impressed the Tenggara to such an extent, however, that we were forced to linger and accept some of their hospitality. Great earthenware jars of sago spirits were brought out with much ceremony and set before us, and plainly we were expected not only to show delight but also to drink. This we did, though as little as possible. I don't know when I've found a smile more difficult to put on than I did with that sour stuff in my mouth.

As is always the case with natives who never before have seen a white woman, the Tenggara people subjected me to the usual amazed scrutiny, inspecting my clothes and fingering my skin and hair, but wholly without offensiveness. The chief, a big fellow with a round head and a jovial laugh, commanded that our visit be properly celebrated, whereupon the men of the village drank long and deeply of the sago, and the women hurried about building fires and cooking rice and yams together with fish, lizard, and monkey flesh in preparation for a feast.

The men wore G-strings of woven bark fiber; the women, knee-length skirts of the same material; the children, up to ten, were naked. Most of them had good, intelligent features, sometimes with a slightly Mongolian look. Their skin was a clear, tawny brown and their bodies, for the most part, were strong and graceful. A disfigurement which we had also found among some people of the Solomons and New Hebrides was the filing of the teeth. Some were filed to points, others straight off. And increasing this unnatural look of their otherwise fine mouths was the stain of the narcotic betel nut, which blackened the teeth and gave a cerise color to the lips.

Martin was delighted with them as photographic subjects and was everywhere with his camera; indeed, he was able to forget his disappointment over Borneo as a place in which to secure wild-animal pictures. Thanks to the Hadji, the natives performed willingly for my husband, the women first with their bark-fiber weaving, the preparation and cooking of food, the care of their children, and the prideful combing of their own and their husbands' straight, glossy hair. And it pleased me very much as I watched these women to see that while they did much of the hard work of the village, nevertheless they were spirited and independent and would tolerate no abuse either of themselves or of their children.

Next, the men demonstrated the use of their blowguns and poison darts, in both hunting and fighting, and the workings of their bamboo fire-making apparatus. This, together with a parang, was carried in a sheath of wood on every male Tenggara's hip. A sinister implication, at least, was the human scalp of long black hair which frequently was used to adorn the parang's handle. Tenggaras, we learned, had been and probably still were headhunters. We gleaned that they had many heads hidden away, but since a penalty of seven years was pronounced by the government upon any man found with one in his possession, a necessary secrecy surrounded what probably was an ancient and, to them, an honored custom.

The sago spirits apparently were very potent, for the men squatting around the big jars and sucking on straws were growing hilarious, and in some instances actually combative.

"Looks as if this might turn into a sort of Saturday-night toot," Martin said in an aside to me.

"Maybe we'd better go," I replied, a bit eagerly. In any case, I'd been feeling rather miserable at the thought of eating monkey meat; it savored too much of cannibalism. Martin consulted first with Mr. Holmes and then with the Hadji, and both agreed that any native under the influence of liquor was something to avoid.

With what must have seemed bewildering suddenness, we put some trade goods into the hands of the chief for distribution, then took to our canoes. Half the village, it seemed to me, followed us, protesting, to the shore, and eight or ten of the younger men piled into a gobong and paddled furiously upstream after us. Angrily flourishing their parangs, they demanded that we return to the village, but their erratic paddling sent them into a mud bank, and we waved them a laughing farewell.

We camped that night a mile or so above Tenggara and prepared for an early-morning trip into the jungle. It seemed to me we had only just fallen asleep when we were awakened by a terrifying, almost human shriek of rage.

Keeping his voice low, Mr. Holmes told us it was a male orangutan, and that he had probably just discovered our camp and was protesting our intrusion into his jungle domain.

"I've got to have a picture of him right now!" Martin reached excitedly for his camera and the flares.

"You'll never get him tonight," Mr. Holmes warned. "He'd be off like a shot the moment you stepped out of the canoe."

"But I've got to do something about him!"

"Don't worry," Mr. Holmes said. "His curiosity will keep him right where he is until morning."

Astonishingly, the men went promptly to sleep. I sat up all night and dabbed coal oil on my face and arms to drive the mosquitoes away, and kept track of the general position of the big orangutan by his hoarse jabbering and the creaking of branches under his great weight. I also remembered "The Murders in the Rue Morgue" and was quite miserable.

We were stirring at sun-up and, to our delight, saw the big, dark shape of the creature in a tree not thirty feet from shore. He was quiet now but watching us sharply.

I don't think I've ever seen Martin more excited, not even when he got his camera ready for his first picture of Nagapate. Ways and means to bring the big fellow within camera range were discussed, and finally it was decided to send a dozen or more of our natives in behind him to drive him, if possible, into the open.

The big orangutan was not to be outwitted quite so easily, for with a yell he was off through the treetops over our heads. He didn't go far, however, and Martin, with a glint in his eye, shouldered his camera and followed him. I followed Martin. Mr. Holmes—very wisely, I afterwards concluded—remained behind with the Hadji.

This went on all day long, the big orangutan keeping just out of camera range. I could have sworn that at times he actually laughed at us. Martin followed grimly and gave up only when the light was gone.

"If the big brute came and sat right on my lens now I couldn't get a picture of him," he said, exasperated.

He gave the order to return to camp. I was so tired even then that it seemed to me if another thornbush snagged me or if I slipped on another slimy root or saw another snake or had to singe off another leach, I'd start screaming and nothing could stop me.

After this, we followed our carriers for perhaps an hour through the dark green undergrowth, when suddenly they stopped and began arguing among themselves as to which direction to take. Then we knew we were lost.

My head throbbed, my body ached, and I was thorn scratches from head to foot. I wanted to cry. Martin gave me a quick, anxious look, so I busied myself cutting a water-vine and getting a drink.

"Well," he said, putting his arm around me, "shall we see if we can get them to agree on a direction, or shall I take over?"

I looked up at him. His ash-blond hair stuck in damp little curls to his forehead. He was anxious and earnest and disappointed over everything, and just as tired as I was.

I had found that there is nothing quite so heartening to a man as knowing his woman has confidence in him.

"You take over," I said.

He smiled briefly. "I—" He broke off and looked carefully in all directions. We might as well have been at the bottom of a deep green ocean. It was dusk by now.

"Well," he said, then took my hand and plunged off at right angles from the course our natives had taken. They protested en masse that this would never get us back to the river, and followed in grumbling reluctance. We arrived at the river in exactly half an hour and found ourselves about a quarter of a mile up from our camp.

I was very proud of my husband over this and told him so, but I doubt that he heard me. He was facing an honest awareness of his inexperience in photographing animals. The jungle and the problems of light baffled him. He was fearfully tired when we headed our gobong caravan downstream for the return trip.

"What's the big smile about?" he asked suddenly.

"Smile? Was I smiling?"

"Yes, sort of mysterious and gloating. You know, little yellow feathers sticking out all around your mouth."

"Oh, I'm a cat now, am I?"

I pretended indignation, but I kept smiling all the way to Sungei Iyau, where, on our arrival three days later, we found our houseboat waiting for us. I shall never forget Martin's face. He shot one keen, startled look at me, then without a word stepped onto the raft and in through the little door. Then, in turn, he stretched out on the bed, sat on one of the rattan chairs, leaned his elbows on the table. He even set his tripod up on the little porch, and then, still without speaking, he hugged me close. Mr. Holmes and the good Hadji, to both of whom I owed the perfect carrying-out of my plan, stood and looked on, and I think they were almost as happy about it as we were.

That night we had a wonderful dinner. I had brought flour in one of the boxes, so immediately I whipped up some biscuits. I had also brought sugar, tea, and condiments. The men netted shrimps and clams right out of the river, and our hunters brought in some green pigeons and an argus pheasant, which I boiled. Wild mushrooms and spinach from the forest, together with yams and rice which we bought from the natives, took care of our vegetable needs, and for dessert we had the freshly picked wild fruits. I put on a clean white blouse with my pants and boots, and brushed my hair and did it up with "rats" and pins as was the fashion of the day. Martin shaved and put on a clean shirt. We had as guests Mr. Holmes and the Hadji, whom we had grown to love, together with the chief of Sungei Iyau.

The trip in our houseboat, when we got under way, was

one of luxurious comfort compared with the gobongs. The kinks in our backs soon straightened, Martin looked rested again, and our little gibbon ape, given the freedom of the raft, was soon fat, saucy, and active. She was a little startled—and resentful too, I think—when, after putting in at a rubber plantation one day, Martin returned with a half-grown titian-haired orangutan named Bessie. They were soon great friends, though, and Martin took some interesting pictures of them and their crazy antics.

I believe that Martin's love extended to practically every creature that lived. He had even taught me to accept two huge hairy spiders that had taken up lodging in the roof of our little floating house. But when, on the morning following Bessie's entrance into our family, I stepped out on our little porch, I knew I would have to draw the line. There, not six inches from where I stood petrified in the doorway, was a basket of squirming, lightning-fanged cobras. Martin pointed out their beauty and said that with their fangs removed they would make fine pets, but I stood firm. Kalowatt jumped to his shoulder and Bessie hid behind him. Both added loud objections to mine, so we had the men pole us into the bank, where Martin reluctantly let the reptiles go.

Reaching Pintasin, the Hadji Mohammed's home, we were both touched and pleased to find that the natives, with some vague idea of what we were seeking in the jungle, had captured some fine specimens of honey bear, several of the native deer (about the size of a fox), and three monkeys. After Martin had photographed all these, we turned them loose in their jungle home.

We continued on down the river to Lamag, the government post, and here once more remained for a few days as the guests of Mr. Holmes, of whom we had become deeply fond. There were reports of an elephant herd in the vicinity, and Martin, hopes high, set out with his camera and hunters in pursuit of them. We got within "hearing" distance, but that was all. The jungle continued to present its green, solid, inscrutable face, and when we took leave of our host, we were still without pictures of Borneo's more important animal life.

Drifting on down the Kinabatangan, we sat on the front

porch of our floating home and contemplated the abundant and sometimes repellent beauties of the Borneo jungle. Trees of strange shapes sometimes tied themselves in complete knots in their efforts to reach the light, and some bore leaves of deep red and lemon-yellow that gave the effect of sunlight where there was none. There were times when my husband and I, hearing the death scream of a jungle creature caught and killed for food by a stronger creature, were oppressed by nature's cruelty.

Arriving at Sandakan and back once more in the hilltop place we had leased, Martin gloomily reviewed the notes he had made of our trip. Kalowatt, now plump as a butterball, sat on his shoulder and pulled his ear. Bessie sat on his knee and studied his hands, one after the other.

"Looks to me," he said, "as though we may have to chalk up this Borneo trip as a failure." He sighed. "Time wasted, money wasted."

I put my arm around him but received a sharp pinch from Bessie for my pains. She was frankly jealous of me where Martin was concerned, and this was her way of warning me to keep my distance.

"You can't help it that the jungles here are so thick," I said, "and that the animals run the way they do. We didn't know it would be like this."

"Well, we should have known—I mean, I should. Any wild animal will run, even a chipmunk, and by the time the camera's set up here and focused, they've put a wall of jungle between us."

"That camera." I was disgusted. "Why, it weighs a ton, and, besides, it's obsolete!"

"Yes, and a new one would cost a lot of money which we haven't got."

"No man can work without proper tools," I said severely, "and before we go on another trip you're going to have a new camera."

"Yes, and what's more, before we're through with this trip, I'm at least going to have some pictures of elephants."

"Well, if you can get any place where you can see them, at least they're big," I said as encouragingly as possible.

With our single, clumsy motion-picture camera, two still cameras, Jack London's old Marlin, and our pistols, we set out once more in the government launch up still another waterway out of Sandakan Bay, this time to a place some twenty miles distant, which from all accounts was elephant country. We took with us four hunters and a half-dozen coolies, the latter to carry food, film, and camp stuff.

Leaving the launch at a designated place along the narrow stream, we shouldered our equipment and struck out through the steaming jungle. Cutting and fighting our way for three days, we finally came just at nightfall to a clear, beaten elephant trail and took to our bed on the ground. While our small tent was designed to keep snakes and insects out, I remembered the python that swallowed the pig and was able to sleep only fitfully. The men disposed themselves in the branches of the banyan.

Martin too was restless. The mosquitoes, of course, had found us. The tent was airless, and the ground through our canvas flooring was both moist and hard.

"Why in the world did we ever pick Borneo?" I said at length, with as much irritation as I have ever permitted myself.

Martin chuckled. I've never known anyone with such steady good nature.

"Oh, I charged that up to just plain dumbness on my part long ago," he said.

"But you still haven't told me how you plan to photograph the elephants."

"Why, the same as we did with the orangutan. Only elephants, being built the way they are, won't be able to escape through the treetops. See?" he added brightly.

"Well, I suppose so. You mean you'll set up the camera in the trail and have the men go back of the elephants and drive them toward you?"

"Right!" Martin yawned sleepily.

I slapped mosquitoes and wondered whether I could still climb a tree. Then I yawned and probably fell asleep, for I was awakened by a great thudding sound that seemed to shake the earth, followed by a thrashing in the brush apparently only a hundred yards or so away. Definitely we were in elephant country. I shivered with delight and woke Martin.

His watch showed that we were within three quarters of an hour of daylight. Our chief hunter, Nangai, good man that he was, had already awakened his men, and, with admirable speed and quiet, they disappeared on a circuitous route that would take them to the far side of the herd. Martin found a vantage point on the trail of his camera, and I fiddled around nervously wishing there were some way in which I could help. It was now daylight, and I remembered suddenly that in the excitement my husband had had no breakfast. The elephants, probably now to windward of our hunters, began trumpeting and thrashing about, but I hurried to our tent anyway and got some biscuits and hard-boiled eggs out of the chop box. I had just reached the trail with these when I heard the shot that meant the drive was on. The tuskers screamed and trumpeted, and looking over my shoulder I saw the lead bull, followed by some twenty others, breaking for the trail. I was between them and Martin. My mouth went dry and I raced toward my husband, who was grinding as steadily and firmly as though this were not one of the biggest moments of his whole life.

"Take the gun and get up a tree!" he barked, never looking at me.

"But what about you?"

"Do as I tell you!"

The thunder and crash of the herd, not fifty yards away, and the shots and yelling of the men to drive them straight at us were all I needed. I snatched up the gun and made for the banyan just off the path.

Martin continued to grind. The herd was no more than thirty feet off when he swept the camera, tripod and all, over his shoulder and made for the banyan I was in, and before the elephants could circle and follow him he had anchored the camera in the tangle of vines and swung himself up. Then, pulling the camera after him to a higher branch, he was out of reach of the angry tuskers, who trampled and trumpeted beneath.

In my excitement I dropped the gun, butt down, in the center of the banyan tree. It went off, angering the elephants still more. Martin managed to unlimber the camera and take some shots of the big beasts through the branches. After a while, seeming to enjoy the whole thing, he took off his pith helmet and threw it among them.

"Well, that was a silly thing to do," I said. "They'll trample it."

Martin grinned. "That's why I did it. If they'll trample it good, it'll make a fine souvenir to take back to Independence."

Our hunters tried to drive the elephants off but were chased for their pains (my enterprising husband got pictures of this), and it wasn't until morning that the big mammals lumbered away and we were able to descend from the tree.

On the whole, Martin was quite pleased with the result of our elephant expedition. We treked jauntily back to our boat, and what was our luck on our way down the river but to see our elephant herd in the water at a bend below having its morning drink and bath. Martin ordered the motor cut. We drifted quietly down toward them, and, before they crashed off into the jungle, some more fine pictures were added to the ones we already had.

Summing up our entire expedition, we hadn't done so badly after all, and at last we were aboard the freighter, headed for home via Singapore. Sir West Ridgeway saw us off with a cordial Godspeed that warmed our hearts, and urged our early return. Sailing with us, and now an indispensable member of our family, was Kalowatt, our little gray gibbon. Bessie, our titian-haired orangutan, a close second in our affections, was also with us. Two cockatoos, one yellow-crested and the other black, completed our little menagerie.

"You know, Osa," Martin said as we watched the lovely tropical bay of Sandakan merge with the general contours of British North Borneo, "you'd never believe it, but I've shot nearly fifty thousand feet of film on this Borneo trip, and I've been thinking that instead of making it just a headhunters picture, we ought to put it together as a sort of study of Borneo—natives, animals, and all. Don't you think so?"

I did, most emphatically. And, happy and proud of my husband, I led the way to dinner. This, a greasy, unnameable stew, was slapped on a rough table by a surly cabin boy, and we ate it by the faint light of a soot-encrusted coal-oil lamp. Roaches and other discomforts too numerous to mention were ours, but I minded them very little. Apparently I was becoming a hardened traveler like Martin—like Charmian London. Perhaps, I reflected hopefully, I had even taken on the look of one.

Our cabin, as well as being lit with a coal-oil lamp, was right over the engine and unbearably hot. We gave up all thought of sleep and devoted the rest of the night to tending our little zoo, which we found, on investigation, was pathetically seasick.

Delivered to us tardily the next morning was a cable from Martin's father with news that left Martin bewildered and grief-sticken. His mother had died nearly two weeks earlier.

We left Singapore, and after stops in Ceylon, Cape Town, and Durban, we continued up the coast of Africa, through the Suez Canal, and finally to London.

I never go back to London that that great and grave city does not have a tinge of the fantastic about it for me, and all because of our experiences there on this trip in 1920. Arriving, as Martin so graphically put it, short on money and long on animals, finding living quarters proved a distinct problem. We went to some five hotels before we found one that would take us in, and then, because of the early-morning chatter of our small zoo, we were asked to move.

Three times more we succeeded in getting into hotels, and three times more we were ejected. At length we found a place in Bloomsbury Palace Street, a dingy place not more than half full, where we were given two rooms on the top floor, a good distance up from the other tenants. The general look of the thing was a little more encouraging, though here also we were warned to keep our menagerie quiet or out we'd have to go.

Martin had looked forward to showing London to me, but so far I hadn't even seen the Tower.

"We might as well be keepers in a zoo and be done with it," Martin grumbled.

"It's all Bessie's fault," I said irritably. "Yes, and yours too. If you'd stop laughing at her, she might stop thinking she's so funny."

"Well, you needn't be smug," Martin retorted. "Kalowatt puts her up to most of it."

Summer in England is colder than winter in Borneo, and Bessie came down with a cough. Martin sat for days holding her and rubbing her chest with camphor oil. She loved it.

"I guess I'll have to go out and buy some sweaters," he said one day after she'd fallen asleep and he had succeeded in detaching himself without arousing her. "Maybe you'd better come along," he added. "You know more about sizes and things than I do."

We closed the door softly on our pets, crept out into the hall, and listened. So far so good, and we rushed and caught a tram that let us off at Selfridge's. I flashed a quick look at the windows as we hurried past. If ever a woman had need of some new clothes, I did, but there was neither time nor money for this now, and we asked our way to "sweaters." We got four soft, thick wool ones at a total cost sufficient to buy me a very nice and much-needed dress. The two for Bessie were size 34, and the two for Kalowatt were of a size to fit a small doll.

Arriving back at the motel, we found a commotion of almost riot proportions. All the people living in rooms below ours were simply hysterical. The hotel was haunted, they declared, and the ghost, screeching and lusty, was up the flue.

We rushed to our rooms and found the inner door still closed, but Bessie was gone and so was Kalowatt. The trunk, which we had pushed firmly across the fireplace, had been pulled away.

"That Bessie!" I said.

Finally, coaxed back down the chimney, they were a big and a little ball of black soot. Bounding past us then and out the door into the hall, they raced from top to bottom of the hotel, scattering panic and soot with equal abandon.

Not only were we asked to leave the hotel in Bloomsbury, but we were presented with a large bill for damages besides. Martin paid it, and except for our second-class passage home, which Martin had put aside, we were down to about five dollars.

Martin was anxious. "I was figuring on something from the South Sea pictures by now," he said. "Maybe not much, but something."

"Have you called American Express?" I asked.

"No point in calling. They've got our address."

"Which address?"

My husband looked at me, then shot to a telephone. Yes, he was informed, there was something for us at American Express. It had been there for days, and they had been unable to reach us.

It turned out to be a draft for ten thousand dollars!

With money magically smoothing the way, we secured rooms in a very decent place where we could live and keep our pets. Inquiry at the zoo led us to a man whom we were able to hire to look after them for a few days, and at length we were free to do London.

"I'm going out right this minute and have my hair done," I said, "and maybe a manicure and a new pair of shoes."

Martin came to me and laid a thousand pounds in my hand.

"This is yours," he said, "and I don't want to see you again until you've spent every penny of it!"

I still had seen nothing of London when, a few days later, we boarded the S. S. *Pan Handle State* for home. A cablegram from Robertson-Cole had suggested an early return to New York with our Borneo picture, and "early" to Martin meant the first boat on which we could secure passage. We traveled first class, and, at Martin's insistence, I had some of the loveliest clothes available in London, topped off by a beautifully matched moleskin cape. We had Kalowatt with us in our cabin, but Bessie and the cockatoos were properly caged and everything possible done for their comfort—and hence ours. I can't think when I've ever had a lovelier or more luxurious time, and to top it all, there was Martin's gift of lingerie—box after box of it—from the finest London shops, dainty and sheer as pink froth—and, as Martin later confessed to me, worth more than three hundred dollars.

"I think it's wonderful," he said a little sheepishly as I opened the boxes, "the way you can wear those overalls and things when we're roughing it. But I like you to have pretty things too, and gosh knows you haven't had many since you married me!"

Early the next morning there was a great commotion on

deck—running feet, yelling and—yes, above all this, Bessie's familiar screech. We looked at each other and rushed out in our bathrobes. Some sailors painting the stanchions on the upper deck had missed a can of paint. Empty, it had been thrown overboard—the contents were in Bessie's stomach.

Orangutans are supposed to be frail and difficult to raise in captivity, but with a pint of vinegar down her as an antidote for the paint, Bessie, lively as ever, got out of her cage at four o'clock the next morning and rang the fire bell. Passengers and crew alike rushed to their lifeboat stations, and Bessie, still ringing the bell, was ordered below and put in chains.

The president of the United States Lines was aboard, and we had spent three most enjoyable evenings with him. He had even said most graciously that he thought Bessie was very bright and amusing. On the last evening at sea, however, he was plainly quite cool toward us—and small wonder. Bessie had got free of her chains, had made her way into the wine cellar, and, when found, was sitting in the midst of some twenty-three broken bottles of extra fine vermouth. At the moment of discovery she was pouring the contents of the twenty-fourth bottle over her head. Thoroughly soaked with the choice and expensive liquor, it seemed probable that this was how she had disposed of an entire case. Martin, of course, footed the bill.

From the boat we went directly to the Hotel Astor, engaging a suite of rooms, one of them for our pets. My parents and Martin's father arrived from Kansas just as we were being asked to leave. Repeating our London experience, we were asked to move once more, but finally we took an eight-room apartment at 39 Fifth Avenue. Here we had one of the bathrooms completely lined with zinc, where Bessie, no matter what she might think up, could do no harm, and we lived at this address in comparative peace and comfort until it was time to leave for our next trip.

It was part of Martin's charm, I think, that he should have been so astonished when we were invited to attend a dinner at the Explorers' Club, of which he was then made a member. He couldn't see at all how his blundering around the South Seas and Borneo with a camera qualified him to join the ranks of men like Theodore Roosevelt and Carl Akeley, the great sculptor and naturalist of the Museum of Natural History.

In all my life I don't think I've ever been prouder than when Mr. Akeley came and had dinner with us in our apartment at 39 Fifth Avenue. Martin's father was visiting us at the time, and though aged by the recent loss of his wife, he was cheerful and made no show whatever of sadness. Little Kalowatt sat at the table, as was now her custom, and did as pretty a job of eating with her small silver fork as anyone could wish to see. Mr. Akeley fell in love with her then and there and came many times to see her. As a matter of fact, Kalowatt was quite spoiled after his second visit, and there was nothing for it but that both Martin and his father must get down on the floor where she could pull their hair and bounce on their chests just as she had done with Mr. Akeley.

"You have a very important mission, Martin," Mr. Akeley said on one of those never-to-be-forgotten evenings. "Even more important than mine."

Martin and his father and I stared uncomprehendingly.

Carl Akeley went on. "I've made it my mission to perpetuate vanishing wild-animal life in bronze and by securing specimens for the museum. You are doing the same thing in film, which is available to millions of people all over the world."

This was one of many long and earnest talks with Mr. Akeley, and through him our plans for the future took shape. He suggested British East Africa as the best place in the world for our film studies of wild-animal life, and so this became our next goal.

The following few months were very busy ones for my husband. There was the editing of our Borneo film, trips home to Kansas—and the problem of raising the money for a properly equipped journey into Africa. While I was busy making the most of my brief stay in Kansas, visiting my family and seeing my old friends—among them Gail Hamilton and her babies— Martin decided that the best and most businesslike method of raising money would be to form a company and sell stock. His father was the first to buy. Not only did his father buy stock, he encouraged Martin to sell stock in Independence. And with the financing of our trip secured, I returned to New York to gather together the things that would insure us more comfort and efficiency on the trip. I likewise engaged in one amusing episode with Bessie.

Mrs. Allan, chairman of the Humane Society, who lived in the apartment below us, was very much interested in our strangely assorted pets and asked one day if I would be willing to appear with Bessie on the steps of the library at Fifth Avenue and Forty-second Street, to assist in a drive for funds. Readily enough, I said yes. The day of the fund drive was very hot. I combed and brushed Bessie and washed her face and hands, then hurried into a white blouse and skirt, pulled a tam over my hair, and called a taxi. Bessie weighed more than I did, and carrying her was quite a job, but being an orangutan, she was built to use her arms rather than her legs, and having once been carried she was utterly spoiled. The taxi driver, of the sort chronically disgusted and impervious to surprise, set us down at the library, and logically enough charged two fares. Bessie, troubled by the sight of so many people, hugged me a little closer than was altogether necessary, and, with her sturdy chest and thick, furry arms cutting off breath and vision, I climbed with considerable awkwardness and difficulty to the platform at the top of the stately stairs—also with complete unawareness that the spectacle of a small woman in the apparent stranglehold of a big ape had stopped the Fifth Avenue traffic.

At all events, Bessie attracted quite a crowd and shook hands nicely with as many ladies as cared to shake hands with her, and, according to Mrs. Allan, the fund, thanks to her, was swelled considerably.

Bessie became quite warm after a while with both sun and excitement, so I decided to take her home. She rubbed the top of her head and, I've no doubt, had a headache, so I gave her my handkerchief and she spread it on, but to her disgust it blew off. There's no doubt that she wanted a hat, because when we slowed at the Thirty-fourth Street intersection, she reached out and with perfect timing appropriated the cap of the traffic officer.

A good Irishman, intent on his duty, he swung around shouting something about the "dignity of the law," and looked into the face of an orangutan. His visored cap was on her head. Bessie's loud protests against parting with the cap snarled traffic

on Fifth Avenue for the second time that day as well as working considerable damage to the cap itself. We were ordered by
the judge to buy the officer a new one, which Martin thought
was reasonable enough.

As the time approached for us to start traveling again, it
became more and more apparent that we simply could not continue indefinitely to fashion our lives around a menagerie. As
it was, they—and Bessie in particular—had made us virtual
prisoners from the moment we acquired them, and so, with
mingled tears and sighs of relief at parting, we placed them in
the Central Park Zoo.

All but Kalowatt. Neither of us could bring ourselves either
to part with her or mention her. We gave her tenderer care
than ever and put off the wretched day as long as possible.
Then, finally, after a sleepless night, my mind was made up. I
would promise to take complete care of her and to keep her at
all times from being a bother—in short, I'd beg Martin to let
me take her with us.

We had sat down to our last breakfast in town and neither
of us ate a bite. Kalowatt, with her little fork and nothing to
impair her appetite, did all the honors.

"Martin—" I began.

"About Kalowatt," he broke in. "I've been thinking about
her. She'd just about die in a zoo with strangers staring at her
all day, and besides that, she's used to us, and—" He scowled
at me. "What do you think?"

I became very intent on whatever I was doing.

"But, of course, we couldn't possibly take her with us," I
said.

My husband glared. "And why not? There's no law against
it, is there?"

Martin had a beautiful little cage made for her, but even so,
several steamship companies refused to take her as a passenger, and we were delayed by the rearranging of our schedule.

And we had reason to be grateful for this delay, because it
gave Martin's father just the little extra time he needed to make
up his mind to go with us to Africa. He had been weighing the
idea for some weeks, it seemed.

"If you'd gone last Friday," he said, "I'd have been on the

shore waving good-bye. But I've made up my mind, and the shore can wave good-bye to me!"

I don't know when I've seen Martin so happy.

"I'll just take a little peek at Africa," the elder Johnson said, "maybe get a look at a lion, then go around home and compare notes with that one hanging in the Booth Hotel."

*Chapter 16*_____

The preparations for our first trip to Africa had tired us all more than we knew, so I took advantage of the leisurely weeks aboard ship to rest and store up energy for whatever might lie ahead. Martin, however, was up early every morning pacing the deck. There was a new restlessness in him, a new anxiety. His father usually joined him, and I contented myself with sitting, Kalowatt perched on my knee, and watching them. Their companionship was a fine thing to see. Martin hadn't told me in so many words what was troubling him, but then it was rarely necessary for us to talk of things that touched us both closely, and I knew I could best help him by being cheerful and confident.

"Now, you stop worrying, son," Mr. Johnson said. They had paused and were leaning on the rail near me. It was just a few days before we sighted the East African coast. "Sure it's a responsibility, other people's money, but—"

"Your money too, don't forget!" Martin put in with a wry smile.

"Yes, and one of the best investments I ever made, or I miss my guess," the elder Johnson replied firmly. "The way I see it," he went on, "there'll be time enough to worry about lighting problems and whether you can get close enough to the animals to photograph them when you've got African soil under your feet and a lion or something out there looking at you."

"You're an optimist, Dad, that's all I've got to say. If they're anything like the animals in Borneo, all we'll see will be their tails."

"Well, I wouldn't say that, son. What about those elephants? Didn't you and Osa have to climb a tree?"

Martin grinned briefly. "We just happened to be lucky that
day." He was thoughtful again. "One thing sure," he said, "Osa
and I aren't going to do any trapping or faking. We're going to
get the animals the way they live in their natural environment
or we aren't going to get them at all."

"Absolutely!" Father Johnson was emphatic. "You're going
to get them honest." Then, after a moment, "You know, son,
there's one thing you overlook and that's you and Osa."

"What?"

"You haven't failed yet in anything you've set out to do, and
as far as I can see, you're a combination that just can't be beat."

Martin flashed a smile at me and winked.

"And me," Father Johnson laughed, "I didn't tell you this,
but along with my Kodak, I brought a little twenty-two popgun,
just in case some of these critters down here don't like the
smell of Kansas!"

Nairobi, principal city in British East Africa as well as the
government seat, was our destination, and there, following Carl
Akeley's suggestion, we were planning to make our headquarters.

Arriving at Mombasa, the seaport to British East Africa, we
immediately noticed the thick and humid heat that lies on this
country's lower lands along the Indian Ocean coast. It took three
days to get our eighty-five trunks, boxes, and crates through
customs and to arrange for their shipment by rail to Nairobi,
though one bright spot in the apparently endless confusion and
swelter was the discovery that refrigerator cars were available.
My husband had our film put in one of these as speedily as
possible, and from that moment on he seemed not to mind the
heat at all. I was at first worried about Father Johnson, but he
declared that it was no worse than summers in Kansas. He
bought a pith helmet and trailed cheerfully around with Martin
from docks to train shed, pencil and pad in hand, doing all the
things I usually did to help check our equipment.

"The boss of an outfit never works," he'd say to me. "You
sit there." If no other shade was available, he'd hire a native to
hold an umbrella over me. The fact that this cost only a few
cents for an entire day had him properly astonished.

"Why, with a few thousand dollars, a man could live like a millionaire around here," he said delightedly. When he learned, however, that it was costing us more to ship our things from Mombasa to Nairobi, a distance of about three hundred and thirty miles, than it had cost to come from the United States to Africa, and that our railroad tickets were costing us eighteen cents a mile, he was frankly bewildered.

On the evening of the third day, with our stuffy hotel rooms and the heat and confusion of Mombasa left behind, we started our journey to Nairobi on the Uganda railroad. Among the pleasant incongruities of travel in this part of the world was finding ourselves in a modern compartment car drawn by a wood-burning engine. The engine, I remember, had a preposterously feminine-sounding whistle which screeched incessantly. The engineer, a bearded, beturbaned Sikh, and the fireman, a black, both with very engaging grins, told us they kept the whistle going all the time to frighten wild animals off the tracks, all of which seemed very silly for the first hour or two out of Mombasa. Cultivated groves of coconuts, mangoes, papayas, and bananas met the railroad bed on either side, and the only animals visible were the monkeys, lively and impudent, that swung through the treetops and chattered at us as we chugged and tooted by. Kalowatt, for lack of treetops, leaped from Father Johnson's shoulder to Martin's and then to mine and, shaking with excitement, pressed her nose against the window.

We decided with some impatience that this certainly was not an express train, for we stopped at every little station along the way. Natives in sketchy and usually untidy costumes swarmed to the train platforms and did a large, if not very profitable, business with the passengers in the third- and fourth-class compartments. Father Johnson was out at every stop and reported that the most popular commodity was milk, sold in every imaginable container ranging from gourds to gin bottles. Other food offered for sale, he found, was some greasy, sticky lumps of stuff with a most revolting smell. He bought some thinking that perhaps Martin or I could identify it. When we failed, he started to put a little of it in his mouth, but Martin seized it and tossed it out the window.

"You're as bad as Jack London," he grinned, not without admiration. "He ate everything too and got a bug they never did figure out."

Thanks to Carl Akeley, we were prepared for the fact that the Uganda railroad did not supply the comforts or the bedding usually found in American Pullman sleeping cars. So when night came I got pillows, sheets, and blankets from our own luggage to make things fairly comfortable. It was ten o'clock when I awoke the next morning, but Martin and his father, both too excited to sleep, had been up since daybreak and said the wild bush through which we were now traveling was alive with animals.

"Looks as if Noah's Ark might have been spilled out right here," Father Johnson cried, his nose, like Kalowatt's, glued to the windowpane.

We stopped for breakfast at a little village called Voi. The eating house was of galvanized iron, and the inside was surprisingly reminiscent of the Harvey restaurants on the Santa Fe line. Even the gong which sounded the call for meals and train-time had a familiar ring. Here the similarity ended, however, for instead of Indians, we saw black Africans wearing only skins and decorated with the most fantastic ornaments, and the shacks huddled around the station had walls of flattened gasoline cans and roofs of grass.

Leaving Voi, the train began the hard, slow pull to the highlands. Here the character of the country changed again, and soon we were out of the bush and traveling through great rolling plains. The air grew fresher and more invigorating, and every now and then we caught glimpses of the snow-covered peak of Mount Kilimanjaro.

The train paused at Kiu, a village very like Voi, where we had lunch. We also took on wood and water. Despite the frequent, necessary stops for fuel and water, the train finally, on schedule, pulled into Nairobi.

Had it not been for the black porters in long-tailed khaki shirts, I could easily have imagined myself in any one of a number of Middle West railroad stations. People in more or less conventional garb hurried to and fro. There was a newsstand and a restaurant, both lively and attractive, and, to my astonishment, a string of taxis stood at the street entrance. These, however, were only the beginning of the surprises Nairobi held for me. For no reason I can think of I had expected to see a somewhat squalid tropical village such as we found in the South Seas, and I was totally unprepared for the clean, white, modern city it proved to be. Our taxi took us smoothly over paved streets flanked by office buildings and department stores and let us out at a hotel which provided all the comforts of up-to-date civilization. Situated nearly six thousand feet above sea level, with a population of more than two thousand whites, Nairobi was the healthful and pleasant seat of the British East African government.

I had pictured all Englishmen in Africa as wearing pith sun helmets and khaki shorts, but here in Nairobi they dressed exactly as they might have done in London, in good, well-cut, tailored woolens. That this was Africa, however, was made sharply evident by the crowds of blacks. There were askaris, the husky native soldiers, proud in their bright-red fezzes; there were house servants in white konzas, a flowing garment that had the look of a nightshirt and is the house servant's livery; and there were market women dressed in skins and carrying flat trays of vegetables on their heads.

The business section of town swarmed with traffic that was at once thick, noisy, and conglomerate. There were dilapidated wagons drawn by mules, rickshaws drawn by blacks, lively bicyclists, slow pushcarts, and impatient automobiles—the latter often of American make—that honked petulantly but without avail. Martin and I were astonished to see this mass move at all, and yet move it did and even with a semblance of order, thanks to the police officer directing it. He was fun to watch. With his air of importance he might have been in the very heart of Piccadilly Circus.

While Martin busied himself with plans for our first safari, his father and I searched for living quarters and had the good luck to find a lovely eight-room bungalow just twenty minutes from town. It was set in the heart of a beautiful garden, of perhaps an acre in extent, that fostered with equal hospitality the flowers familiar to our western eyes, as well as the brilliant, unfamiliar blooms of the tropics; and tall, straight evergreens

stood sentinel on all four sides. At the back of the house we
found an oblong patch of fine pineapples, together with a large
square plot, freshly spaded, that clearly was the kitchen garden.

Delighted with our find, Father Johnson and I hurried back
to town, searched out Martin, who was deep in figures that
had to do with safari Fords, ox carts, porters, and the like, and
rushed to the little real estate office just a block up from the
hotel, where we signed a lease.

"And you've no idea how beautifully arranged the house is,
Martin," I said excitedly on our way back to the hotel. "Why,
one servant in the house and another to take care of the garden
will be all in the world I'll need."

That I wound up with ten servants never has ceased to
amuse me. It began the next morning. Martin had left early
with his father, and I was packing our things, eager to get out
to the bungalow, when there was a tap at the door. I said
"Come," and in walked a big, fine-looking black in spotless white
konza and skullcap. He carried a breakfast tray which, with
utmost respect and deftness, he set before me.

I said, "Who are you?"

He replied, "Aloni, your room-boy."

I said, "Oh, you belong to the hotel?"

He replied, "No. Aloni belong to you."

As simply as that he hired himself to us, which, as we afterwards realized, was our good luck, for together with his small,
neat wife he proved invaluable, and before we ourselves had
moved into the bungalow, he had set up housekeeping in a
grass hut in a corner of our garden.

The rest attached themselves to us with almost equal directness. On the morning of my first encounter with Aloni, I
discovered a score of natives squatting outside our hotel and
watching our windows. By this time I was ready to leave for
the bungalow, and I thought that if their intentions were similar to Aloni's, I would simply ignore them. No sooner had I set
foot outside the door of the hotel, however, than they swarmed
about me, each thrusting anywhere from six to fifty letters of
recommendation under my nose. Most of them were written in
neat enough script, but their contents were little short of aston-

ishing. "Mohammed is a fairly good cook," read one. "I never saw him stealing." "Kimani was my houseboy for three months," said another. "He does as well as he can."

Bewildered by all this ambiguity, I shook my head and ran for a rickshaw, but I wound up, as I've said, with ten servants. Two or three at most would have done very nicely, but I found that they had an undeclared code of division of work, as effective as any trade union, and that the cost of all ten was less than the wage of one servant at home.

Once settled into a routine, we found that our cook, as in every part of the world, was the aristocrat of the servants, and, as such, was paid something like four times as much as the rest. He was an enormous man with a wide grin and strong, white teeth. We thought his name, Joanna, a trifle too feminine, so we called him simply Mpishi, meaning "cook" in Swahili. His costume, over which apparently we had no control, was somewhat startling, consisting as it did of a shirt-like smock, khaki shorts, tattered socks, and a pair of cast-off shoes. On Sundays, however, he was almost splendid in starched white trousers, a mess jacket minus sleeves, and a too-small straw hat perched slantwise atop his head. When he hired himself to us, he said he was a cook—and he was. Mpishi let us know without preliminaries that he had two assistants—one to prepare the vegetables, the other to clean the pans.

Aloni also introduced an assistant, a sort of apprentice roomboy. "This one, Toto," Aloni announced. Actually, I found out later, *toto* is the Swahili word for child or infant and can be applied to elephants and rhino babies as well as human beings. In a household such as ours, *toto* often becomes a substitute as a proper name and designates the youngest member of one's domestic staff. If there is a youngster in the culinary department, he is invariably "Kitchen Toto."

Toto was twelve years old and, from what I could make out, was Aloni's son by another wife. Toto wore a grin of perpetual delight and was spotless in khaki shorts and starched white shirt and cap. Whenever he went to market with me to carry my basket, he tied a jaunty cerise sash around his waist.

Zabenelli, who understood English, was houseman, also acting as butler, messenger, and general utility man. Two gar-

deners also hired themselves to us, as did a watchman. All were
Kikuyus, who still wore animal skins dyed with red clay. The
gardeners didn't know anything about planting and tending
anything new, but the soil was fertile and the rains frequent,
and soon we had all the free corn, peas, lettuce, tomatoes, and
beans that we could eat, while every bowl and vase in the house
bulged with fruit and flowers.

In short, keeping house in Nairobi was downright fun, and
knowing I would have a chance at it only between safaris, I
made the most of it. Almost daily I would go to either the "white
market" of the British and Boer farmers, or to the native market where the native and East Indian gardeners sold their produce. There I would buy, for practically nothing, white-skinned
potatoes, alligator pears, strawberries, asparagus, and whatever
else our own garden lacked. Clean, orderly butcher shops supplied us with wild game as well as with the standard cuts of
meat. Father Johnson often accompanied Toto and me on these
shopping excursions, and we both developed what amounted
to a secret passion for the "white market." It was just as much
fun as a crossword puzzle, and almost as exciting as backgam-
mon, for everything—butter, eggs, flowers, fruit, vegetables,
tinware, and furniture—was sold at auction.

Running Father Johnson and me a close second in the matter of getting sheer fun out of our new life was Kalowatt. All
the climbing she had ever done—with the exception of her es-
capade up the chimney with Bessie in London—had been within
the narrow limits of our New York apartment, where the chan-
deliers were the closest substitute she could find for trees. Here
we gave her the run of the garden, and she kept carefully within
the limits, swinging from tree to tree and gorging on fruit. When
stuffed to capacity, she sat on a high branch and performed
monkey antics for an always-increasing audience of natives.
Given her choice, I think she would have slept in a treetop
rather than in her pillowed bed. No amount of coaxing would
bring her down, even when it grew dark, until Martin had the
idea of getting some of our natives to make a pretense of hitting us with sticks. The effect was magical. Kalowatt, screaming with rage, leaped among them, cuffing, scratching, and
biting, and not until she had accomplished a complete rout was

she satisfied to be taken into the house, where she then strutted for the greater part of an hour, proud of having rescued us. In this land of so many types of primates, Kalowatt became noted for her intelligence and antics, and we, in turn, became known as "the people with the gibbon ape."

Martin, it seemed to me, had the least fun of any of us, but as his father pointed out, work and fun were one with him when they combined the things he loved to do. With characteristic directness, he had surveyed the possibilities of our eight-room bungalow and then had a clause added to the lease to the effect that certain drastic alterations could be made, but that on the expiration of our tenancy the house would be restored to its original condition. We had brought with us from New York several fifty-gallon developing tanks and drums on which to dry the film. When these were set up, together with several long, narrow tables, and the windows of the darkroom made lightproof, we had as fine a laboratory as any to be found outside of New York or Hollywood.

The city water presented a problem. Coming as it did from various swampy lakes and rivers, it was muddy and thick with vegetable matter and in that state could not be used for developing. Filtering was a slow and complicated process, so Martin had a tinsmith build wide gutters around the roof of the house to catch the rainwater. These were connected with fifty-gallon tanks which in turn were piped into the darkroom, and even during dry seasons enough water was available in this way to meet all developing needs.

Carl Akeley had written various people letting them know of Martin and his mission in this part of the world, with the result that our house—or, rather, the laboratory—became the gathering place for everyone in Nairobi interested either in photography or in the animals of British East Africa. Major A. Radclyffe Dugmore, the famous explorer and photographer, who made some of the best still pictures ever to come out of Africa, developed hundreds of his photographs in Martin's laboratory.

Major General Sir Edward Northey, the governor of Kenya Colony, often was a visitor. Intensely alive to the problem of preserving the wildlife of British East Africa, he was most enthusiastic in his approval of our plan to hunt with a camera instead of with a gun, and gave us his unqualified support.

Sir Northrup McMillan, a member of the legislative council, lived just up the street from us. Extremely interested in photography, he spent many hours in the darkroom, and his kindly advice and understanding of our problems did much to smooth our path.

Then there was our good friend Mr. Stanley Taylor of the fingerprint department of the Bureau of Native Affairs. In addition to giving us much useful information about the natives, he solved what had been a major problem for Martin by allowing him to store his negatives in the vault of the department— the only fireproof storage space in Nairobi.

Blayney Percival, of course, occupies a niche all his own in my affectionate regard. Twenty years as game warden in British East Africa had made him an unquestioned authority on the animals of the country. He knew all the various species and their habits and haunts, and he was extremely generous with both his knowledge and his time. He had a brusqueness of manner that at first was a little disconcerting, but this wore off after a little and we saw that it grew out of a downright exasperation with the so-called big-game hunters who came, in increasing numbers, to fatten their egos with trophies, no matter how obtained, and whose lust to kill would in time become a menace to African wildlife.

Blayney came one night carrying a thin, worn book. I had made a cake, which we served with some coffee in the living room. Martin had opened the windows wide, and the garden was fresh and fragrant following a hard tropical shower. Kalowatt chattered excitedly at a large red admiral moth on the screen.

Martin looked tired but happy. That day he had completed plans for our first safari, which, on Blayney's advice, was to be a more or less experimental one to the shores of the Athi River, just thirty miles from Nairobi and easily accessible by automobile.

"Well, Blayney," Martin said, "I've got my headman finally. About the best to be had, I should say, and the funny thing about it is, he just walked in and, in so many words, said 'Here I am.' "

Blayney accepted another piece of cake and smiled enig-
matically.

"A big fellow, too," Martin went on. "Good-natured, but with
an air of authority that packs a real wallop."

"Yes," I put in, "and he was headman for Colonel Roosevelt
a couple of years ago!"

Blayney looked up. "Flat nose, wide mouth?"

"Biggest mouth I ever saw on any man," Father Johnson
said.

"I know." Blayney nodded. "Jerramani. A good man. Comes
from Tanganyika and knows this country as well as I know
London."

Martin laughed suddenly. "Why, you old son of a gun, I'll
lay a bet you sent him to me!"

"It's important," Blayney said, "to have the right headman,
especially when you're new to the country. Another thing: When
you start on your long trips with a lot of porters, you'll be glad
of a headman the porters will respect." Then, after a moment's
thought, "You'll need a second man, and I'd suggest Ferraragi.
The only thing is that he's almost as good as Jerramani—feels
himself of equal importance—and there probably will be a bit
of rivalry."

His thoughts seemed divided as he ruffled the thick yellowed pages of the book he was carrying. "Twenty-five dollars
a month each is all you should pay," he said. "Spoils them to
pay too much."

"Thanks for the tip, Blayney," Martin grinned. "Overpaying
is a sort of weakness of mine and—oh, by the way, I haven't
any porters so far. Thought I'd better leave that for the headman."

Blayney thought a minute. "As a matter of fact," he said,
"on a short trip such as this one, I don't think you'll need porters. Just take some of your house servants along." Then, "You
say you have two safari Fords?"

"Yes, Newton Limited here fitted me out. A new one, and
a secondhand one on which they put a safari body for my cameras and supplies."

"Can any of you shoot?" Blayney asked suddenly.

Martin laughed. "Well, Osa did a neat job of killing a cobra when we were in Borneo. Took its head right off."

"Yes," I said, "and two minutes after that I missed a wild pig the size of a young cow."

"Well, this trip to the Athi River will give you a chance to practice up, and I'd suggest you go at it in earnest."

Martin stared. "But we're not interested in killing anything, Blayney. I told you that."

Blayney nodded. "I know, you're not here to shoot game, but you can't safely carry that ideal to extremes. There are times when almost any wild animal is dangerous, you know—when hungry, during mating season, or guarding its young, sometimes even when you disturb it in its sleep—and every now and then it will be a question of its life or yours. That's to be expected."

Martin nodded, "I see that, of course."

"Funny thing," Father Johnson put in thoughtfully. "Martin never was one for killing. Why, when he was a boy, he beat the tar out of another young one his age just for killing a garter snake." He scratched his head. "And I guess maybe I'm partly to blame for encouraging him to feel that way."

Blayney Percival nodded. "I know. It's just that there's a bit of a problem here that'll take some figuring out."

"Well." Martin hesitated. "I'm not bad at target practice."

"Not the same thing at all as a moving, living object, and besides, it's going to be up to you to provide meat for your headman and porters. They're forbidden by the government to carry guns, you know, with the exception of your picked gun-bearers, and if you can't provide meat, you'll have to hire a white man—professional hunter—for the job. Cost you more than all your porters put together."

"Well—" Martin hesitated. "How much?"

"Around a thousand dollars a month."

"A what?" I gasped.

"Great Jupiter!" said Father Johnson.

Martin looked more troubled than at any other time.

"Fact is, Blayney," he said, "we've got the expenses of this thing to the bone now." He smiled a little sickishly. "But if it's got to be done, that's that."

Blayney nodded. "I'm afraid you'll have to." He lit a cigarette and took a turn about the room. "Martin," he said abruptly, "I'm going to take you three into my confidence on something that I'd—" he gave a short laugh. "Well, with the exception of telling Carl Akeley about it, I'd sworn I'd never confide it to another living soul." He pushed the thin book into Martin's hands. "It's all in there," he said.

I looked at the book over Martin's shoulder. The paper, as well as being yellow with age, was stained, and the old-fashioned type made it difficult reading.

"You can study it later," Blayney said. "Point is that the old Scotchman who wrote that book back in the early part of the nineteenth century described a crater lake which is on no map ever made of this country."

Martin stared at him. "You mean there's a lake around here nobody knew about?"

"Nobody, and you may be certain I've kept my ears open."

"But you'd think some of the natives would have run across it," I said.

"It's probable, but if they have, they've guarded the secret just as carefully as I have, and probably for the same reason."

"A lake," Martin said with mounting excitement. "Why, animals must go there by the thousands!"

Blayney nodded. "Yes, and probably from hundreds of miles in every direction—a sort of sanctuary, undisturbed by the white man and his gun. That's why I'm telling you about it, Martin. I'd like to see you go there some day with your camera and come back with a record of what animals are really like in their natural, undisturbed state."

Father Johnson was now on his feet. "Well, see here," he said, "where is this place?"

"If it isn't even on the maps," I put in doubtfully, "perhaps the Scotchman was sort of romancing."

Blayney Percival shook his head. "From the description in that book of the surrounding country, he wasn't romancing, and I believe that, barring the difficulties which the country itself may present, I could go straight to it."

Martin was beside himself with excitement. "Well, man alive," he shouted, "let's go! Why waste time on the Athi River? Why waste time on anything?"

Blayney smiled rarely, but he smiled now. "If you're wise, old chap," he said, "you'll take a lot of experimental trips before you attempt this one. Assuming that my reckoning is approximately correct, the lake is up to the north in an uncharted region near the Abyssinian border, perhaps five hundred miles as the crow flies, and without a doubt the country we'll have to cross to get to it will be both hard going and dangerous."

I had picked up the book, and I'm sure my eyes were bulging at what I saw. "Why, it says here that an animal called a camelopard was seen at the lake, and a two-horned unicorn!"

Blayney smiled. "I think that refers to the giraffe and oryx," he said.

"But I agree with Martin," I cried excitedly. "We mustn't waste time—we must go right away!"

"No," he replied. "A trip with the hazards of this one should only be made following careful preparation."

"But we don't mind hazards," I protested. "We're used to them. The Solomon Islands, South Seas, Borneo. . . ."

He shook his head. "I'm positive," he said, "that the lake must be almost inaccessible. Otherwise hunters, natives, someone since this man," he laid his hand on the book, "would have run across it." He was thoughtful for a moment, looking at me. "There's no question in my mind but that it's going to be a very hard trip, even a hazardous one, as I said before, and I'm inclined to think, Mrs. Johnson, that"—he smiled again— "if I were you, I wouldn't set my heart on going. It will be no trip for a woman."

"Oh!" It seemed to me I must explode. "No trip for a woman! That again!"

Chapter 17 _____

"Well, I guess that's everything," Martin said anxiously eyeing our heavily loaded safari Fords. This was about a week after our long talk with Blayney Percival, and we were at last ready to leave for our first experimental trip to the Athi River. The cars stood in the driveway outside our bungalow, and every inch of space was piled high.

"No, it isn't everything," I replied. "Here's Kalowatt's bed."

"Kalowatt's bed!" he stormed. "Can't we go anyplace without Kalowatt? I didn't come to Africa to be nursemaid to an ape!"

We both were as tired and nervous by this time as if we'd never before gone on a safari.

"All right then, we'll leave Kalowatt behind," I said with sly promptness. "And have her run off or be poisoned or stolen or something! That's a fine idea!"

They both laughed, and Father Johnson settled the whole business by perching our little gray gibbon, together with her bed, on his knees.

I drove one car, Martin the other, and with us we took the two headmen, Jerramani and Ferraragi; our cook, Mpishi; our room-boy, Aloni; and our all-round houseboy, Zabenelli. None of them trusted me as a driver and so they rode with Martin. Father Johnson rode with me.

The roads out of Nairobi were of smooth, hard-packed clay. Within twenty minutes we were in the open plains, and not more than an hour from Nairobi we began to see gazelle, ostrich, and zebra.

"Martin! Martin!" I screamed, as if he could hear me. "Look!"

"Hey, watch out," Father Johnson shouted. "That critter ran across the road right in front of us—you pretty near took his tail off!"

"But this many animals close to Nairobi—look at them! Why, a little farther out there's probably everything—we aren't going to have any trouble at all!" In my excitement I was pushing down on the accelerator. We clattered and roared over the road.

Father Johnson touched my arm. "Aren't you going a mite fast?" he asked anxiously.

I nodded. "Sure. Want to get there right away. Why, all Martin will have to do, practically, is set up his camera and turn the crank. And as for meat for the porters, look at that bunch of antelope over there! We can just shut our eyes and shoot!" I bounced the car off the road and bounced it back on again. Everything rattled and shook.

A small herd of zebra, up ahead, stared at us, ears pointed forward. Then, as we came abreast of them, they leaped to a gallop and started to race our cars. This went on for perhaps two hundred yards, when suddenly they swerved to cross the road. I jammed on the brakes just in time. I also heard Martin's brakes screeching behind us. The zebra now gathered in a tidy group on the other side of the road and stood calmly regarding us, with nothing to explain their purposeless dash.

"Hey!" Martin yelled.

I stuck my head out the door.

"We're not going to a fire, you know," he shouted, "and I don't know of any hospitals in this direction either!"

He looked cross, but I grinned and waved to him and went off at a somewhat moderated speed until we came to a flock of ostrich. They too decided to race us and looked very earnest about it. They had a crazy, half-running, half-jumping gait which also included the elegant crossing of one foot over the other— like a fashion model on parade—and I speeded up to keep pace with them, expecting any minute to see them trip. Martin's honking warned me to slow down again, so I gave up the race. The ostrich were too fast for me anyhow.

In about four hours we came to the place Blayney Percival had suggested for our camp. It might have been a lovely scene in a park, with the gnarled trunks of great mimosa trees fram-

ing the gently sloping banks and lively stream, and to the north
a dark, jagged cliff for contrast.

Martin scolded me a little for fast driving, but he gave me
a hug besides, and I could see he was every bit as excited as I
was over the animals we'd seen and the apparent brightness of
our prospects.

Jerramani and Ferraragi proceeded to order the setting up
of our modest camp, and the air of disdain which accompanied
this made clear that each was remembering the important men
he had served and the impressive camps he had supervised—
men of Theodore Roosevelt's caliber, Carl Akeley's. The other
men seemed similarly minded, all rebelling at taking orders,
whereupon Martin took command and, in words that had the
sting of a lash, sent them sharply and with increased respect
about their work.

Next, Mpishi, our cook, presented himself to my husband
and, standing helplessly, arms hanging at his sides, asked for
firewood. Twice he declared, with an effective air of personal
injury, that he could not cook without firewood.

Martin said firmly, "There's enough wood for six fires within
twenty yards of here along the riverbank. Go and get it."

Mpishi stiffened. "Me cook," he said. "Me not porter."

Father Johnson jumped up. "I'll get the firewood," he said.
"And I'll build the fire too. I'm good at building fires."

"Stay where you are," Martin barked tersely, though not
meaning it that way. "When a white man loses face with a
black, his authority is gone."

Mpishi went for firewood, then presented himself shortly—
same manner, same tone—saying he needed water. By this time
he had food in preparation which in all fairness he shouldn't
be asked to leave, so Martin told Jerramani and Ferraragi, both
of whom were completely idle at the moment, to fetch water.
They stated loftily and in duet that such work was for porters.
Sharply Martin reiterated his order. The two big natives looked
at each other; Jerramani drew himself up and glared. Ferraragi
stooped for the bucket, handling it as if some contamination
were suddenly upon it, and went for water. Jerramani's dignity
and authority remained intact.

After dinner we sat about the fire in front of our shelter. It was our first evening in the African open and I was fit to pop with excitement. I was even shivering a little.

"Cold?" Martin asked. He took my hand and pressed it hard. The firelight was on his face, and I could see he was smiling; he knew I wasn't cold.

Father Johnson sat on the other side of me, his little .22 across his knee.

"There might be a lion snooping around someplace," he suggested hopefully.

All we could hear at first was the soft rush of the river close at hand and the plaintive cry of night birds. It was a clear, moonless night. Then suddenly, on the opposite bank of the river, we heard a ghoulish, mirthless laugh. From what Blayney Percival had told us, that would be a hyena. Then, as our ears became accustomed to the vibrant silence, we picked out the grunt of the wildebeest and the sneeze of the hartebeeste, and then, difficult at first to identify, a low, steady rumble and a faint vibration in the earth.

"Antelope, I think," Martin said, "stampeding across the plain."

If they were stampeding, fear was driving them—no doubt of that. Sharp pity turned me a little sick; the weaker creature everywhere was the victim of the stronger.

We were awakened before dawn the following morning by Father Johnson.

"Hey, you two kids," he whispered sharply through the flap of our tent. "If you want to see something, you'd better get up!"

Still half asleep, we got into our things and stumbled outside.

"Where? What?" we asked.

Father Johnson pointed through the thick morning dusk to the river, and there we saw the dim shapes of hundreds of animals. It was still so dark we couldn't make them out, but some were already at the river, drinking; others, following the beaten trails, were on their way to the water's edge.

Martin rushed into the supply tent for his camera; I rushed for my gun and, rushing out again, sprawled flat over a guy rope. My gun went off, fortunately without killing anybody, but even before I could pick myself up I heard the startled rush of the animals away from the river's bank. Martin said nothing, but I could see he was distinctly disappointed in me.

"Well," he said, "maybe they won't run more than a mile or two. I guess we can go after them."

The sun came up, and I suppose it was a very beautiful morning, but I was aware only of my disgrace. Martin and I gulped our breakfast in silence, and even Father Johnson's recital of how he once fell flat in an Elks' parade didn't help a bit. Mpishi, still on his dignity, said he hoped we would supply him that day with fresh meat to cook. This, it seemed to me, considering all the food we had brought from Nairobi, was an unnecessary demand on our first day out, but Martin nodded, remembering what Blayney Percival had said, and whether we liked it or not, the job was ours of killing something before we returned.

Gloom was still heavy upon me as we started out, and it wasn't lessened particularly when Ferraragi showed clearly that he wasn't in the least honored to carry my gun. Martin saw this and punished him by giving him the camera to carry besides. Ferraragi started to balk, but Jerramani reasserted the authority won the night before by snapping a command, and we started on our first African hunt.

We had gone little more than a mile from camp when we spied a herd of small animals grazing peacefully. I guessed from the description I had read they they were Thompson's gazelle, sometimes called Tommies. Martin motioned Jerramani to hand him his gun.

"Well, aren't you going to try to photograph them first?" I asked.

Martin shook his head. "Background isn't interesting, and besides, we might as well get this killing business over so we won't have to keep thinking about it."

I reached for my gun and we crept forward, keeping well to leeward of the cute little animals, and in a few minutes we were close enough to hear the soft sound of their feeding. I glanced at Martin. He was raising his rifle. Father Johnson and I did likewise, and as one man we all fired, whereupon the gazelle leaped straight into the air and sped away—every one of them. We avoided looking at Jerramani and Farraragi when we handed our guns back to them.

Some distance farther on we caught sight of nine Grant's gazelle, which are larger than Tommies and have beautiful, curved horns. This was in a gully, the background was good, and Martin decided he'd like a picture of them. He told the men to circle the animals and drive them toward us, but his voice, too loud, apparently carried down the gully, so the gazelle threw up their heads, saw us, and galloped away.

And so it went all day long, game on every side of us which we could neither photograph nor hit. At one time we were so close to some Tommies that it seemed to me we could almost touch them with our hands, and yet our shots went wild. This was at the end of the day, we were returning to camp, and the porters looked very sad and discouraged. It didn't help our feelings very much, either, to remember what Blayney Percival had said: that a native headman or gun-bearer is only as great as his white bwana (master), and that if a white hunter fails to live up to a certain standard, then his servant in turn becomes the laughingstock of his fellows. An African servant, Blayney had informed us, "is faithful, humble, and admiring," and asks but two things of his master: one, that he never run away; two, that he be a good shot. Well, so far we hadn't run away—there had been nothing to run from.

This went on for three days, with an enormous amount of ammunition being shot and not a single hit. A deep gloom settled on the camp. In an effort at being funny I reminded Martin that in western movies the hero was always being shot at by fifteen or twenty men—crack shots, supposedly—and none of them ever hit him. Martin merely looked at me. Father Johnson, as usual, viewed the whole situation quite cheerfully and told us many stories of rabbit hunting in Kansas.

On the morning of the fourth day, Jerramani came to Martin and, with something very close to a sneer, said he and the rest of the porters were hungry. He asked for a gun to go and kill some meat.

Martin knew in that moment that unless he did something, his failure as a hunter would be spread among the blacks all through British East Africa, and his authority from that point on would be lost. Springing to his feet in a rage, he not only refused Jerramani the use of a gun but told him that if he ever dared to presume so far again he would "beat the tar" out of him. Jerramani seemed both impressed and pleased by this display of temper and retired with mumbled apologies. Martin winked at me then, and I saw he wasn't nearly as angry as he had pretended to be, but when he picked up his double-barreled elephant gun, a .470 Bland, I also saw that he intended to solve the meat problem, and alone.

He came back in a little while, though, mad and limping, and with the sight broken off the new, five-hundred-dollar rifle. Unfamiliar with the gun, it seemed that he had aimed at a Tommy and accidentally pulled both triggers. The recoil from one barrel of a .470 Bland is enough to set a strong man back on his heels. The concussion from two had hurled him backward, and the rifle had soared through the air, landing muzzle down.

Rubbing some ointment on his twisted ankle, Martin then took a long drink of water, picked up his .405 Winchester, and grimly started out again. I begged to go with him, but he said "No," violently, and once more strode off across the plain.

I suppose I have spent longer days in my life, but I can't remember when. At any rate, it occured to me that if I caught some fish the meat situation might be relieved a little. I wasn't at all hopeful, certainly, that Martin in his present mood would bring anything down; so, saying nothing to anyone—not even to Father Johnson, who was in his tent getting a much-needed rest—I got out my fishing tackle and went around a bend in the river to try my luck. The Athi River simply teemed with a fish resembling the Mississippi catfish, but a sense of failure must have been strong upon me or I wouldn't have scurried out of camp before dropping my bait in the water. I'm not a bad fisherman—indeed, I'm considered a very good one, for a woman—but all I could catch that day was a four-foot crocodile.

Five o'clock came. Martin had been gone seven hours, and even Father Johnson, who always tried to put the most optimistic face possible on things, admitted to being a little worried.

"I can't stand it any longer," I said. "We've got to go and look for him. Maybe he ran into a lion or something."

Father Johnson nodded and we went to get our guns, when

we heard a blast from Martin's police whistle a short distance away. We raced to where he was, on the far side of a clump of thornbush. At his feet lay a beautiful impala with long, curved horns. Martin was completely exhausted. For more than an hour he had dragged the hundred-pound buck across the plains.

"I couldn't leave it," he said. "As it was, a pack of hyenas followed me most of the way."

I was so happy I almost cried. Certainly this should reestablish Martin in the eyes of the porters as well, of course, as supplying them with meat. I couldn't understand why they didn't look happier about the whole thing, though clearly they were impressed when they discovered that a single bullet in the center of the animal's forehead had brought it down.

Martin and his father and I walked off quite as if expert marksmanship and bringing fresh meat into camp were an everyday affair, but when we were out of earshot of the porters, Martin confessed that the kill was sheer luck. He had started dejectedly back to the camp when he ran into the gazelle and, desperately anxious, had knelt and taken careful aim. To his astonishment, the buck at which he had aimed galloped blithely off, but another lay on the ground, bored neatly in the skull.

"But it's wonderful anyhow," I said, "and for goodness' sake, don't let the men know!"

Arriving at camp, we discovered to our astonishment that the porters had followed us in and left the gazelle where it lay on the edge of the plain. Martin demanded an explanation.

"No good," they said discouragedly.

My husband was dumbfounded. "What's the matter with it?"

They told him it had not been "hallaled." Being Mohammedans, they were forbidden to eat the flesh of an animal that had not had its throat cut before it was dead. They would make a slight compromise, it seemed, and eat the flesh if the ceremony were performed immediately after the animal had been killed, but obviously this one had been dead at least two hours, and they could not touch it as food.

Father Johnson, Martin, and I withdrew to our tent that night and had a serious discussion.

"It's been the same story day after day," Martin said glumly.

"Everything we've done has been wrong. As a matter of fact, the whole trip here to the Athi River has been a total loss."

"If I remember rightly," Father Johnson said in his sometimes brittle, humorous fashion, "experience was what you came for, wasn't it?"

"I guess so," Martin replied vaguely. He wasn't listening.

"More failure than success in it, sure," Father Johnson went on. "That's what makes it valuable. Keeps you working. Makes you learn."

Martin was intent on a gloomy review of our failures.

"We came to get pictures, and what have we to show for it?" he demanded. "Nothing! I'm throwing other people's money away for—nothing!"

"Well, it hasn't all been our fault," I said. "Whenever we left the heavy cameras behind to make the hunt for meat easier, we usually found conditions perfect for photography. And when we went out to get pictures, either we couldn't find animals or they kept out of range or the light was bad." I thought about this a minute, then added, "All of it hasn't been bad judgment; a lot of it's been plain bad luck."

"Bad luck nothing," Martin shouted in exasperation. "I've turned into a meat-hunter for my porters. I'm no longer a photographer!"

"Hold on, now, son—listen to me." Father Johnson pulled his chair a little closer to Martin's.

Martin listened, with the result that we decided to stick it out at least another week. Experience was what we needed—no doubt of that. As for the meat problem for our confounded men, we decided to go into Nairobi and buy some, all properly "hallaled."

We were up for an early start the next morning. I chanced to look off across the plain and there, perhaps three hundred yards away on the crest of a hill and silhouetted against the rising sun, were two large elephants. I called excitedly to everyone to look. Martin rushed for his light camera.

"It will be a perfect piece of photography!" My heart was thumping like everything. "Maybe our luck's changed," I added hopefully.

Keeping in the cover of thornbush, we crept to within about

a hundred yards of the hill, only to see our two elephants suddenly dissolve into four zebra and run away.

Martin pulled in his lips the way he always did when he was mad, and we trudged back to camp.

"It was the way they were grouped," I said, "and the sun behind them and everything—and besides, you thought they were elephants too, or you wouldn't have taken your camera."

Leaving Father Johnson in charge of the camp, we got into the new Ford and started for Nairobi. Neither of us spoke for quite a long time. We had gone only a little more than three miles when, at a bend in the road that gave a view of the plain, we saw a large herd of antelope. They made a beautiful picture. The early-morning light and the background were exactly right. They were quite a distance off, but Martin had brought his long-focus lens and ground out a picture of the beautiful creatures grazing peacefully.

"Maybe if you shot your gun we'd get a little action," he said. He hadn't looked so happy in a long time.

I thought a bit. Perhaps I could stir up the herd and put an end to our meat problem at the same time. I picked out the largest buck in the herd, took a long and careful aim, and fired. To my complete astonishment, he fell where he stood. The rest of the animals galloped away.

"Hey," Martin cried excitedly. "That was a piece of luck. I guess we're better when we don't take aim than when we do!"

"What do you mean?" I was indignant. "I took aim, and that's the one one I picked!"

"All right, Annie Oakley." Martin laughed. "If you can pick 'em off at four hundred yards, our troubles are over, and that's all right with me!"

"That's the one I aimed at, I tell you!"

Martin laughed as we drove over the rough ground toward it. "The thing for us to do from now on," he said, not believing me in the least, "is pick a big, well-bunched herd. Can't very well miss that way."

I was so furious with him I couldn't speak, but when we stopped at the side of the sleek, tawny animal, I forgot about being angry. The soft eyes of the lovely creature were wide open, and they seemed to look straight at me with reproach for taking his life. I turned away and burst into tears.

"I wish I hadn't killed him!" I sobbed in Martin's neck. "He's so harmless—and so beautiful!"

Blayney Percival threw back his head and laughed. We were at home again in Nairobi and telling him the troubles, thick and varied, that had crowded about us in the Athi River region.

"I should have told you," he said when he was able to get his breath, "but everybody who ever comes to Africa, either with a gun or camera, has the same devilish time of it. I don't know whether it's the light or atmosphere, but whatever it is, it's almost impossible to aim or focus accurately until you're accustomed to it."

"Well, at any rate," Martin grinned, "you've given us something to blame beside ourselves!"

"Probably accounts for those elephants turning into zebra, too," I said with relief.

"Well, one thing you don't hear me asking now, Blayney," Martin said, "is when we're going to push off to that uncharted lake of yours. I know we're not ready."

"Right," Blayney said, rising to go. "Just knock around here for a while longer—fifty or sixty miles out of Nairobi. I'll be the first to tell you when you're ready for the long safari."

Waterhole scene. Note that both the common and Grévy's zebras are present, as well as beisa oryx.

A visitor drops in for breakfast at Lake Paradise.

Air view of massive herd of bush elephants in Lorian Swamp

Common zebra grazing

Giraffe on the Northern Frontier

Lion on his rock resembles sculpture.

This lioness seems to have spotted a potential meal. Generally lionesses, not their mates, make the kills.

Ample supper for the whole clan

Adult female gorilla

Two gorilla youngsters

After capture, the two young gorillas adapted quickly to new surroundings.

Two young friends, gorilla Snowball and chimpanzee Beebee

Martin, with Snowball on his lap

Chapter 18 _____

We met John Walsh in Nairobi at one of the native markets. His occupation was "killin' meat," and he was completely matter-of-fact about it. Weathered and hard as a knot of hickory, nevertheless his sandy hair was sprinkled with gray, and his back was quite bent. He was very sensitive about his age and tried to straighten his round shoulders whenever he caught us looking at him.

"Totin' bucks like them's what's done it," this with a jerk of his thumb two fine impalas lying on the floor of the market, both properly "hallaled." When he got to know us a little better, he confessed to sixty years, but he was probably well over seventy.

Martin eyed him with proper respect. A man of his age who could make a living that way must know his business.

Mr. Walsh concluded his dickering with the native market owner—grumbling out of habit, I'm sure—and, pushing whatever money he had collected into a greasy snap purse, was about to climb into his old Ford when Martin stopped him.

"I'd like to talk to you, Mr. Walsh," he said.

"Shoot," replied Mr. Walsh. "I ain't got much time."

He scratched his back impatiently through the rips in an amazingly clean blue shirt and squinted at us speculatively under the stiff brim of a tattered helmet. I think he had the narrowest, sharpest pair of eyes I'd ever looked into.

The upshot of this talk was that John Walsh put himself and his old Ford at our disposal, together with his place on a plateau near the edge of the Athi Plains some forty miles from town. His price was five dollars a day, we to supply our own groceries and kill our own meat. He sketched a rough map which he shoved into Martin's hand, then put his Ford into a sort of standing jump and was off down the street in a cloud of blue stench that hung on the air long after he had gone from sight.

We left early the next morning, Father Johnson, Martin, and I—and Kalowatt, of course—but no porters. We'd had our fill of them for the time being. Mr. Walsh's map, while apparently haphazard, was accurate, and we drove up to his place around nine o'clock. I don't know when I had seen anything as bleak, unless it was Mr. Walsh himself. A two-room shanty of galvanized sheet iron was about all there was to it. No trees or garden. The house inside, while clean enough, was cluttered with rubbish that had in it everything from old boots beyond repair to empty gin bottles, tattered shirts, trousers, and hats of assorted sizes, a dozen or so tin harmonicas, and a broken feather fan. Moreover, every corner was piled high with London newspapers and "penny dreadfuls," all yellowed with age and, in some instances, dating back as far as the nineties.

One of the many intriguing things about Mr. Walsh was his ability to conceive a fantastic idea and stick to it. His chief notion concerning us was that we were rich Americans—most likely actors in the movin'-picture business, since we had a camera with us—and that we were in Africa to collect some antlers, skins, tusks, and such to take back to Hollywood.

He always talked very rapidly and never listened to anybody. We knew he wasn't deaf because we'd tested him to find out.

"I'll go git 'em," he said, all ready to jump into his Ford early the next morning. "You set here. Five dollars an antler, twenty-five dollars a skin."

"Hey, wait a minute!" Martin yelled, and tried carefully for perhaps the tenth time to explain that less than anything else did we want trophies of animals, that we wanted pictures.

Mr. Walsh nodded impatiently. "All right, all right—twenty dollars a skin."

The old fellow shifted into gear, but before he could get

away, Martin and I jumped in beside him with our guns and light camera. Never had I had such a ride. John Walsh crouched behind the wheel, his old helmet pulled forward, his red-whiskered chin stuck out, and away we flew. In no time at all we were in animal country, and here we found that roads seemed a matter of complete indifference to this demoniac Ford, which, though apparently falling to pieces in every vital part, nevertheless seemed capable of outrunning any animal on its own ground. Up hill and down dale we went until we sighted a herd of kongoni. This was all old John really needed to start him moving. Pulling his helmet almost to the bridge of his thin nose, he jammed the throttle to the floor and catapulted us into the middle of the startled beasts. Then he turned to Martin.

"Well, here you are, Mr. Johnson," he said.

Naturally, by the time Martin had his camera set up and focused, there wasn't an animal in sight.

Mr. Walsh shrugged. "Well," he said, "I done my part," and with that rushed us back to his place again.

"Craziest hunter feller I ever seed," he confided to Father Johnson about Martin.

Poor Father Johnson was in no mood for confidences, however. He had his hands full with Kalowatt. For an hour, it seemed, she had chased John Walsh's skinny chickens around among the thornbushes and, catching them, had, each time, turned them about, held them firmly, and carefully plucked out their tail feathers.

I laughed—I couldn't stop laughing—and it served me right that in that instant Kalowatt was off again. This time I chased her, but not before she had caught a terrified rooster whose tail feathers were already half gone and applied herself with utmost thoroughness to pull out the other half. John Walsh bounded toward her, cursing. She leaped to my arms for protection and looked surprised and hurt when I spanked her soundly. It was no use, however, for by the time we left for Nairobi a week later, I doubt that there was a tail feather left among all twenty chickens.

Martin decided that night to experiment with building a camera blind near a water hole about two miles from Mr. Walsh's. We all went to work on it the next morning—Martin, his father, and I—and I thought when we got through that we had done a very nice job, since there was nothing at all to distinguish the blind from the clumps of growing thornbush in the vicinity. We went back late that afternoon and crouched hopefully behind the camera. After a long wait, the animals began to come one by one—zebra, impala, kongoni, ostrich. For no reason that we could figure out, however, they didn't go down to the water but kept just out of camera range, milled around for about two hours, and went away. Martin had much more patience than I, for after three days of this I had none left, and besides, my knees gave out. I simply couldn't crouch any longer. Father Johnson went with him the next afternoon and I remained home. Mr. Walsh had washed his hands of us by this time. We could stay in his place as long as we liked, he said—five dollars a day, payable every morning before breakfast—if we kept our ape away from his chickens. This declaration made, he went about his business of bagging meat for the native market in Nairobi, and we were left to our own devices.

On the day I stayed home, I mixed up a nice big meal out of our own stores for old John's poor skinny fowls and sat lazily inside the doorway with Kalowatt—now forcibly restrained— watching them eat it, when right into my vision, not fifty yards away, walked a beautiful Tommy gazelle. I ran and got my gun and aimed carefully at his proud head.

"How pleased Martin will be," I thought, "when he comes home and finds gazelle chops for dinner." My aim wavered, however, for there were no porters now demanding meat. I shot into the sky and the Tommy galloped off—warned, I hoped, against coming around when Mr. Walsh was at home. All I was able to give my husband and his father for dinner that night was tinned meat and vegetables and some dried fruit. Martin said he guessed we'd go back to Nairobi in the morning.

"Any luck in the blind this evening?" I ventured to ask after a while.

"Warthogs!" Martin replied disgustedly.

I thought the pictures of the warthogs were extremely interesting. We were back at our home in Nairobi. Martin had developed and printed them and was projecting them along with some other odds and ends of things he'd photographed at the Athi River.

"Why, that's simply wonderful photography, Martin," I said. "Just look how the cross-lighting hits the bumps on these hogs."

"Yes," Martin growled, "and just look at three months in Africa with nothing but warthogs to show for it—look how that hits our pocketbook!"

The little bit of film ended, he snapped off the projection lights.

"Warthogs," he muttered to himself.

Blayney Percival saw the warthog picture a few days later and thought it fine.

"You're getting on to the peculiarities of the atmosphere now, old man," he said to Martin. "Another short trip or two and you'll be ready for anything."

"We were thinking we'd like to get into big-animal country this next trip," Martin said.

Blayney Percival nodded and spread a map on the table.

"Here's the place I suggest." He pointed to a spot northeast of Nairobi. "The Ithanga hills. They rise right up out of the plains, and because there's plenty of shelter and water, animals are drawn to them from miles around."

"Lions too?" Father Johnson asked hopefully. "I was sort of hoping I'd see one before I went home—a wild one, I mean."

Blayney smiled. "They're there, all right. Lions, rhinos, leopards, and especially the buffalo."

I shivered a little. Carl Akeley had pronounced this big creature the fiercest animal in all Africa.

"Around in here," our game-warden friend continued, pointing to a spot on the map in the southern part of the Ithangas, "is the Whitehead plantation. I've already told Mr. Whitehead about you—he and his wife are charming English people—and they'll be more than happy to have you as their guests any time you care to go."

"The sooner the better," Martin shouted jubilantly. "That's what we want, big-animal country!" Then, after a moment's thoughtful study of the map, "I appreciate it a lot, Blayney, the invitation of the Whiteheads, but I think we'd better make this a real safari. You know, try out our equipment, take a dozen or so porters—go in for a real workout."

Blayney nodded. "You're right. A trip or two done that way and you'll be ready for anything. Trial and error, in other words."

"And how about your uncharted lake?" I put in. "When do we start on that trip?"

He looked at me reflectively a moment, then smiled. "When you've added up the errors of this trip," he said. "And don't forget before you go to sharpen up on your marksmanship."

The next morning, and every morning before we left, found all three of us up at five o'clock for rifle practice—a bit of preparation for which, later, we were to be very glad.

We left Nairobi for the Ithanga hills in about a week, just before the "short rains." In addition to Martin, his father, and me, and our personal servants, we added a dozen porters who within a few months were to be the nucleus of a safari company of a hundred and ten men.

It took us only a few hours in our safari Fords to reach Thika, a small settlement at the foot of the hills. Here we were joined by two ox wagons sent on, the night before, with our camp equipment and chop boxes. These wagons were clumsy, springless affairs and might have been patterned after the covered wagons of our own pioneer West. In charge was a noisy, youngish, red-faced Boer who carried a flexible black whip more than thirty feet long which he cracked neatly, constantly, and with apparent relish. But the placid oxen didn't seem to mind, and their speed at best was fifteen miles a day.

Martin, his father, and I—and Kalowatt, of course—began the slow ascent of the hills in the Fords. The porters plodded alongside, and by early afternoon of our second day we arrived at the cool, comfortable Whitehead bungalow. This lovely home was set in a flower-filled garden and reflected the culture and charm of our host and hostess. They urged us to make their place our headquarters, but, much as we were tempted to accept, we pushed on over increasingly rough roads to a site some four miles to the north.

Leaving Father Johnson to superintend the making of camp,

Martin and I, with Jerramani, set out on a preliminary scouting expedition. The peaceful hill country was very like New England, with tall, straight trees and little underbrush.

We hadn't gone far when we came to a deep ravine which, dark, cool, and mysterious in the setting sun, looked capable of harboring any or all of the animals mentioned by Blayney Percival. Bravely, with Martin in the lead, we descended the steep, rough bank and took up our march along the side but near the bottom. The low sun, cutting lance-like through the trees, picked out the brilliant coloring of rock, flowers, and foliage.

"Isn't this lovely, Martin!" I exclaimed, forgetting all about animals.

"Hssssh!" warned Jerramani sharply.

Suddenly, as if they had sprung out of the earth, a herd of buffalo appeared on the opposite bank. They stood in a sort of battle formation and stared at us, their great heads thrust forward and their rope-like tails straight out behind. There must have been thirty of these beasts across the narrow ravine. The sun glistened on their black hides and turned their eyes to blood-red balls of fire.

It took no learned naturalist to see that these powerful brutes would not, like the impalas and Tommies, leap gracefully into the air and run away. An African buffalo is a none-too-friendly-looking animal at best. Its huge bulk stands about five feet at the shoulders; its great curved horns, spreading three to four feet at the points, are mounted on a huge head; and it has a peculiarly diabolical eye set in a protruding ring.

"Martin," I managed to say, "are they going to come after us?"

"I don't know," he said. His voice was just as shaky as mine. He ignored the gun which Jerramani with more than a hint of challenge held out to him. "We'd better get out of here," he said, and seizing my arm he literally dragged me up the rough side of the ravine. Finally, at the top, we broke into a run and were still running when we reached camp.

Jerramani followed far in the rear at a sad, dignified pace, and his manner showed all too plainly to Ferraragi and the rest of the men that he considered himself a marked man. He who had so proudly boasted of the prowess of Theodore Roosevelt now served a bwana who not only could not shoot, but who also ran away. It was a disgrace not easily to be borne.

Martin and I withdrew to the shelter of our tent.

"We'll never run away again, Osa," he said resolutely.

"N-no," I said, though without much conviction.

Even though we couldn't be very proud of ourselves as hunters so far, we at least had every right to be proud of our camp. This, our first expedition with full safari equipment, was contrived for efficiency and comfort, and achieved both to a gratifying degree.

Our sleeping tents had double roofs lined with red cloth to keep out the terrific heat, and there were mosquito nets for our beds and—greatest luxury of all, I think—a roomy canvas tub. The big dining tent was a single, heavy tarpaulin with netting at the sides, and a third tent, also with a double roof, protected our photographic supplies, ammunition, and guns from both heat and rain. Light but sturdy canvas chairs, together with cots made up with good mattresses and bedding, contributed more than comfort, we found—they meant proper rest and steady nerves for our work.

At a distance from our group of tents the porters were put to work building a grass cook-tent, and grass huts for Jerramani and Ferraragi. Too lazy to build huts themselves, the porters lay around a campfire with only one thin blanket each to protect them from the cold nights. They didn't seem to mind, however.

Our complete dining-room equipment of white enamel fitted into a huge bucket and weighed just sixty pounds, the legal weight of a single porter's load. Mpishi, we found, was cheerful and an excellent cook on safari when he had his two assistants. He made the most of anything supplied him. On this occasion, we had fresh eggs from the Whitehead plantation and vegetables from native gardens to supplement our own canned beef, dried fruits, and coffee. Martin even had his favorite American cigars, which he carried in heat-proof, zinc-lined boxes.

The headmen and our personal servants received a daily ration of rice, the porters two pounds each of mealy-meal—a coarsely ground dried corn—and all were given meat when their master supplied it. The meat problem was one we were grimly determined to master on this trip.

Our porters were a picked lot of strong, experienced men. When I first saw them, with their spindly legs, I doubted that they could even lift their sixty-pound loads, much less carry them, but, as it turned out, they could maintain a slow, steady pace with marvelous endurance. If hurried, as was sometimes the case on a forced march, however, they were soon utterly exhausted.

The Bureau of Native Affairs has laid down very definite rules governing both master and man. Every black employed by a white man is registered at the bureau and must carry a kapandi, or identification card, bearing his fingerprints and description. To desert his master is an offense punishable by imprisonment, unless the native can prove treatment contrary to the regulations. The white employer, on the other hand, is bound to provide each man with a canteen, a blanket, and a daily ration of two pounds of mealy-meal. When there is meat, the porter is given but one pound of mealy. A safari porter is not required to carry more than sixty pounds or to travel more than fifteen miles a day.

On the morning following our first encounter with the buffalo, we started on a march just as the sun came up. It was a fine, bracing morning, with a touch of the night's chill in the air. Martin decided to take all of the porters except two, whom he left behind to guard the camp. Father Johnson was right up in the lead, carrying his own .22 rifle.

We struck straight up into the hills and in about an hour were on the rim of a huge, natural stadium some ten miles across and twenty-five miles long. In every direction we could see game trails, crossing and recrossing like a gigantic crackle. Toward the bottom of the bowl, Jerramani pointed out some rhinoceros spoor and said the big, two-horned animals had been there within the last twenty-four hours.

"I'd just about as soon see one of them as a lion," Father Johnson said eagerly.

"And there's nothing I'd like better to get in my camera. Which way do you think they went, Jerramani?" Martin asked.

The rhinos were forgotten, however, when we came on nine

buffalo asleep under a tree. I saw Martin's jaw harden. Quickly he estimated the direction of the wind, then, motioning us all to be as quiet as possible, he led the way with his camera bearer to the lee side of the big animals.

For a moment I was in complete panic. Here we were, fourteen or fifteen of us, with Martin wholly intent on getting pictures, and Father Johnson and I (he with his little .22) the only ones with guns ready in case of a charge. I think the thing that got me over my panic was my pride in Martin, for he had moved to within a hundred feet of the buffalo, had set up and focused his camera, and with a firm hand was turning the crank. Suddenly the great beasts scrambled to their feet, and it was a bad moment for all of us. Our porters knew what bad shots we were—we all knew. The animals pushed their great heads toward us and pawed the ground, their tails straight out behind them, but Martin kept on grinding.

"Steady, Osa," he said, very quietly. "Remember what we said, and if they start coming try to pick off the leader. I think that will head them off."

Suddenly I remembered Borneo and the water buffalo—how when they charged I screamed. Whether or not there was a concerted movement of the big black animals toward us now, I don't know, but I fancied there was, and I screamed, shrill as any train whistle. The beasts looked startled, shook their heads as if it had hurt their ears, and, wheeling, galloped away.

"Gosh," was all anybody said, and that was Father Johnson. Martin looked ridiculously nonchalant—I think he even whistled—and it seemed to me that both Jerramani and Ferraragi eyed us with just a hint of respect for having stood our ground. What they thought of my screaming was something else again.

On our sixth morning in the Ithangas we were in a little donga (valley) that opened out of the bowl, when we sighted a large herd of buffalo.

"More buffalo," said Father Johnson disgustedly. "Where are some of the other animals Blayney Percival was telling about—rhinos, leopards, lions?" He tried to tell Jerramani about all the American buffalo he had seen and hides he had hauled when he was a young man, but these two never did understand each other very well, and anyway, Jerramani was trying to get through his head the astonishing directions Martin had just given him. He was to take eight of his men, my husband repeated, move carefully around behind the herd, and drive them straight toward us. There were all of fifty of the big animals in the herd, and the whole idea must have seemed to Jerramani— and undoubtedly was—the ultimate in foolhardiness. I remembered Borneo and the elephants and the tree we climbed. There were no climbable trees just here.

Martin set up his camera. Ferraragi and I stationed ourselves to cover him. Father Johnson stood ready with his .22. A thicket of brush, none of it big enough to climb or offer much protection, was off to the side, and it was understood that we all would dash there for cover should the buffalo herd appear too intent on running us down.

"And you remember to scream, Osa," Martin grinned. "It's the best ammunition we have."

All was ready. We heard Jerramani and the men yelling, and then we heard the buffalo beginning to stampede in our direction. They were coming straight at us. I found myself both pleased and terrified. Martin was turning the crank. They were perhaps two hundred yards off when I heard a crash in the brush just behind us and saw Father Johnson's face take on a fixed, frozen stare. I whirled. Not thirty feet away, a huge buffalo was coming out of the thicket, head down, straight at us. I fired. Two more appeared. I pulled the trigger as fast as I could, emptied my gun at them, then turned and ran to Martin. When I recovered from my panic, I found that I had killed two of the charging beasts, that the third had run away, and that, fortunately or not, the big herd had veered and thundered off down the valley.

"Anyhow," I said, my teeth still chattering, "the meat situation's taken care of for a few days."

Jerramani and Ferraragi were proud and jubilant. Martin's feelings were mixed.

"I guess we won't have to worry about this shooting business anymore," he said, giving me a quick hug, "but why did those three brutes have to bust in just as I was getting pictures of the big herd!"

"Good girl, Osa," Father Johnson said, patting me on the

back. "You did so good I didn't have to fire a single shot."

We thoroughly enjoyed our first meal of buffalo meat, and our boys, that night, seemed practically hilarious. Around the big campfire were three or four smaller fires, and suspended over each was a gasoline can which served as a common cooking pot. (We found it difficult to keep the men supplied with these cans because they were always letting them boil dry. Promptly, of course, the bottoms would melt out and their food would drop into the fire.) Into this crude pot they put their mealy-meal and water, then added what they considered the choice cuts of the buffalo—the brains, lungs, hooves, and entrails. They waited only until this mess was little more than warmed through, then ate it half raw and saltless. The firmer flesh of the animal was cut into strips and dried on sticks before the fire, and I found that the men carried these bits of hard, blackened meat (biltong) for days and chewed on them the way children, when I was a little girl, chewed on licorice sticks.

Great men have adventured and explored in British East Africa and left rich and permanent memories. At one time or another we paused at the places where Paul Rainey camped, where Theodore Roosevelt shot his first lion, where Major Dugmore made his first flashlight picture of the king of beasts. The next day after our buffalo kill, we journeyed to Mackenzie Camp, so named for Lady Mackenzie, one of the few women to head an East African safari.

Just before we reached camp, we found a little group of bright brown bushbucks feeding. Pretty animals, less than three feet high at the shoulders, they had short horns that curved gracefully in the shape of a lyre. Jerramani suggested that they were very good to eat, which rather annoyed us since he and the rest of the men were already as full as ticks with buffalo meat. Martin ignored him and, setting up his camera, made some lovely pictures of the little animals in the cross-lighting of the setting sun.

Father Johnson seemed to be up to something at a green thicket on the edge of a narrow donga. I didn't pay much attention to him at first; these were the first bushbucks I had ever seen, and I was thinking I'd love to have one as a pet.

Then I heard a curious snarling sound and, turning, saw the elder Johnson poking into the bushes with the barrel of his .22. I took my gun from Ferraragi and ran to him. His eyes blinked rapidly with excitement.

"What in the world are you doing?" I asked.

Continuing to poke, he said, "I saw something kind of yellow through the bushes, and I thought maybe it might be a lion."

I heard another snarl.

"Get Martin quickly," I whispered. "Whatever it is, he'll want a picture."

Father Johnson frowned as if he wished I hadn't crowded in on his fun, then nodded and sprinted off. I signaled to some of the men to move around to the other side of the donga. Martin picked up his camera, tripod and all, and came running. When he was all set, I moved along perhaps thirty feet to a little open spot in the thicket and had a clear view of Father Johnson's "lion."

It was a big leopard on the low branch of a tree, perhaps fifteen feet back from where Father Johnson had been poking with his gun. Seeing me, he turned to spring in the direction of Martin, so I raised my gun and fired. He leaped from the tree and ran out of the thicket directly toward the camera. Halfway there he crouched snarling under a small thorn tree, and I saw blood running down his flank. Either I had made a mis-shot or the bullet ricocheted. In a panic for Martin's safety, I fired again; the leopard stiffened and fell.

I don't know when I've seen Martin so angry.

"What did you have to go and spoil my picture for?" he shouted. "Couldn't you have waited? We'll never get any pictures if that's what you're going to do all the time!"

The men sang and danced with joy. The bwana and bibi (mistress) were becoming real hunters, and, as it turned out, Father Johnson's "lion" proved to be the finest leopard ever taken by us in Africa.

"Well, see here," Blayney Percival said, plainly puzzled. "I didn't expect you two back from the Ithanga hills just yet. Didn't you like it up there?"

"We ran out of salt," I said brightly. "Can you imagine me? I didn't put enough in the chop boxes, and for three days the food was so tasteless and horrid we just couldn't stand it."

"But I'm sure the Whiteheads would have helped you out with some—"

Martin laughed. "We could have got salt easily enough— just made it an excuse to come back." He was completely serious now. "We've put your trial-and-error system to a pretty good test, Blayney, and feel we'd like to push on to that uncharted lake without wasting any more time."

The game warden shook his head slightly. "I've been thinking a lot about that," he said. "For all I know, my uncharted lake, so-called, is nothing but a phantom lake."

"Man alive," Martin said explosively, "you don't think we mind taking chances, do you? Why, that's all Osa and I have ever done."

The result of this chat was a compromise: Martin and I went with Blayney Percival for a brief trip through the Southern Game Reserve, where elephants were said to be in migration, and where he said we would see an interesting variety of animals, if nothing else.

Part of the reserve, we found, lay on a shadeless plain. Again I was reminded of the Dakotas and the wide, flat lands of Texas. Here, however, instead of domestic cattle, we saw herds of zebra, antelope, wildebeeste, and eland, and, similar to the bleached skulls of our American bison, the skeletons of rhinos wantonly slaughtered by soldiers during the war. Next we passed through a wooded section covered sparsely with mimosa and acacia, and a little later we reached the dry bed of the Ol' Garai River.

Following this for a time in search of a suitable campsite— we had brought forty porters with us on this trip—we ran onto elephant tracks. Blayney said they were not more than twenty-four hours old. Luck was with us, we decided, and felt very gay. Too gay, in fact, for when Blayney in the most casual manner possible said something about this being a good section for warthog, and that he'd enjoy some fresh pork, Martin and I picked up our guns and thought we'd show off a bit. While the boys were pitching camp, we'd go pick off a warthog, just like that.

Two hours later—it was nearly dark—we returned, empty-handed. To our astonishment, just outside Mpishi's tent, there hung one, all neatly skinned, cleaned, and ready for cooking. He too, it seemed, had heard Mr. Percival's lightly expressed wish for a bit of pork and, armed with a hatchet, had strolled down the dry river to a spot perhaps three hundred yards distant where the verdure suggested the presence of a small swamp. A swamp there was, and a warthog in it. Mpishi threw the hatchet, tomahawk fashion, and fresh pork, deliciously cooked, was served for dinner that night.

It was no sooner dark than all about us lions began roaring. Somehow it had never occurred to me that there would be so many in one place, not even in Africa. I hoped I didn't look as nervous as I felt, but at any rate Blayney tried to reassure me and said there weren't really very many, that it just sounded that way because they were circling us from curiosity, trying to figure us out.

Tired as I was, I couldn't sleep for their racket, and after a while I began to identify them by their roars. One had a particularly deep, long-drawn, sepulchral tone of which I'm sure he was very proud. It had a rain-barrel quality that was magnificent and spine-chilling, and I visualized him as a great, tawny beast sporting a fine, heavy mane and surrounded by a coterie of admiring lionesses. Perhaps he was even putting up a bluff of protecting them from some danger which they as mere females were incapable of combating or understanding. With this bit of whimsy I got over the uncomfortable feeling that I was a sort of female Daniel. Martin had long since fallen asleep, and, not to be outdone in either bravery or bravado, I composed myself and followed suit.

From dawn to dark the next day we followed the tracks of the elephants is a winding trail that crossed and recrossed the dry river bed. This carried us deeper into the interior, and we passed through countless herds of animals. On this trip we saw the largest single herd of giraffe we had yet seen. There were thirty-seven of these awkward, strange-looking beasts. Martin set up his camera, but they caught our scent and were off, making excellent speed in spite of an odd gait that seemed about to trip them at every step. Martin succeeded with his telephoto lens in getting one fine shot of them against the sky as they disappeared over the crown of a hill, and this alone, he said later when he had developed it, was worth the whole trip into the Southern Reserve.

The elephant trail took us finally into deep bush country, and the natives in a village there shook their heads when we expressed our hope of catching up with the big herd.

"A week ago," they said—Blayney interpreted for us—"you could not count the elephants here, there were so many, but now they have gone back to the mountains and will not return until the next rains."

We gave up our elephant hunt.

Scientists and hunters, most of whom have spent much time in Africa and know a lot about elephants, cannot agree on the migration question. Some believe that years ago, before civilization restricted their movements, the great herds were in constant migration, and that today the old habit persists and keeps them moving, sometimes seeking shelter from rain and winds, or keeping a rendezvous during the breeding season, or merely following an instinctive urge for change. Others, equally wise in the ways of elephants, say that the big animals live and die within a comparatively restricted area.

On our way back to Nairobi, we had rare luck in securing some fine pictures of eland, the largest species of the antelope family, which fast is disappearing under the gun of the ruthless hunter. Blayney Percival said this was the biggest herd he had seen in recent years, and he doubted that we would ever again see so many, all in one group. Beautiful creatures with widespread horns and sleek, fawn-colored coats shading to gray under their bellies, they are valued as trophies above any of their kind. This, together with the fact that their meat is sweet and tender, probably accounts for their slaughter.

Chapter 19 _____

Blayney Percival came to say good-bye and wish us Godspeed. After four weeks of preparation we were ready to start on the long safari that would take us north across the Kaisoot Desert and into the unknown lands along the Abyssinian border. We were standing in the driveway beside our safari Fords.

"Don't take any unnecessary risks to find that blasted lake, will you?" Blayney urged. "I don't know what possessed me to tell you about it until I could go with you, I swear I don't!"

He was so distressed and reluctant to see us go that Martin thumped him on the back and shook hands at least five times before we got in our cars to leave.

"We'll not only find your 'phantom' lake, Blayney," he said, "we'll bring back pictures to prove we found it!"

Our good friend studied us both for a moment and then nodded. "I believe you will at that," he said.

"That's what I always tell Martin," Father Johnson said, joining us. He was wearing his pith helmet and a new khaki outfit and boots, and carrying Kalowatt on one arm and his faithful .22 on the other. "They're a pair that can't be beat."

Blayney looked at him, startled. "Stop a bit," he said almost sharply. "You're not going on this trip, are you?"

Father Johnson twinkled. "I'm going till I see a lion," he said, "or anyhow a rhinoceros."

Martin explained then that his father had consented to turn back at a place called Rattray's.

"Yes," the elder Johnson sighed, "and then I guess I'll have

255

to start home." He shook his head regretfully, "I kind of wish now I hadn't told everybody down in Independence that I was going home by way of Paris and China. Rather stay here a while longer—but you know how folks are: They'd be disappointed if I didn't do the whole thing up brown."

Blayney stood back and raised his hand in a sort of salute as our heavily burdened cars started to roll.

"Give my regards to Rattray," he called out to Father Johnson, "and tell him I said he was to take good care of you!"

The preparations for this safari had literally staggered us.

"It's a good thing," Martin had said one day, sitting for a moment on the edge of a provision box and wiping his sweaty, grimy face, "it's a good thing Blayney told us about that lake of his." He grinned. "You know, sort of like a bunch of hay on a stick in front of our noses?"

And so it was as we had worked day and night, parceling our stuff out, weighing it, and packing it into sixty-pound loads. There were tents, ammunition, photographic equipment and supplies, food, clothing, and items too numerous to mention that would be needed on the long journey. On Blayney's advice we had planned for a six-months' trip, and the itemizing of the food supplies alone—a responsibility which I assumed—would have taxed the ingenuity, or so it seemed to me, of a well-organized commissary department. My list of provisions was many pages long, and for days on end, big trucks from town unloaded groceries at our bungalow sufficient to stock a good-sized store.

We had added a truck to our motored vehicles and an eager, resourceful young man by the name of Cotter to drive it, but most exciting of all, it seemed to me when I first saw them, were the four ox wagons, each drawn by twelve beautiful oxen. We had rented these, together with experienced drivers, and had sent them on a week ahead of us, carrying the bulk of our supplies. Their journey was to end at Meru, a government station two hundred miles north, where we were to meet them. The load from that point on was to be transferred to the backs of a hundred porters, most of whom would be drawn from the hills in the vicinity of Meru. In addition to our headmen, Jerramani and Ferraragi, and the rest of our men, we also included twelve experienced safari men from Nairobi.

Our cars were so heavily loaded that they sagged on their axles, and we were obliged to curb our impatience and drive slowly. Martin was at the wheel of one of the Fords with Zabenelli and Jerramani as passengers, Cotter carried Aloni and Toto in his truck, and I drove the other Ford, accompanied by Father Johnson, Mpishi, and Ferraragi.

All of our experimental trips had been to the south and east of Nairobi. Now we were going straight north, and by late afternoon we were in country entirely new to us. So far we had seen very few animals, and Father Johnson voiced the opinion—humorously, of course—that there were no lions in Africa, or rhinos either, for that matter. This started a somewhat disjointed argument with Ferraragi, who apparently felt it his duty, and quite passionately, to defend Africa. Father Johnson baited him on in a Swahili that was purely experimental, and I, on the sidelines, had a lovely time. Presently we came on a stream of natives trudging along the side of the road. That is to say the women trudged, with great loads of garden produce on their heads. The men, painted, decorated dandies, were completely unburdened and dawdled idly. Father Johnson was hotly indignant over this and for the time being forgot all about his lions.

Native villages along the way, sometimes of no more than four or five huts, arrested his scornful attention. Men lolled in these flimsy shelters of leaves and grass; women everywhere tended the children and did the work.

"I thought it was only Indians made their women do all the work, like I saw when I was a young man back in the States. Why, these fellows are lazier than they were," Father Johnson fairly sputtered. Ferraragi and Mpishi tried to make out what it was that gave him so much concern, and stared at the villages we passed as hard as he did, but everything was perfectly normal and all right to them, so they merely shook their heads and fell into a pleasant doze.

At dusk we came to hill country, and rolled through native markets where blacks squatted along the roadside and swapped skins, vegetables, and gossip. This was the land of the Kikuyu tribe of Kenya Colony. A pastoral people, they live mainly on goat's milk and vegetables. A one-piece skin and a G-string complete their costumes.

Toward noon of the next day we ran into a powwow. Some

three hundred warriors were seated in a wide circle by the side
of the road holding what seemed to be a serious executive ses-
sion. They wore headdresses of ostrich plumes that were at
once fierce, handsome, and enormous, and they carried six-
foot metal spears topped with a ball of ostrich feathers. This
ball, we learned, signified that at the moment the warriors were
at peace with the world. Their bodies, crudely decorated with
red clay, glistened and smelled of castor oil.

Martin, delighted with this as picture material, stopped his
car, set up his camera, and started to grind out some shots of
the group. He had taken but a few feet when still another crowd
of Kikuyus came rushing down the road and surrounded us,
making great gestures and a lot of noise. Zabenelli translated
for us and said an old chief had been deposed and a young one
put in his place. We had been taking pictures of the latter's
group in conference, it seemed, and the old chief and his ad-
herents had come to warn us against having dealings with the
impostor. The young chief lost his temper, snatched the ostrich-
feather ball from his spear, and made a lunge at his predeces-
sor. There was a wild, savage uproar as six hundred natives
became a whirling mass of resentment. Martin and I ran for
our cars and started the motors. Looking back, we expected to
see the ground littered with dead and dying. Apparently there
was not so much as a scratch among the entire six hundred.

We started on our way, whereupon their political differ-
ences were forgotten and they raced after us demanding bak-
sheesh. Martin threw them a handful of coppers, and when we
last saw the battling braves they were scrambling for pennies
in the road.

Mount Kenya rises almost abruptly out of the plain to a
height of 17,040 feet and has the distinction of being the only
snowcapped mountain straddling the equator. At its foot we
found Fort Hall, a group of government rest houses constructed of split bamboo plastered with mud and having mud
floors and high grass roofs tapering to a point. The half-dozen
white officials who made this their headquarters were very cordial, and presented us with milk and eggs.

Our ox wagons, they said, had passed there in good condition the night before and by now doubtless were circling Mount Kenya to the west. Eyeing our heavily weighted cars doubtfully, they were of the opinion we would never get through to Meru on the rough mountain roads. They advised us to leave part of the load behind and make a return trip, but since we were impatient of delay, they then suggested that we take the road on the eastern slope through Embu. It was a little longer than the road taken by our ox wagons but less hazardous for motored vehicles.

How we reached Embu with springs and axles intact I never shall know. We consoled ourselves, however, with the idea that the eastern slope was the lesser of two evils, and we were thankful we hadn't attempted the road on the west. Here we found mountains that were wilder and more rugged than our own Rockies, with roads that twisted and turned and seemed to follow the most astonishing caprices.

We passed within inches, it seemed to me, of waterfalls that tumbled a thousand feet; we crept up spiral inclines miles long with the great weight of our loads dragging us back; we coasted down precipitous grades with our loads pushing us almost out of control, across narrow, flimsy bridges that seemed to sag under us and around hairpin curves that left no room for bad judgment or error of any sort.

We were all day in reaching Embu, a distance actually of only thirty-three miles from Fort Hall. My knees crumpled under me as I got out of our car. My muscles set up an involuntary shaking and were numb at the same time.

Father Johnson was white as paper through his recently acquired tan—and, bless him, hadn't offered a single word of advice on the whole trip. He had just sat quietly and in a soothing monotone had said over and over again, "Good girl, Osa. Good girl."

The next day we twisted and turned a tortuous but less hazardous course toward Meru. Once we climbed for ten miles through the forest and when we emerged into the open saw, not more than a hundred yards across the deep valley, the road we had left an hour before.

We traveled through what might have been fairy-tale forests with foliage of such brilliant and varied greens as I have seen nowhere else in the world. Then clearings gradually took the place of forests as we neared Meru.

We passed several squads repairing the roads. These were made up for the most part of plump, pretty native girls from twelve to sixteen years of age—happy young tomboys who shouted to us and hitched onto our cars wherever they could find a brief hold.

In the late afternoon we arrived in Meru, which is by far the loveliest of all the beautiful government stations of British East Africa. There were neat lawns of close-cropped grass, a polo field, and a golf course, and the forest in the immediate neighborhood of the station was cleared of underbush and clean as an English park. This was all the work of a former official named Horne who went to Meru many years ago. He had pacified the warring natives and put them to work planting and landscaping. When he was transferred to another district, he left to his successor in office, Mr. Crampton, one of the most orderly regions in Africa.

We didn't expect the rest of our safari for several days, so we borrowed tents, engaged experienced Meru porters, and for a week searched the forest for elephants, but with no luck whatever. The recent chill rains had driven them southward.

Our safari, covered with a thick coat of red dust, caught up with us just two weeks after our arrival at Meru, and we pitched a temporary camp just outside of town. Mr. Crampton sent some of his native aides into the hills for porters, and they returned with seventy strapping young men, all in the gorgeous feather headdresses of their tribe and a brand-new coat of red and blue paint. With the thirty-odd porters we already had, these new men brought our safari company up to a hundred men. I was a little staggered when I saw the Johnson personnel all gathered together around our campfires that night.

"You know, Dad," I said, slipping my arm through his, "a hundred people are a lot of people." Then I laughed. I guess I was a little nervous at the size of the whole thing. "To feed and everything, I mean."

"Gosh, yes," he replied. His eyes popped with excitement. "It's a lot of people anyplace, and—well, just think, this is all yours and Martin's!"

"And yours," I reminded him, "and Chic Sale's and some more people back in New York."

Martin joined us, and there was a look of such happiness and quiet competence about him that all my fears left me. He said nothing, just put his arms around us both where we stood. The firelight was ruddy on his face.

"Only trouble is," Father Johnson said, shaking his head, "I don't know how I'm going to make the folks in Independence believe it! Here I am, looking at the whole thing, those natives and all, and I can't believe it myself!"

We were planning to move on to Isiolo in the morning, so we went to bed early that night. A marrow-chilling drizzle set in somewhere around nine o'clock, and I called to Aloni to take some extra blankets in to Father Johnson. I threw three extra ones over Martin and heaped probably five on my own bed, then crawled in shivering and proceeded to worry about the natives lying outdoors on the bare ground. With no more cloth among the entire seventy than would make a pair of trousers, they simply built a fire and lay beside it, miserable and shaking.

I was both sorry for them and annoyed. If they hadn't been so lazy, they would have put up some grass shelters for themselves. The more I thought about this, the more annoyed I became. They'd probably be down with pneumonia in the morning, the lot of them, but they'd get no sympathy from me.

As a matter of fact, there wasn't so much as a sniffle among them. For my own peace of mind, however, I persuaded Martin to go to the store in Meru and buy them a blanket apiece. He did so; they cost a dollar apiece and the color he had chosen, unfortunately, was bright red. The hill men were delighted, not because the blankets represented protection against the elements but because of their garishness, and our seventy good dollars, we soon found, had gone to ornament the porters, not to keep them warm. Martin also stocked up with a supply of flour, potatoes, and mealy-meal before setting out for Isiolo.

Isiolo is a quarantine station for the control of the many cattle diseases which, if not checked, play havoc with both the domestic and wild animals of Africa. Dr. Macdonough was the veterinarian in charge, and we notified him by runner that we were coming and asked his permission to store our extra supplies in his care. This he cordially granted us.

We were all very gay and confident as we left Meru with our picturesque caravan. The skies had cleared, and we assured one another that all our troubles were behind us. After traveling ten miles through the forest, we came to an open plain literally covered with game. Here we saw oryx for the first time, graceful gray animals with long, straight, black horns that glistened in the sun. In profile they had the look of the legendary unicorn. We also saw our first gerenuk, a grotesque little animal with a giraffe-like neck and long, thin legs, which lives in waterless country and, so far as I was able to find out, has never been seen to drink.

In addition, we saw many game birds—quail, sand grouse, guinea fowl, spurfowl, bustard, vulturine guinea fowl—all of them good eating. We thought it would be a very nice gesture to take a few to Dr. Macdonough, and we were quite proud of ourselves when we presented him with an assortment of twenty-five. Then we learned that he had done the very same thing for us, going out himself and bagging nearly sixty. This was but one instance of his thoughtfulness on our behalf, for he had tents up and ready for our occupancy and a big, new, grass storehouse for our supplies.

It was the last week in December, and Dr. Macdonough, together with Lieutenant Douglas, the only other white resident at Isiolo, pooled with us on Christmas Day, and on our community table there appeared an amazing assortment of tinned delicacies, some that had been sent only recently from England to this forsaken outpost and treasured for association as well as contents. In addition to game we had fine, juicy steer steaks, we introduced our British friends to hominy grits, and the royal feast wound up with English plum pudding ablaze with choice brandy.

The day after Christmas, Major Pedler, head of transport of the East African Army, came to Isiolo on a tour of inspection, and we decided to go with him on a lion hunt. Father Johnson was beside himself. At last he was going to see a lion, but all day long, astride government mules, we followed various trails and saw no sign of one. We had gone farther than we thought and had to make the last half of our homeward journey in total darkness.

I felt worried about the men on foot but was comforted by the fact that they had our guns in case of an emergency. About a half hour after we had reached camp, one of the men rushed up to us with the news that Ferraragi had shot himself. With lanterns we took the back trail and found Ferraragi, covered with blood and his clothes in tatters. We took him, moaning and groaning, to Dr. Macdonough, who found his wounds were caused by gravel. It seems that as the men trudged along in the dark they heard, quite close at hand, the roar of a lion. Ferraragi cocked the gun to be ready for an emergency, then stumbled. The muzzle of the gun went into the ground and both barrels went off, sending a shower of sharp gravel flying through the air. It was almost like shrapnel, and one pebble went clear through Ferraragi's arm. He was sure he was going to die. Dr. Macdonough cleaned and dressed his wounds, and the next day Ferraragi was playing the role of an interested invalid when Martin discovered that the stock of a brand-new gun (he had never shot the second .470 Bland, which had cost us $500) was broken. He was furious and fired Ferraragi on the spot for carrying a cocked gun. More than that, he didn't hire him back for three days! I felt really sorry for Ferraragi as he moped about the camp, the image of grotesque despair.

Not wishing to admit it, Father Johnson was nevertheless just a little stiff and tired after our unsuccessful lion hunt. More, he was actually skeptical by now whether there were any lions in Africa.

"Maybe they're getting extinct or something," he said gloomily the next morning in camp as we sat having breakfast. His back was stiff, and Martin was rubbing it for him.

"Remember," he went on, wincing a bit as Martin struck a tender place, "we've covered a lot of territory."

We decided on one more hunt before we left Isiolo. We simply couldn't led Dad down, so once more we set out on mules. Dr. Macdonough joined us on this trip together with his gun-bearer, and I heard Father Johnson boasting to him as they jogged along together that we had just as fierce animals in

America as they ever hoped to have in Africa.

"Why," he said, "just a plain ordinary domestic bull is fiercer than anything I've seen so far in these parts, and you ought to see our bears and wild cats and panthers—yes, and a kind of lion, too. We call it a mountain lion."

"Yes," acknowledged Dr. Macdonough politely, "I understand that America is a very wonderful country."

"You're darned right," punctuated Father Johnson.

We stopped for lunch beside a small donga, and here, as luck would have it, Dr. Macdonough's gun-bearer stirred up a rhino that was taking a nap in a thicket. It charged straight out toward us and we all dashed behind trees. The big, horned beast stood there and seemed to consider a moment; he even looked inclined to go and find another shady spot and finish his nap. Suddenly I saw Father Johnson craning his neck for a better view of the big fellow. Some brush screened his vision and apparently he decided on a better vantage point, a tree some thirty feet distant.

He sprinted for it. The rhino saw him and was off in pursuit. Dad and the rhino got to the tree at about the same time. Dad skinned around it, the rhino after him. Around and around they went and each had the appearance of chasing the other. I was terrified. I didn't dare raise my gun to shoot, for with one right on the other's heels, I was just as likely to hit Dad as to hit the rhino. I glanced at Martin; he was white and completely frozen.

Then I watched Major Pedler raise his gun and take careful aim. I closed my eyes and didn't open them until after the shot had been fired, but the rhino was down, and then what I saw— to my complete astonishment—was Father Johnson coming toward us in a positive rage.

"Who went and shot him?" he demanded accusingly. "I could have outrun him—and shot him too if you'd just given me time!"

Chapter 20 _____

"Well, I suppose there's something about every job that a man doesn't like," Martin said. He had just shot a fine Grant's gazelle.

I nodded, and, with Dr. Macdonough and Father Johnson, we stood looking down at the lovely animal.

"It's an exceptionally fine specimen," the doctor said, "and I don't think that in all the years I've been in Africa I've seen one with longer or more nearly perfect horns."

My husband pumped the empty shell from his gun. "At that," he said with a touch of morbid whimsy, "I suppose the poor fellow would just as soon be in belly of a native as in the belly of a lion."

"Lion!" snorted Father Johnson.

This was to be our last hunting trip out of Isiolo. In a few days we were moving on to Rattray's, just seven miles up the Isiolo River, and there we would say good-bye to Dad as we pushed northward into increasingly rough country. We had made three trips hoping to find lions. Martin wanted to photograph lions just as badly as Father Johnson wanted to see them. But so far, we'd had no luck.

On our way down a slope overlooking the plains, Jerramani stopped suddenly and pointed off. We halted our mules—and there, perhaps four hundred yards away, with the low sun highlighting their tawny backs, were six lions, two males and four lionesses, running in single file toward the herd of Grant's gazelle out of which Martin shortly before had picked his fine specimen.

"Lions, Father Johnson. Look!" I squeaked in my excitement.

The elder Johnson squinted off, frankly skeptical.

"You mean those six animals over there?" He shook his head. "Couldn't be—not six lions. Must be something else."

I pushed the binoculars into his hands. They were powerful glasses that I knew would bring the big cats up almost into his lap.

Father Johnson sighed happily; his smile was positively ineffable. "Lions," he said. "Six lions, running one right behind the other."

That night the meat of the gazelle found its way quickly into the cooking pots of the natives, and the skin and horns were put on the roof of the grass cook-house to dry. Japanda, our strange, gnome-like little skinner, engaged especially for this trip, twittered happily as he worked on the fine pelt, and went to great pains to stretch it carefully. Martin made a gift of both skin and horn to Father Johnson, who was to take them back with him to Nairobi and ship them from there to Independence.

We had reckoned, however, without Africa's hijacker, the hyena. With the coming of morning we found our trophies gone, both pelt and horns, and except for the clear tracks just below that slope of the roof where the skin had been stretched, we might have cast our suspicions in other and wholly wrong directions. Nevertheless, an element of mystery continued to surround the incident, for our porters, a hundred of them, had slept on the ground that night so close about the cook-house that to pick one's way among them, however carefully, would have been practically impossible.

Both Martin and I developed what amounted to positive loathing for the hyena. He is an ugly, sneaking coward and apparently knows it, for he slinks along on his yellow belly with his tail between his legs and with never a show of spirit or clean, honest fight. A pack of hyenas will attack the weak or wounded, the newborn or feeble, and apparently kill for the sake of killing.

The scavengers of the animal kingdom, they will follow a lion or leopard and finish what is left of the kill. As a matter of fact, there's nothing they won't eat, for we've had them steal from us leather boots, jackets, and even the leather upholstery of our cars.

"Worse than coyotes," Father Johnson said.

Mr. Rattray, a man of squarish build and firm expression and perhaps fifty years of age, turned out to be one of those people who do strange things in the out-of-the-way places of the world. His hobby was breaking Grevy zebra to harness. They were immune to the tsetse fly, he said, and the feeding problem was simple, because they could live on the dry, sparse vegetation of the plains. The sight of them pulling a plow seemed to fascinate Father Johnson.

"I keep looking for the rest of the circus," he said, chuckling.

"What circus?" Mr. Rattray asked. He was quite literal-minded.

Father Johnson tried several approaches. He had imagined there just wasn't anybody in the world he couldn't be right friendly with in no time at all, but here, apparently, was a man of different fiber from just plain folk. He decided that his encounter with the rhino—being a distinctly local event—might arouse Mr. Rattray's interest. As a matter of fact, he was frankly pleased to have been the hero of so narrow an escape.

He awaited a favorable moment following a meal which Mpishi and I had cooked. Mr. Rattray seemed in an almost mellow mood, so Dad told him all about his rhino. Mr. Rattray listened attentively enough—almost too attentively for Dad's comfort. In addition, however, he looked bored. Dad was plainly exasperated.

"Well," he said, "a man doesn't get chased by a rhino every day, does he?"

Mr. Rattray took his pipe from his mouth. "No, why should he?" he replied.

This left Father Johnson out on a limb, and Martin moved in to the rescue.

"Certainly is a nice place you have here," he said. "Orderly—really marvelous."

Our host squinted at him as if about to speak but changed his mind.

If Blayney Percival's calculations were correct, Rattray's place lay just about halfway between Nairobi and that part of the Abyssinian border near which we hoped to find the uncharted lake. Martin sounded out Rattray to see if he had ever heard of such a lake, but the mere suggestion was met with an impatient snort. Fiction, he called it. Nothing up that way but the Kaisoot Desert and beyond that a big, barren, saltwater lake that extended right across the border into Abyssinia. He thought the name was Rudolf.

From that point on it was simple for Rattray to reach the decision that somebody had glimpsed the south tip of Rudolf at some time or another and jumped to the conclusion that they had made a discovery. Indeed, he was so emphatic about it—loose thinking or loose talking of any sort were his particular aversion—that he had us almost persuaded against continuing the long and hazardous trek north.

"If it's pictures of animals you want," he said, "you'll find them in abundance up in the Shaba hills: elephant, rhino, buffalo, lion, and even the reticulated northern giraffe."

Martin and I talked this over. The Shaba hills were a little off our course, but we might be wise to spend a few weeks there, get a few thousand feet of good animal pictures, and send them back to Rattray's for shipment to the United States. Neither of us voiced the doubts that were to haunt us from that day forth, nor did either of us suggest abandoning our original plan. Martin referred to it just once.

"I don't care what anybody says," he declared. "Blayney Percival is no fool."

The memory of our camp in the Shaba hills will always bring back mixed memories. It was one of the most beautiful and rewarding campsites we ever had, but the trip there . . .

We had gone but a few miles toward the hills when we found ourselves on the edge of a great river of lava. "I guess I must have been crazy to let you come on this trip," Martin said. The country seemed to grow rougher at every step. Scattered bits of volcanic slag cut our shoes.

He stopped abruptly and turned me toward him.

"Won't you please go back?" he pleaded.

I was both angry and ashamed of being angry, as I realized his concern for me.

We had gone on for probably another mile, and still, stretching as far as we could see, was lava, smooth and slippery in places, sharp and jagged as broken glass in others.

"I'll send Ferraragi back with you and half a dozen of the men," my husband urged. "Go back to Rattray's. He'll take you in to Nairobi—maybe Dad's still there, and you can go in with him."

All I did was to shake my head. He looked at me a moment, then sighed and turned to the men, ordering a halt. Then followed a consultation with our headmen in which Martin said he thought it would be better to find a way, if possible, around the volcanic field rather than to attempt to cross it. Jerramani and Ferraragi talked this over together, then discussed it with the men, but they all voted otherwise, saying they would rather go the shorter way, across it.

Reluctantly Martin yielded, but he insisted that the men rest until some of the sun's heat had gone out of the slag. The day's fifteen miles being still uncompleted, the porters balked a little; change in routine always troubled them. Martin also ordered that the men fill their canteens at the stream about half a mile distant. His next concern was the feet of the Meru porters. They had no sandals, never wore them, and were astonished, apparently, when my husband examined their horny soles. Their own headman saw no cause for concern, so Martin decided he was worrying unnecessarily and we sat down to rest, ate a light meal, and waited for the sun to go down.

The stars were shining when my husband, with some misgivings, gave the word to start across the rough slag, and the men, picking their way skillfully, swung into a singing, noisy line. At the end of the fifteen miles, however, they drew to a halt, and the sun was up before they could be induced to move on again. The lava soon was blistering hot with the sun on it, and the air had a searing intensity.

Only once before in my life can I remember torture that even approximated what followed, and that was on the island of Malekula, when the natives put their guns to our backs and drove us up the mountainside. My skin burned, my eyeballs ached, and there was a drum-like pounding in my head which I seemed able to endure only when, by some curious quirk, I kept pace with it.

Slowly my thick boots were being cut to ribbons. I looked at Martin's; they too were cut. I looked up at his face and knew that this was just as horrible for him as it was for me. It was worse, because he had the worry of his cameras, chemicals, and film, and the worry of the men as to whether they could keep going under their burdens of sixty pounds each. And, too, he had the worry of me. I should have done as he asked and gone back. His face was flushed and wet, and a pulse beat hard in his throat. He smiled. "You're doing fine," was all he said. No reproaches—confident that I wouldn't let him down.

Shortly after noon, he called a short rest and looked the men over. He was shocked to find their lips swollen with thirst and to learn that they had not filled their canteens. The order which Jerramani had passed on to the headman of the Merus had been airily dismissed as a vagary of the white 'mbwana.

At the end of another hour of pushing ahead, Jerramani came to report to us that some of the men were dropping out of line. I saw Martin's mouth tighten as he looked back over the wretched natives, and then he gave an order which I knew was the most difficult he had ever issued—to use a whip if necessary to keep them on their feet. Left behind, death of thirst on the searing rocks would be a matter of only a few hours.

It was about four-thirty when Jerramani, desperate this time, came up to us where we led the straggling procession and told us the Meru porters were throwing down their loads. We went back along the line and found most of them sobbing, some of them apparently half out of their minds, others in a half stupor, dropping face down on the slag.

Nightmare seemed added to nightmare. Martin was now confronted with either lashing the men unmercifully and forcing them on, or letting them proceed without their loads. He chose the latter course, sending Ferraragi on ahead with them while we stopped and, with the help of Jerramani and five of our men, gathered our stuff into a compact pile and built a rough barricade of rocks around it.

We soon caught up with and passed the wretched Merus, and in something like an hour we came to the end of the slag. A sandy stretch dotted with thorn trees lay ahead of us. The Merus straggled in and stumbled from the hot, rough lava onto the sand with crazy shouts of relief, only to find that the tiny particles dug into their bleeding feet and gave pain greater than before.

Kalowatt, in her comfortable, airy, carrying case and with a porter assigned especially to her, apparently had not suffered at all on the tortuous journey. On the contrary, she was ready for a frolic the moment she saw me and scolded lustily when I merely pushed a banana into her box and let it go at that.

Martin picked three of our best men and set off across the valley in search of water. He refused to let me go with him, and this time I heeded his wish. I must have fallen asleep in the hot sand, for I awoke to find Jerramani beside me; he had brought my cot from our cache.

My husband and I had decided on a signal of three shots in quick succession in the event that he found water, and it seemed to me that I listened for these even as I slept. But for hours on end there was nothing to be heard except the moans of the poor Merus, the occasional hollow roar of a lion, or the nearer dry cough of a leopard.

When Martin's signal finally came, I was too deep in sleep to hear it. Morning was just breaking, and I was awakened by the almost hysterical shouts of the Merus as, heedless of their swollen feet, they stumbled off in the direction of the shots. I followed with our own men and, guided by the shots which Martin continued to fire at intervals, found him a little over a mile from camp.

His eyes were red-rimmed and strained. We said little, but his smile made me very glad that I had not gone back to Rattray's, and I was glad again when I was able to help him establish a temporary camp at the water hole and direct the doctoring of the porters' feet. Next came the retrieving of our supplies and checking of cameras, chemicals, and film. My husband allowed himself no rest until this was done, and I think I awaited the verdict as anxiously as one might await word from an operating room of a loved one. His smile again was all I needed.

I knew everything was all right, and then out of sheer relief, I suppose, I began to boss him.

"You go and get into bed this very minute," I stormed.

"Why should I go to bed?" he demanded irritably. "It's broad daylight!"

"Yes, and look at you," I scolded, quite as if it was his fault. "Eyes way back in your head, lips cracked. You'll be down sick next thing you know, and then what'll we do?"

I had pushed him into our tent by now, and while I took off one gashed and mutilated boot, Aloni took off the other. Finding that his feet had been bleeding, I sent Aloni for water and an antiseptic. While we bathed Martin's feet he carried on hilariously.

"I feel wonderful," he mumbled. "Never felt better in my life." He dropped back on his pillow. "Everything's fine," he repeated over and over. "Photograph stuff's all right; everything's all right!"

He slept the clock around.

We set up camp in the Shaba hills. Martin insisted that the porters build grass huts for themselves, and that they place them in orderly rows, and these, together with our cook-house, storage-house, and our own tents, made a cozy little village. A strong barricade of thornbush was built around it, on advice of Jerramani, to keep out the lions, leopards, and thieving hyenas, and, altogether, nothing could have been more comfortable. Martin and I regretted that Father Johnson was not with us to enjoy it. We missed him frightfully.

The nights were cool, and each morning, refreshed and eager for the day's work, we sat down to Mpishi's breakfast of good coffee, eggs, ham or bacon, and toast. After breakfast I frequently accompanied Martin to the blinds. Frequently also, it being my wifely duty to keep the larder filled, I went either fishing or hunting accompanied by Ferraragi. Africa has comparatively few streams, but those few are full of good fish, and the Guaso Nyiro (river) near our camp was no exception. It was quite usual to catch more than two hundred pounds of fish in a day, and it was quite usual too to see our men eat most of the catch at one sitting, drying the rest over their fires to nibble on until the next treat.

The routine life of the camp was similar to that of any well-regulated household. Aloni and Toto made the beds, cleaned the tents, and washed the dishes and the clothes, while Mpishi and his assistants did our personal cooking. The natives, of course, did their own. It was my job to arrange the menus, but inasmuch as I had taught Mpishi our way of cooking, this was simple.

We always bathed and changed into fresh clothes for dinner. I made it an invariable rule to keep my hair well brushed and arranged, and to give as much attention to manicure and beauty treatments as though we were in the heart of New York rather than in the depths of so-called darkest Africa. It always seemed to me that I owed it to Martin to look my very best no matter what the circumstances.

The two things we really did miss, though, were fresh fruits and vegetables. There were no gardens in the remoter sections of Africa, and no wild fruits except an unpalatable, warty fig which Kalowatt alone would eat.

We might have been much happier without Mr. Rattray's very logical surmise that the uncharted lake we sought was, in fact, the salty, barren, hundred-mile-long Lake Rudolf. Nevertheless, we were grateful to him for suggesting this trip to the Shaba hills. On entering them we saw countless fresh trails and knew there must be a number of good water holes somewhere about.

Our men found the water holes just two hours from the campsite we had chosen. They came back to report the good news, and early the next morning they led Martin and me to the place where they were. There were five water holes in a sandy depression some two miles long and a mile wide, and crowded at every one were not only the animals with which we were now familiar but also the stunning reticulated giraffe which Mr. Rattray had told us we would see.

All the porters except our personal help were put to work building blinds at the water holes. Martin had long since come to the decision that only with the use of these shelters could he hope to be really successful with his wild-animal photography and with characteristic thoroughness he had questioned hunters who had used them. His needs differed, of course, from those of hunters, for he had lighting to consider, and position and time, and it was necessary to make allowances for these.

His plan now was to experiment with two blinds at every water hole, one on either side to take care of shifts in wind. These were placed about a hundred yards back from the holes. Four-foot-high walls made of piled-up stone encircled a space seven feet in diameter. Supports and a roof made of thornbush completed our practically airless chamber. A narrow aperature running lengthwise for about four feet served as both peephole and an opening for the camera lens. The interiors of these little hotboxes were almost dark, and yet any quick movement betrayed our presence instantly to the sharp-eyed and sharp-eared animals. We also learned that while these animals quickly forgot the scent of a man, they remembered an inexplicable movement and kept clear of the water holes for sometimes a week.

A day in the blind was a long one, because we had to take our positions before daylight. Up at three, and with twenty or more porters carrying chairs, guns, cameras, and lunch, we set out with high hopes, no matter how disappointing the day before might have been.

Those early walks through the thickly wooded hills were unforgettable. Often it was still dark, and yet we smelled the morning, fresh and cool, and on it the sweetness of the foliage which we couldn't see. We walked noiselessly on the broad, hard-packed rhino trails. All about us were the waking sounds of the wilderness: birds chirping, zebra barking, lions exploiting their deepest bass notes, and rhino crashing, with angry snorts, through the underbrush.

By the time we reached the blinds, dawn was in the sky, and we arranged ourselves as quickly and comfortably as possible. Our men then returned to camp. They would come back for us only when the light was gone.

And there we would sit, hours on end, Martin often in one blind and I in another, but we forgot our cramped quarters as we watched.

The animals came for their morning drinks. Zebra, gazelle, giraffe, ostrich, rhino, buffalo—down from the hills they came, sometimes as many as three or four hundred crowding amicably around one hole. We were amazed at the extent to which they respected one another's rights. I never did get over a sort of Noah's Ark unreality about the whole thing.

We ground out thousands of feet of film and would have remained for several weeks longer if suddenly the animals hadn't thinned out. One morning we heard shots and knew what had happened. A party of hunters had taken possession of the Shaba hills. We even found that they were using our blinds at the far hole, so we tore these down, scattering the stones and burning the brush, and when we resumed our trek, every blind had been destroyed.

When we pushed northward again, it wasn't necessary to urge the Meru porters to fill their canteens. In addition, they made it known that they'd like to have some buffalo hide; tardily, they wanted to make some sandals to protect their feet. A few days later we ran across buffalo spoor on the edge of a tinga-tinga (swamp) and decided to pitch camp for a few days.

We set out the following morning to explore the swamp but found no buffalo. We did, however, come suddenly on a grazing rhino. Martin set up the camera and stationed me behind it.

"You keep on grinding no matter what," he said. "I'll go toward him and see if I can get him to charge." So far, the big beast was unaware of us.

Behind a camera, Martin was completely cool, and I've seen him face animals of every sort as they charged toward him— all with perfect steadiness and even delight in the knowledge that it meant a fine picture. But stalking an animal with a gun was something else again, and what happened to him was similar, it seemed to me, to what is familiarly called buck fever in the States. He shook all over, his eyes bulged out, and then, as if to contradict these apparent evidences of fear, his jaw stuck out with a degree of determination that was almost comic.

"Keep grinding," he whispered hoarsely back to me. "This is a rare, one-horned specimen!"

He now shouted to attract the rhino's attention. The huge animal turned with a start, charged halfheartedly, then stopped in a stupid perplexity as Martin stood his ground. Apparently he was pondering what to do next.

"That's enough unless I can get some action out of him," Martin called.

At this point the rhino seemed to weigh the desirability of moving; then, with a snort and a puff he made for us.

My husband took aim and fired, wounding the animal. As it started off, he prepared for another shot. Just then I heard the pounding of hooves in the brush behind us together with the startled grunts of our men. There, coming directly at us, was a herd of zebra, another of oryx, and, bringing up the rear, a herd of what must have been close to a hundred buffalo. Apparently Martin's shot had stampeded the big animals in the narrow donga, and the smaller ones were racing ahead to keep from being trampled.

Martin rushed to where I stood. It seemed certain that we would be run down unless we could turn aside the pounding avalanche. Waving our arms and screeching, we turned the smaller animals, but the buffalo came straight on. My husband aimed for a big one in the center of the herd and brought him down. I dropped another. Martin dropped a third and then we stood while, miraculously, the herd, seeing the leaders fall, divided within a few feet of us and rushed past on either side, while small stones kicked up by flying hooves pelted and cut us and we were choked with dust.

We had forgotten all about the wounded rhino until some of the men gathering firewood found him dead. We sent Japanda to get his hide and single-horned head but found that instead of being a rare specimen, he was nothing but an ordinary rhino that somehow had lost one of his two horns.

Again we pushed on north and saw so many of the ugly and unpredictable beasts as we went that I grew tired of them. I even decided that I actually disliked them and was a little afraid of them too. That one of them had been close to goring Father Johnson certainly hadn't added to my love of them. I tried to persuade Martin that we had enough pictures of rhino for the time being. Then one day we saw a beautiful specimen, perfectly posed, with both background and lighting exactly right for a picture. His Roman nose and splendid horns were clearly outlined, his heavy shoulders and muscles rippled magnificently in the sun. Martin set up his camera and turned it over to me; at a signal I was to start grinding.

"Keep on grinding no matter what," he whispered as he'd done so many times before. This time he moved recklessly close to the unsuspecting beast before he gave me the signal to start turning the crank. The rhino turned, and I knew from the way he lowered his head that he was going to charge. Just then another rhino moved from behind a rock where he had been concealed, and together they charged my husband, gaining excitement from each other in the chase.

Martin was long-legged, sure-footed, and level-headed, but it seemed impossible to me that he could escape this time. He ran at an oblique angle across the camera, then turned sharply out of the path of the snorting beasts, who kept right on going.

I was shaking until my knees did actually knock together.

"Well, Osa," he said excitedly, "I'll bet that's the finest picture of charging rhinos that's ever been taken!"

I thrust my gun into Ferraragi's hands and ran and kept on running until Martin caught me. It seemed to me that I had forfeited all my rights, all his confidence, everything, for I had neglected to grind the camera.

"Next time," said he, "I'll get the action; you get the picture, and don't you worry about me."

We camped at Laisamis, a water hole which had been used by both Paul J. Rainey and Major Dugmore as a site for photography. We spent several days there before continuing our trek to Marsabit.

What lay ahead proved to be a grueling trek, as we crossed the Kaisoot Desert which lies south of Mount Marsabit. The road across the desert seemed impassable, and indeed there were many places where we had to unload the car and let the porters almost carry it for long stretches.

When we reached Marsabit, we stopped for a few days' rest, and it was there that we found Boculy. A little, wizened old man with sore eyes and a jaw that was curiously lopsided, he seemed to appear out of nowhere and, presenting himself to Martin, signified his wish to join our safari. There was a curious dignity about him, a sureness that we needed him more than he needed us. We engaged him on the spot. I set about doctoring his sore eyes, but with little effect, for every two or three days he seemed to go totally blind. His jaw, it seemed, had been broken when he was a young man and, never having been properly put in place, had mended askew, which made both speech and eating difficult. He accounted for the disfigurement with a fantastic tale of an encounter with an equally fantastic elephant which at first we were inclined to doubt, but after he had been with us for a while I was ready to believe anything he said. I had the feeling that Boculy had been born old, and certainly he had a wisdom concerning elephants that went beyond mere knowledge. He was known among the other natives as the "Little Brother of the Elephants."

This strange little man became literally Martin's shadow. It was clear that he knew this northern country better than did our own men, and my husband sounded him out one day with regard to a probable uncharted lake in the area. Boculy looked vague, and whenever Martin raised the subject he seemed not to hear or understand. Either he knew of such a lake or he was being mysterious, as became an oracle of his proportions. Another curious manifestation, whenever the lake was mentioned, was the manner in which he rubbed the top of his head and patted his stomach, an old test in coordination which I remembered trying as a child.

At all events, it was this strange old man who led us, with a minimum of hardship and effort, on the next, very important part of our trip.

"I wish I knew where to go from here," Martin said to me on our fifth evening in camp. We had made trips in all directions hoping to come on some sign of the lake, but without result. Boculy had disappeared within an hour after we had pitched camp days before, and we hadn't seen him since. Then suddenly he appeared, as usual out of nowhere.

"Tembo, 'mbwana, tembo mingi sana," he said. Translated, this meant, "Elephants, master, very many elephants."

Martin and I talked it over and decided our trip wouldn't be a complete loss if we could photograph "many elephants," so we set out early the following morning in the wake of our strange guide. I think we had both hoped that if and when Boculy returned, it would be with news of the lake.

For days we marched behind our ancient guide in some very rough country. For another day we climbed steadily and

then, completely without warning, we were at the edge of a
high cliff overlooking one of the loveliest lakes I had ever seen.

Martin and I stared down without speaking, and then at
each other, and then at Boculy. He stood with an almost unhappy perplexity on his face, and again he was rubbing the top
of his head and patting his stomach. Apparently he had warred
with himself about bringing us here. He had wanted this hidden paradise to remain a sanctuary for his beloved elephants,
but his devotion to Martin had prevailed.

The lake was shaped like a spoon, about a quarter of a mile
wide and three quarters of a mile long, and it sloped up into
steep, wooded banks two hundred feet high. We stood at the
tip of the spoon, which was a high cliff. Opposite, a deep cleft
served as the handle. It lay in the center of an extinct volcano,
and the beach which ran back a hundred feet or so to the edge
of the forest was of hard, washed lava.

A tangle of water-vines and lilies—great, blue African lilies—grew in the shallows at the water's edge. Wild ducks,
cranes, and egrets circled and dipped. Animals, more than we
could count, stood quietly knee-deep in the water and drank.

"It's paradise, Martin!" I said.

He nodded.

That was how Lake Paradise was given its name.

Chapter 21 _____

"Do not be afraid," said Boculy. "The elephants are only eating." We had pitched camp on a cliff overlooking Lake Paradise, and behind us the great trees seemed to have gathered all the blackness out of the night to screen the advance of a mighty and noisy foe. In every direction the trumpeting of elephants blasted the silence and shook us where we sat under our flimsy canvas roofs. The creaking and snapping of trees went on without pause.

"Do they always tear down the forest when they eat?" Martin demanded of Boculy.

"And scream?" I asked. "Do they have to do that?"

A crash nearer at hand had my husband on his feet and reaching for his gun. I had visions of the lot of us being squashed flat.

Boculy was completely calm, however, and, pitying out ignorance a little, I think, explained that the trumpeting was only friendly conversation and that the crashing had merely to do with the manner in which the big animals fed. They liked the tender shoots at the tops of young trees, he said, and bent and sometimes broke the slender trunks to reach them.

Our camp survived the night without damage, and by morning Martin and I felt a positive affection toward the huge animals for being so kind as to spare us. We sat out under the trees having breakfast, and already my husband was envisioning a complete record on film of elephant family life.

"Why, this place is their home," he said excitedly, "and they've let us move right in!"

Just then, over Martin's shoulder as he sat facing me, I saw three large elephants shuffling lazily along the path that led past our tents down to the lake. Apparently in a genial, playful mood, they stopped every now and then to blow trunkfuls of dust over one another's backs.

Martin slipped into the tent for his camera, set it up to leeward, and cranked happily. So far they hadn't noticed us, and my husband signaled me to move into the picture. The big fellows were so exactly like the elephants I'd seen in circuses that I wanted to go right up and feed them and pat their wrinkled trunks. To walk toward them seemed the most natural thing in the world to do. I even decided the big one's name was Jumbo. Ten or eleven feet high at the shoulder, they loomed gray and solid above me, but, so far, it hadn't occurred to me to be afraid. When they wheeled suddenly and faced me, however, and their trunks went up in alarm and their ears stood straight out from their heads, that was something else.

"Osa!" I heard Martin shouting. "Come back here!"

I stood where I was, my feet heavy on the ground. A shivery feeling began in my stomach and darted in all directions to the surface of my skin where it became goose bumps, and a nightmarish sort of fear held me completely immovable. Martin said afterwards that the elephants and I, all equally motionless, might have been a stuffed group in a museum.

Suddenly then, as if by some occult signal, the three elephants turned tail and lumbered off. I'll never know what possessed me, but I chased after them yelling at the top of my voice.

Martin's roar of laughter stopped me and I retraced my steps, feeling very silly. He was still laughing.

"What would you have done if you'd caught them?" he asked.

"That part doesn't matter," I answered with as much dignity as possible. "I had to show them they couldn't bluff me."

We stayed three months at Lake Paradise, and Martin planned our short expeditions so methodically while there that when we left for Nairobi and the States we had a thorough working knowledge of the surrounding country. Hard-packed elephant trails, apparently centuries old, crisscrossed the great virgin forest with the orderliness and purpose of as many city streets. Exploring them, we found they led straight and clean to the lake, to feeding grounds, to desert, to plain, and to water holes, and that animal traffic increased or lessened according to season. Cool, rainy weather saw the four-footed travelers heading for desert and plain; hot, dry weather found them returning to forest and lake.

"Palm Springs in the winter, Lake Saranac in the summer," Martin said flippantly. It always pleased him to find similarities in human and animal conduct. "People think they're so smart!" was a favorite and telling dig.

When we assembled our safari for the return trip to Nairobi, our money was practically gone, we were at the end of our film supply, and nerves and muscles were weary, but during the three months at the uncharted lake Martin had conceived a plan that both delighted and staggered me.

"Won't it take an awful lot of money?" I asked cautiously.

"Of course it will, but we'll pay it back the way we've always done, out of the pictures we make."

My husband's plan was to spend at least four unbroken years at Lake Paradise, with enough money and equipment, including the latest and best in cameras, to photograph the family life of all the wild creatures that assembled there. Of first interest, of course, would be the elephant, with as many of his wise and sometimes mysterious habits as we could capture. According to Boculy, there must be many thousands of these prehistoric survivors in this unmolested section of British East Africa.

With Boculy to guide our safari, the return trip to Nairobi was made with a minimum of effort and strain. The little old man's sure instinct even led us clear of the sun-baked lava field, and when we reached Meru our porters were very nearly as fresh as when we left Paradise. Here we discharged them, and after deducting their advance and hut tax, we paid each man about ten rupees (five dollars). This was spent promptly, of course, for sugar, rice, unspeakable coffee, and gaudy calico, and the last we saw of our Merus, they were marching happily toward their native hills. Thankfully, we resumed the journey to Nairobi in our cars, with motor lorries and ox carts now carrying our equipment and precious film.

"Good. Good work," said Blayney Percival. With the usual

restraint of the Britisher, he said little more than this as we ran pictures for him showing the beautiful crater lake which we had named Paradise and the unharassed animals drinking quietly at its shores.

"But aren't you excited?" I demanded.

Mr. Percival permitted himself a little smile. "Frankly," he said, "I believe I am. As a matter of fact," he added, "I doubt that even a score of wild horses could keep me from joining you on your next trip."

We could very well have gone straight on to the States without stopping in Nairobi to develop the film which we had exposed on our thousand mile journey. Martin had sealed it carefully, and the additional time spent in travel would have affected it not at all, but it was impossible to wait the additional weeks to see what photographic luck we'd had and, more, we wanted to share with Blayney Percival some of the joys of our discovery. After all, the lake, or rather the possibility of its existence, had first been his dream.

Martin then told Blayney our plan to spend at least four years at the lake when we came back from the States.

Blayney thought a moment. "Splendid idea, I should say. Take some financing, of course, but what you've shown me on the screen here ought to solve that problem. Those animal pictures you took from the blinds at the Shaba hills, your rhino stuff—they're corking, all of them and, of course, your Lake Paradise pictures are superb."

My husband shook his head. "Whatever we realize from this stuff," he said, "belongs to the people who financed our trip here. Most of it, anyhow."

Maybe they'd agree to take the interest and put the principal back in," I said, feeling quite bright.

Martin brushed this aside. "Wouldn't be nearly enough," he said. Then he went on. "What I did have in mind, though, was showing what we have here, especially the Paradise stuff, to a man like Mr. Eastman of the Kodak Company, for instance."

"Mr. Eastman!" I stared at my husband. "Did you say Mr. Eastman?"

"Yes, George Eastman. I have a feeling that this would interest him."

"But, Martin, you don't know Mr. Eastman."

"I've never met him, if that's what you mean." He eyed me with sudden, almost hostile, challenge. "Is that what you mean?"

"Why, yes. It seems silly, a man you've never even met."

"Well, you don't always have to meet a man to know him, do you?"

The sky was leaden and a cold drizzle slanted against the train window, distorting the landscape. I might as well have been looking at it through tears, and the fact that this was early spring and that the trees wore a fresh green dress did not make the upper New York scene one jot more attractive. Martin sat opposite me in the observation car of the train that we had boarded at Rochester for Manhattan. His lips were pulled in, and he made a great show of reading the morning paper.

All that trouble for nothing, I thought to myself. Martin's determination to see Mr. Eastman had taken us to Rochester. We had been admitted to the great executive's presence, but after a five-minute audience with the slim, tired man, in which we presented everything just about as badly as possible, we found ourselves being politely escorted to the door.

With utmost courtesy Mr. Eastman had said, "I have seen some of your interesting pictures, Mr. Johnson, and I've no doubt but that as you go along your work will be of increasing importance, but unfortunately I have made it an inviolable rule never to invest in private enterprise. Good morning—and thank you very much for coming to see me."

In the taxi on the way to the train, and while waiting in the station for the southbound express, Martin and I had spoken to each other only in monosyllables, though I found it very difficult not to point out to him that if one must be so foolish as to build up a big and illogical expectation, one must also expect to take a big and very logical fall. But I managed to keep perfectly still. We rode along for a while, and then the conductor opened the door and said something about Albany being the next stop. He could just as well have said Poughkeepsie for all I cared, but as we were pulling into the station the fact that we were stopping suddenly mattered very much to me. I bounced to my feet.

"Come on," I said vigorously to my husband. "We're getting off."

I was off the train before Martin could catch up with me. "What do we want to get off at Albany for?" he demanded crossly. "We don't know anybody in Albany."

"We're going back to Rochester," I said.

"What?"

"We're going back to see Mr. Eastman."

"But that's crazy. We can't do that!"

"At least the man has a right to know what he's missing, hasn't he?" I demanded over my shoulder as I led the way at a fast clip toward the northbound tracks.

"But we shouldn't have gone to him in the first place. You were right all along," he said.

"Mr. Eastman isn't going to pass this thing up until he knows what he's passing up. Why, the way we told it to him, both talking at once, he probably couldn't make head or tail of a thing we said. And besides," I added, "he's going to let us show him the pictures of Lake Paradise."

"But he told us he didn't have time to look at any pictures. He said his whole day was tied up!"

"We'll wait till he does have time."

I pushed Martin aboard the Rochester-bound train, his face puckered and flushed with perplexity. "He'll think we're crazy, going back," he said. "Why—I bet he won't even let us in!"

"Mr. Eastman will see you now." The quiet, lovely woman who was Mr. Eastman's secretary opened the heavy door into the inner office and stood aside for us to enter. Martin looked at me wildly, I squeezed his hand, and once more we were in the big man's office and the door was closed behind us.

"Won't you sit down?" Mr. Eastman said with extreme courtesy—so extreme, in fact, that I had a picture of his patience being all tied up tightly with thin white string.

I flashed a look at Martin. His nervousness had left him, and he was perfectly composed—the way I've seen him when a lion or rhino was charging the camera and he kept on turning the crank.

"I'm not very good at talking about things that mean a lot

to me," he said, "but I want to get it straight that I didn't come just to put over a money proposition. I don't pretend to be that kind of spellbinder."

Mr. Eastman nodded slightly.

"I was so anxious to make it clear that you couldn't lose by investing in a motion picture to be made of the animals at Lake Paradise that I guess the whole thing had the sound of a money proposition, but what I wanted to do was to interest you in the idea and not in a mere business deal."

"Naturally," I said, putting in my bit, "we know you have plenty of ways of making money without suggestions from us."

Mr. Eastman seemed to be trying not to smile. "Am I to understand then," he said, "that you're not promising me a super-colossal return on my investment?" I thought to myself that his eyes were like pieces of blue ice with the sun on them.

Martin shook his head. "I promise only to return your money with a nominal interest for its use. The expense of a four-year safari to this lake—it's up near the Abyssinian border—will be very large. Only someone who sees the idea and not the returns would consider backing me."

"I must say I like your frankness, Mr. Johnson." Mr. Eastman rose and walked to the window. Martin and I sat very still. We didn't even look at each other.

Mr. Eastman turned toward us very suddenly. "I'll invest ten thousand dollars in your idea," he said, "and you may use my name freely in securing more."

It was still raining when we boarded the train for New York, but I decided that it was a very nice rain, and that this was a very remarkable world.

"He said he believed in us both," I said to my husband. "He said that."

Martin looked as though he couldn't stop smiling even if he wanted to. "He also said he likes people who have dreams and the gumption to carry them through. I liked that part too," he grinned.

"Good-bye! Good-bye!"

"Well, do you have to let them see you crying?" Martin demanded. "They'll think I beat you or something."

"Nobody's crying. Who's crying?" I said crossly. "Good-bye,"
I screamed over the side of the ship's railing to the pier below.
"Good-bye!"

Their faces were blurred, pink discs in the frosty air, and
they stood all in a row pushed against the ropes by the crowds
behind. Everybody was screaming and throwing confetti. It was
December 1, 1923, and once more we were setting sail for Africa. There were my mother and father—his hair a little gray
at the temples now. Next to them stood Freda, tall and fair,
very like Martin, and at her side, Father Johnson.

"Plant those Kansas watermelons and let me know how they
turn out." Mr. Johnson's voice came thinly through his cupped
hands.

I saw my pretty mother reach into her bag for a handkerchief, and I also saw my grandmother poke her brusquely in
the ribs, and then poke my father, for good measure. My father
was a passenger-train engineer now, an erect, distinguished,
kindly looking man, and I felt very proud of him—proud of
them all. Suddenly it seemed a little cruel that our work should
take us so far away from them, and this time for four years
without a single return trip.

"Good-bye! Good-bye!" we all said senselessly, over and over
again.

I don't know when my feelings had been as mixed as they
were on this sailing, and instead of waiting to watch the New
York skyline fade, I ran to our stateroom and indulged in the
biggest cry I'd had in years. Martin followed me and sat uncer-
tainly on the edge of a chair. I blew my nose and peered at him
through the flowers and baskets of fruit that stood along with
our hand luggage piled in the middle of the floor and saw that
he was anxious, perplexed, and annoyed, all at the same time.

"What's the matter anyhow?" he demanded finally in complete exasperation. "Here everything's better for us than it's
ever been, and look at you!"

"I don't know," I said.

"Huh!" said Martin.

I just sniffed for a while.

"Lake Paradise and all," he mumbled to himself. Then he
began adding up the many wonderful things that had hap-

pened to us since we had been in the States, and my tears seemed very silly indeed.

"Take Mr. Eastman," he said. "Why, that man's our friend, he isn't just a financial backer. Sent those flowers, didn't he?" For emphasis, my husband bunted the huge basket of chrysanthemums with the toe of his shoe.

"Yes, I know," I said in a small voice. "Everything's wonderful."

"And all the rest of the people that are behind us with their money and their faith—Daniel Pomeroy, George D. Pratt, Mrs. Henry Pomeroy Davison, Trubee and Harry Davison—what more do you want?" My husband almost shouted this last at me.

"You make it sound as if I didn't know all those things."

My husband went right on, piling up such a weight of masculine logic against my wholly feminine, illogical tears that I should have been crushed with humiliation.

"And the official sponsorship of the Museum of Natural History, signed by Henry Fairfield Osborn the president, F. Trubee Davison, and all the officers—what could be more wonderful than that, or a greater incentive?"

"I feel wonderful," I said.

"Well, that's fine," my husband said with immense relief. He came and sat beside me. "You see," he said after a while, "I guess I'm sometimes awfully afraid you're going to get tired of living the way we do among wild people, wild animals—no home. It's tough on a woman—it must be."

He was trying so hard to understand my tears, but since I didn't understand them myself, it was all pretty confused.

"And when you cried just now, I began to be afraid all over again that maybe you'd rather have stayed behind with your folks than go with me."

"Why, that's the silliest thing I ever heard," I said. I was very indignant.

By tripping a photo-flash wire, this leopard took his own stunning portrait.

The blind. Not shown are the stifling heat, absolute silence from dawn till dusk, stale sandwiches, and always the possibility of a charge that could effectively demolish the blind and its occupants.

Martin considered this dynamic photograph to be one of his best.

Flash shot: striped hyena, the rarer of East Africa's two species

Flash shot: black rhinoceros. (Editor's note: this species is now on the brink of extinction.)

The Johnson home in Muthaiga, a suburb of Nairobi

One of the Johnsons' most useful campsites: Nanyuki Forest with Mount
Kenya rising in the distance

Martin lounges in a tent in the Belgian Congo.

Osa is not exactly lounging as she waits for help.

The Johnsons relax after a tense moment, a buffalo charge that was definitely
not a bluff.

Chapter 22 _____

It was the afternoon of April 12, 1924, when once more we looked down on Lake Paradise. The sun broke through an overcast sky just as we trudged up the last hundred feet of the incline to the rim, and there it lay, two hundred feet below us in the hollow of the extinct crater, quiet as a pond and with the blue water lilies on its breast. Brilliant butterflies flitted above the lilies. Heron and egrets, ducks and coots, storks and cranes strutted, and animals stood in the clear water up to their bellies, sleepily content with their lot. A lip of pale green marsh-reed edged the lake. Wild olives festooned with Spanish moss grew up the sloping banks. Dark-leaved mahogany trees swept in thick ranks to the crater's rim, and beyond, magnificent in its vastness, ominous in its reddish-gray nudity, lay the great Dida Galgalla desert stretching clear to the Abyssinian border.

I stole a look at Blayney Percival, who stood beside us; his eyes were suspiciouly moist. He caught my look and reddened a little.

"I'm bound to confess," he said, "that this is rather more astonishing than I had expected it to be."

Old Boculy rubbed his ebony pate and looked very proud. Martin pressed my hand tightly and said nothing, but we both knew that this moment was the fulfillment of one dream and the beginning of another.

Apparently for our benefit, a note was struck that, half comic, nevertheless emphasized the lavish beauty of this animal sanctuary. A big elephant knee-deep in the water with other members of his family seemed to decide that his bath was complete and that he had had enough to drink, so he turned to lead the way up into the forest. Wound firmly around his switching, ropelike tail at a most decorative angle was one of the blue water lilies.

Two hours after our arrival at Lake Paradise, the "long rains," which we had dreaded for weeks, began to fall.

Unexpected difficulties, I think, are at once the challenge and the charm of the lives of all explorers. When we had puffed into Nairobi on the Uganda railway with our two hundred and fifty-five crates and cases of equipment, we thought complacently, this safari is going to be wonderful; this time we have every last thing we could possibly need to make our expedition a success. We didn't realize that the weight and bulk of our supplies would hamper and almost defeat us. At best, the five-hundred-mile journey northward was beset with difficulties, and something like half the distance would be virtually impassable once the heavy rains set in. Certainly, should the Guaso Nyiro be at flood when we reached it, our safari would end on its southern bank.

Had we traveled light, we could have been under way within possibly two weeks after our arrival in Nairobi. This would have given us a safe margin before the "long rains" were due. As it was, five weeks raced by before the last case was unpacked and made up into the usual sixty-pound bundles for the porters to carry. Eighteen guns, twenty-one cameras, six Willys-Knight cars with safari bodies—water tanks, hardware, staple foodstuffs, clothing, ammunition, photographic supplies—these and hundreds of items had been assembled to be transported, over a country largely trackless, to Lake Paradise.

In all, our cavalcade comprised the six Willys-Knights; four motor lorries; five wagons, each drawn by six mules; four ox carts, each drawn by four oxen; two hundred and thirty-five natives, two hundred of whom were porters; together with gunbearers, cooks, house servants, and the like.

As rapidly as possible we loaded the slower-moving vehicles and sent them on ahead to Isiolo, but when we ourselves left Nairobi, we were obliged to face the fact that we were three weeks behind schedule and only by the rarest good luck could get through ahead of the rains. At all events we were cheered by the fact that Blayney Percival, who had retired from his position as game warden for British East Africa, would join our expedition at the Guaso Nyiro.

Martin rarely worried, but I saw that the responsibility of this undertaking weighted heavily upon him. For one thing, his was the task of being commander, judge, physician, and provider for more than two hundred natives. We had been told, and also knew from experience, that before the end of the long and harsh trip a certain percentage of this number was almost sure to die. Picked carefully, these men always appeared to be of equal strength and fitness when we started out, but fevers, illnesses, accidents, or wounds of one sort or another almost invariably took a toll. And even graver, if possible, than this responsibility was the one we owed to the Museum of Natural History, to George Eastman, and to all the others who had invested confidence and money in our undertaking.

Although the skies were leaden when we reached the Guaso Nyiro, the rains had not yet fallen and we crossed it, singing gaily. Blayney, according to promise, joined us there, and his presence in our safari was of itself reason for rejoicing.

Arrived at Archer's Post, Martin made a reckless decision to which I gave enthusiastic support. This was to attempt a short-cut through the mountains. Blayney was doubtful that we would succeed, and he was right. The mountains proved impassable, and we were obliged to turn back to Archer's Post, a distance of some sixty-five miles. Precious days and energies were lost, and, added to this, an unrecognized ailment reaching almost epidemic proportions spread among our porters. All of our efforts at doctoring them proved unavailing, so Martin put the worst cases into ox carts and sent them back to Meru. A day or two later, while we were still at Archer's Post, our ranks were further depleted by the desertion of some twenty porters. With the help of Blayney, however, we reorganized our safari, and March 29 found us pushing northward across the now familiar Kaisoot Desert, a vast expanse which under threatening skies had the look of a gray, sleepy sea.

Scattered rains began to fall, and with the men—both black and white—grunting, sweating, and swearing, we were obliged to fight every foot of the way. Our cars, lorries, and wagons bogged repeatedly, and more times than I could count we were obliged to get out, unload our supplies, and dig, haul, and push and carry before we could go on again.

Old Boculy joined us at Kampia Tembo, a godforsaken government station which was made up of a few mud huts and some scrawny cattle. With this strange old fellow to lead us, our spirits lifted, and we started out on what he assured us would be a short, quick route to Lake Paradise. A bit distrustful by now of short routes, nevertheless we followed him into wholly unfamiliar territory. Fifty men with axes and crowbars cleared a sort of trail along which our heavily burdened safari moved at best little faster than a slow walk.

After about ten days of this we came to country so rough that we were frightfully discouraged. Boculy, however, nimble and cheerful as a little gnome, waved his bony arms and urged us on, and because there was nothing else to do we followed him once more, skidding over boulders, creeping through high, tough grass, crashing down ravines, and straining up steep grades until abruptly and to our complete astonishment, late on the afternoon of April 12, we found ourselves at the foot of the crownless mountain which we knew cradled our lake.

Rain! I have been in many tropical regions famous for their heavy downpours, but never had I dreamed that rain could take on the proportions of the deluge that fell from the skies just two hours after our arrival at Lake Paradise.

As soon as the wagons arrived with our camping equipment, we of course put up our tents, but no canvas that was ever made could keep out the water that poured upon us as if tipped from the shore of some celestial sea. Our men, having no shelters whatever, were completely miserable. I did what I could to keep them cheerful by giving them extra sugar and coffee, and Blayney shot buffalo to provide fresh meat. We also managed to keep great fires going at least part of the time so that the poor fellows could be warm even though wet.

We were close to panic on April 15, three days after our arrival, when we discovered that the instructions accompanying our electric-light plant stated plainly and uncompromisingly that the batteries must be in use before April 11.

Martin's generalship in this emergency was a joy to watch. Picking some sixty of our best men, he rushed to completion in a single day the fourteen-foot-square building which for nearly four years was to house both our electric plant and machine shop. The men were divided into groups, and the work was done with little or no lost motion. One group brought clay and dung, another group mixed, another cut poles, others cut grass, some twenty of our best craftsmen put up the actual building as the raw materials were brought in, and eight men, expert thatchers, added the roof the moment the walls and roof poles were up.

Blayney helped Martin install the plant, and we tried not to remember that we were four days behind the deadline for putting the batteries into operation. Our porters stood banked three and four deep outside the windows and the open door. Boculy, being a privileged person, stood just inside the door. There even seemed to be a lull in the pounding of the rain, but actually there was no dramatic delay whatever when the big moment came. The three of us shook hands solemnly, I crossed my fingers, Martin seized the wheel and gave it a spin, and the lights were on. It was as simple as that. Martin smiled. Blayney said, "Stout fellow." Boculy rubbed the top of his head, and the natives in chorus said "Ahhhhh." I remembered noticing how their wet, ebony bodies glistened in the sudden blaze of man-created light.

In spite of the discomforts and hardships of working in the rain, we rushed work on the rest of our permanent buildings. These, we were determined, should be of more durable construction than the mud-and-straw shacks usually found in British East Africa. We built the huts of stout logs for permanence, standing the logs upright in African native fashion, and plastered them inside with a mixture of dung and mud that dried eventually to the hardness and firmness of concrete. The whole was then stuccoed with a mixture of buffalo, elephant, and rhino dung mixed in exact proportions with clay, and the result was a surface the color of Chinese punk and very like Mexican adobe. This, topped with a thatch of dried yellow grass, was very attractive against the pale and darker mahogany greens of the forest.

Martin wisely provided for a double-air-space thatching for all our permanent buildings. This was very puzzling to our native thatchers, but certainly it provided greater coolness than the single thatch and was an added protection against the seasonal rains.

We covered the interior walls with rough, unbleached sheeting—pasting it on, wallpaper fashion, with a mixture of shellac and glue—and were rewarded with an ivory tone and a soft dull texture that gave a very pleasing effect. The wooden cases which had boxed Martin's photographic materials and our foodstuffs were taken apart very carefully and made into good, smooth floors.

Our living room was fourteen by seventeen feet, with a big screened veranda across the front, and our bedroom, fifteen feet square, boasted a large pink stuccoed bathroom which opened off the end wall. I was delighted to find the clay which gave us this delicate shade. In no time at all, of course, I had put frilled sash curtains at all the windows.

The most important building of the lot, of course, was Martin's laboratory. A room eighteen feet by twelve housed the big drying drums, storage cases, table, and racks, and the darkroom, ten by fourteen feet, was equipped with the special lighting, running water, developing vats, storage tanks, and all the rest of the paraphernalia that go to make an up-to-date motion-picture laboratory.

Clear water was all-important for the developing of our negatives, and eight hundred gallons a day was brought up from the lake on the backs of mules. This water was filtered repeatedly through charcoal and sand, and finally was put through cotton. In the rainy season, Martin simplified the problem with the same method he used so successfully at our bungalow in Nairobi—he built roof gutters.

An always-present problem on our safaris was keeping the highly sensitized film and chemicals in perfect condition, but my husband managed this very well by using special drying compounds and having continuous shipments of fresh stock sent from the Eastman Kodak plant in Rochester. And, of course, after the films were dried on the big drums, they were patched in 200-foot lengths, wrapped in special chemical-proof paper, and then placed in tins which, in turn, were made completely airtight with a coating of paraffin wax.

In due time, of course, we added guest houses and landscaped gardens. On the far side of the garden, like a row of barracks, stood the huts of the porters. Our buildings, several acres of vegetable gardens, a regiment of employees, our motor trucks, cars and ox wagons, flocks of chickens (which multiplied with astonishing rapidity), and herds of donkeys, humpbacked cows, and camels were all enclosed in a stockade of palings and thornbush thirteen feet high. It was quite an impressive village.

Whenever we settled long enough anywhere, I always planted a garden, and this time, knowing that we were establishing ourselves for perhaps four years, I had brought garden tools, seeds, and bulbs enough—Martin said—to cultivate all the land clear to the Abyssinian border. This was a slight exaggeration, of course, but I did have enough surplus to start most of the water holes blooming with flowers in and around Lake Paradise. Wherever there was running water, too, I always popped in some watercress seeds. The elephants loved watercress.

On the second day after our arrival at Paradise, I got out my big bundle of seeds, put on overalls and boots, and, with a dozen or more men carrying picks and shovels and wearing puzzled expressions, went hunting for a likely garden spot. I found a well-drained plot with good soil on the side of the hill, not too far from our camp, and put the men to work. It was a very muddy business, and Martin and Blayney stood around and scoffed. At any rate, they were quite skeptical.

"I should be inclined to think that most of the seeds would rot," Blayney offered reflectively.

"That's my guess, too," Martin contributed. "And, of course," he went on, "any that don't rot will naturally be gobbled by the birds."

I went right on slopping around and putting seeds in the ground.

"I seems to me," my husband next said—winking at Blayney but addressing me—"that you'd have a lot more fun if you just sat down and made mud pies."

In spite of these pessimistic predictions, however, I managed to raise a fine crop of beans, peas, sweet corn, carrots potatoes, cucumbers, turnips, squash, salsify, cantaloupes, and watermelons, and fairly popped with audible pride every time any of these came on the table.

"Never argue with a woman," my husband grumbled to Blayney. "Nine times out of every ten she's right."

Much as I enjoyed the vegetables and fruits out of our garden, I think I relished even more the wild delicacies I found in the forest. Often I've returned home with armfuls of wild asparagus and spinach. There was a black cranberry, very sweet and good; a native coffee; abundant mushrooms; a fruit that seemed a cross between an apricot and an apple; a bitter wild plum that made fine jam; and a wonderful brown honey. Darkest Africa!

It would be impossible for me to set down in chronological order the things that happened at Lake Paradise. Time, as we know it in the city, doesn't exist in the wilderness, for there are no newspapers, scheduled events, or social calendars to set one day, week, or month apart from another. The seasons alone marked time for us and governed our goings and comings and our work.

During the rains, when water was available on desert and plain, we could be found there in our blinds, photographing gazelle, antelope, giraffe, zebra, warthog, and lion. During the drier weather, we divided our time among the marvelous water holes and the forests about Lake Paradise, where steadily we built up a film record of the buffalo, the rhino, and, most important of all, the elephant.

Martin and I often laughed, remembering our first expedition to the South Seas. It, like all our other expeditions, had been a photographic one, but our only camera was an old reconditioned hand-crank Universal, and our film totaled a few thousand feet. On this safari to Lake Paradise, we had a battery of twenty cameras—ten motion picture, ten still—and our lenses, bought in America, England, and Germany, had been ground to order and thoroughly tested.

Five of the motion-picture cameras were designed by Carl Akeley especially for photographing wildlife. Two of these were mounted together, one taking regularly timed pictures while the other took the same action in slow motion. A third Akeley camera was fitted with four lenses of different focal length that could be switched and adjusted in a fraction of a second.

Still another camera—Martin called it his "fire department" camera—was mounted on a heavy unipod and designed to take pictures from our car as we traveled. This was great fun, as it could be swung into position and focused before even the fleetest animal could get out of range.

Another series of cameras was operated by an electric motor and could be set up and controlled from a distance by wires. All of these cameras, equipped with wide-angle lenses, portrait lenses, landscape lenses, and diffusing lenses, prepared Martin for any photographic emergency.

Anyone seeing the arsenal with which we arrived at Lake Paradise would have been justified in assuming that we were out to kill animals quite as much as to photograph them in their wild state. It was merely a precautionary measure, however, and took into account the series of emergencies that might arise over a period of from four to five years. I list this arsenal roughly.

3 English Blands, .470, double-barrel

1 English Bland, .275, Mannlicher action

1 American Springfield, .303, Mauser action

1 English Rigby, .505, Mauser action

3 American Winchesters, .405, lever action

1 American Winchester, .32, lever action

2 English Jeffries, .404, Mauser action

1 American Winchester shotgun, .12, double-barrel

1 American Ithaca, .20, double-barrel

1 American Ithaca, .20, saw-off shotgun, called riot gun

1 .38 Colt revolver

1 .45 Colt revolver

On these jaunts, lasting sometimes for ten days, we usually took with us the following men:

2 camera bearers

1 tripod bearer carrying two tripods

1 bearer with lens case

1 bearer with press Graflex and tripod

1 bearer with a case of loaded film magazines

1 bearer with two cases of loaded plate holders

1 bearer with 4 × 5 Graflex and tripod

1 bearer with case of odds and ends: filters, tools, oil, first-
aid kit

1 bearer carrying lunch

Martin's gun-bearer

my gun-bearer

Boculy, the guide, and Bukhari, our headman.

Martin had worked out a fine system that made for almost
split-second timing and efficiency. Each case was boldly num-
bered and each bearer was thoroughly rehearsed until he knew
both the sight and sound of the number, with the result that
with a single command, and wholly without confusion, any one
of the score of cameras could be brought forward and put within
reach of my husband's hand.

In case of danger, our gun-bearers crawled up close and
were ready with our rifles. These men were always of higher-
than-average intelligence and acted both on knowledge of the
various animals and on clear judgment rather than on orders
from us. It was generally accepted, I think, that Boculy, the
little, brown, lop-jawed man, knew more about elephants than
any other native in the whole of Africa. Neither he nor his
methods were particularly convincing at first glance, for much
of the time he shuffled along muttering to himself and apparently was more than half asleep. Aware of the doubts which
we felt concerning his self-boasted cleverness, he sometimes
put on quite a show of examining the earth and looking for
signs where I'm sure there were none, but after a while we
came to have a complete and almost fatuous confidence in him.
I have seen him scent, or perhaps "sense," game with the sure-

ness of a bloodhound, and his methods, while often meaningless to us, were certain of result. It developed that we almost
hung on the negative or affirmative shake of his head, and this
was all the more amusing when one considered that often the
object under consideration in his clawlike hand was nothing
more nor less than a small piece of mud. Just that. While he
turned it over and over, examining it with his half-blind eyes
and making funny little noises, we waited breathless on his
decision and accepted it as absolute.

The condition of a few blades of slightly bruised grass held
tremendous import for him, for he knew by the angle at which
a single spear was bent just how long a time had passed since
the heavy foot of an elephant had trod it down. By studying the
little fellow's methods, we caught on a bit. It seems that a blade
of grass trodden flat requires something like three hours to pull
itself erect again, and the different angles in between have an
almost precise hourly, half-hourly, and even quarter-hourly sig-
nificance.

A bent branch told this uncanny old man of the passage of
a herd to within five minutes; it also told him the kind of herd
and the probable direction it had taken. A mere glance at the
trees, and he knew from the way the tender buds had been
cleanly nipped that giraffe were so-and-so near or far away.

If this astonishing old black failed for a time to find traces
of elephants or whatever other animal we were most interested
in photographing at the moment, he would shrug philosophi-
cally and say one of three things: "*Shauri ako*" ("Business caused
by white man"), "*Shauri mungu*" ("Business caused by God"),
or "*Shauri mvua*" ("Business caused by rain").

And whenever Boculy made up his mind for any or all of
these reasons that we would be wise to quit for the day—we
quit for the day.

Our many encounters with elephants during the four years
we spent at Lake Paradise endeared the splendid creatures to
us and helped us, I think, to understand Boculy's reverence for
them. Dignified, conservative, intelligent, with an apparent
awareness of his place in life, this fine animal attends strictly
to his own business and lets other creatures severely alone.

Elephants fight little among themselves, are intelligent parents, and have an instinct for tribal loyalty. They have their own leaders and follow and wait upon their decisions.

There were times when Martin and I were so interested in the animals themselves that we almost forgot our job of getting pictures of them. At the end of one very hot day spent in a blind (I remember we both had splitting headaches and were on the point of gathering up our things and going back to camp), we saw a herd of some twenty elephants ambling toward our water hole. We were to leeward, but the big fellow who obviously was the leader sensed, if not our presence exactly, something warning him that all was not as usual. Perhaps at some time or other on one of his migrations he had heard the explosions of guns, had seen a companion fall, had caught the scent of man. At any rate, he stopped abruptly, his troupe halting instantly in their tracks. His ears stood out, his trunk lifted and waved exploringly, and he advanced alone to the water hole, a slow step at a time. Here, fully conscious of his responsiblity as a leader, he did not so much as look at the water; instead, he drew away and went back to his herd and apparently held a conference. As I have said, it was a frightfully hot day and the big animals probably had come a long distance to quench an almost overpowering thirst. Taking this into consideration, it would seem, the leader returned once more to the water hole to investigate. A little fellow, probably his son, started to follow, whereupon the father paused long enough to smack him sharply with his trunk and send him back into the herd. This second investigation proved no more satisfactory than the first—I could have sworn the big fellow sighed and shook his head—and, returning to his family and companions, he led them quietly but firmly away.

Martin and I loved baby animals of every kind, but baby elephants were simply irresistible. There was one little fellow— he couldn't have been over a few weeks old—who was being led for perhaps the first time down to a water hole. It was another of those very hot days, and the baby lagged behind the herd and whined and complained bitterly. As a matter of fact, I felt certain that if we could have been close enough we would have seen big tears rolling down his face. His mother lost patience finally, seized him by the ear with her trunk, held him firmly with her huge foot, and then proceeded to squirt water over him. The infant squawked and struggled in vain and wasn't released until his mother was satisfied he had had enough both to cool and discipline him.

My husband and I almost laughed aloud when the baby got to his feet still squawking—his pink mouth wide open—only to find that he felt refreshed and almost happy. He took hold of his mother's tail with his trunk, quite as one of our own babies would take his mother's hand, and stood complacently while she had her drink. Then he followed her quietly into the tall grass, still holding her tail.

I suppose it would sound very silly for anyone to say that elephants conduct schools for their young ones, and yet if it was not a school, or class, that we came upon in the forest about eight miles from our Lake Paradise home, I'm sure I don't know what it was. Four mothers with as many youngsters apparently had chosen this quiet retreat—a discreet distance, I assume, from the male members of the family—to go into the intricacies and art of trumpeting. Fortunately they were so busy and earnest about it all that we were able to watch them for quite a long time without being observed. The procedure seemed to be for each mother in turn to lift her trunk and let forth a mighty blast and then for her young one to set himself also for a mighty blast, only to emit a thin squeak somewhat resembling a tin whistle. This disappointment and despair of the mothers and the abashment of the babies over all this had us laughing out loud, finally, and school was dismissed promptly and in some alarm.

Thanks to Boculy, we were able to secure many fine pictures of elephants in herds, but I think we were equally interested in coming on single animals at close range. In these circumstances, the big animal was without the guidance of leader or herd, and his reactions, if anything, were sharper. His great ears would push straight out from his head, his long trunk wave exploringly, and he would squint his small eyes in our direction in an effort at identifying us. After a long look then and a great sniff, he would usually decide that while we were nothing to fear, neither were we familiar to him, and, backing off a few paces, he would turn around and stroll dignifiedly away.

There was one mammoth old lady whom I should have liked to spank for her habit of breaking into my garden and systematically eating ten square feet of my sweet potatoes. We set up our cameras, one night, with wires and flashlights, and just as we were getting into bed we heard the boom of flashlight powder.

"Good," I said, as I heard her crashing into our stockade paling. "Perhaps this will teach her a lesson."

The photographs turned out sharp and clear, and Martin was delighted. He liked sweet potatoes, but he liked photography even better and hoped she would come back. She did, repeatedly, in spite of booming flashlights, and one night, to prove how completely unafraid she was, she proceeded to strip the thatching from one of our huts. A little tardily, I decided that the best way to please the old lady, as well as to stop the destructions, would be to plant a bed of sweet potatoes for her outside our stockade.

Martin and I have heard "big-game hunters" boast of killing elephants, and there's no doubt but that to bring the animals down requires fine marksmanship or luck—or both. The need for either skill or luck is that the only vulnerable places in the creature's noble head—other than the tiny eyes, of course—are a spot no larger than a dollar in the center of the forehead, a similar spot at the temple, and another behind the ear.

Our only boast with regard to killing elephants is that in all our years of association with them we have taken the life of only one. We were having lunch in camp on that occasion, and Boculy, much excited, came running.

"Big elephants," he cried, "all together very quiet."

Within a half an hour our gun-bearers and porters had carried our cameras to the place indicated by Boculy, and there they were, a small but complete herd of six or seven big females, several young ones, and four big bulls. They were in the open, grouped closely together, with the babies playing tag around the legs of the older ones, and the lighting, atmosphere—everything—was right for a perfect picture.

It was I who usually "stirred up" the game to get action, but this time Martin insisted that inasmuch as there was little or no cover to run to in case of a charge, he would take over my job and I would take his place behind the camera.

My husband moved slowly toward the herd. They were unaware of us. I cranked steadily, admiring the magnificent creatures and wishing it were possible to photograph in color the rich shades of their big gray bodies against the tawny yellows of the veld. With too great suddenness, perhaps, the largest bull saw Martin. Startled, he spread his ears, raised his trunk, shifted uneasily, snorted—and charged!

Martin ran. In similar circumstances, my husband and I had often stopped a charge by simply yelling and waving our arms, but this animal, apparently angered at being taken by surprise, refused to be either swerved or halted.

Martin dodged, doubled, and swung about, but the beast took every turn with him and was gaining fast. True to our pact, I kept on grinding; I kept screaming too, and my gunbearer stood ready at my side with my rifle. Terror then was added to terror as the rest of the herd tore after their leader. One part of my brain told me that this would be a magnificent picture; the other told me that unless I brought the lead elephant down, Martin would be trampled. I snatched my gun and fired. I have no recollection whatever of even stopping to take aim—and the big animal faltered and fell not fifteen feet away from where we stood. The rest of the herd, startled at seeing their leader pitch to the ground, swerved and lumbered off.

Released from the tension and excitement, I started involuntarily to run and fell into a pig-hole. Martin came and fished me out—covered with mud!

Chapter 23 _____

"Martin! Martin!" I shouted one bright morning, and ran across the garden to the laboratory building. The darkroom door was closed and the red warning light was on, but completely heedless of consequences I dashed in, even leaving the door open.

"Hey, what's the idea?" my husband yelled. "Do you want to spoil all this negative? You know better than that!"

I hurried back and closed the door. "We've got to go to Isiolo right away," I said, "and we've got to dress, too!" I was already on my way again. "And you be sure to put on your best shirt."

Martin caught up with me halfway across the garden.

"What is all this, anyhow?" he demanded.

"The Duke and Duchess of York!" I said.

"What?"

"They want to meet us! They sent a runner! Come on, hurry!"

My husband grinned. "Well, gosh," he said.

This was somewhere along in 1925. At any rate, Blayney had gone on a long-deferred visit to England, and I regretted so much that he wasn't with us.

In the midst of a sketchy but much-needed manicure—in which I did more damage than good—it occurred to me that even a duke and duchess on safari might grow tired of tinned vegetables, so on the spot I went to the window and called to some of our men to go into the garden at once and pick a few of the choicest of everything there. There were tomatoes, lettuce, celery, cucumbers, radishes, green onions and beans, watermelon, cantaloupes, Country Gentleman corn, and even

312

potatoes—and all washed carefully and laid in a box with sweet, clean ferns from the woods, they looked very nice indeed.

I did my hair as best I could in all the excitement, dressed in my nicest white silk shirt and tie and English riding breeches and boots, and set off in my fresh-polished, country-club car, determined to make as respectable a showing as possible in spite of our long absence from civilization. Of course, I took three of my best men with me, together with my boxes of lovely, fresh vegetables. When I left, Martin was supervising the loading of his camera truck, for, naturally, we never stirred without our photographic equipment.

I made splendid time. The road down from Paradise and across the desert was a very decent one by now in all except the rainy season, and in something like five hours I had reached the Guaso Nyiro.

We had forded this river so often that I thought nothing of it. Then I saw a group of people on the opposite shore: a dozen or so native men and, presumably, two white men. Hunters, I concluded, and plunged my car into the river. The river was higher than usual, and halfway across I found the water rising about me. Perhaps I had driven into a hole. At any rate, I sat there in a helpless rage, with the water rising rapidly to my chin.

After what seemed to be a consultation on shore, a native swam out to us with a long, stout rope. This he tied to the axle of my car, and then the people on shore all pulled like mad and hauled us in.

I'm sure I said my thanks with all the earnestness I felt, but I was concerned about my vegetables and was busy making sure they were all right when the tall white gentleman of the group asked if I wasn't Mrs. Martin Johnson. I said I was, and asked him if he thought my car would start, that I had to hurry on to Isiolo.

Then the second white person—a lady, in khaki breeches like myself—said, smiling, "You've had a rather wet crossing, haven't you?"

I said yes and thought what a mess my nice white blouse was and my hair and everything, and told my men to hurry up and do something about starting the car.

"May I present my wife," the tall gentleman began and then,

because he smiled, I recognized him. We laughed and shook hands all around, but I felt very silly that the Duke and Duchess of York should have had to haul me, dripping like a half-drowned puppy, out of the river. Both were still panting a little from the unwonted exertion, and I told myself that I ought to feel terribly embarrassed, but there was something about them that simply made embarrassment impossible.

I still was puzzled, however. "I had expected to find you in Isiolo," I said, "not out here in the wilderness."

The duchess, dear and little and young, with the loveliest blue eyes I ever saw, nodded and said that since they had rather expected us down they had decided to come as far as the lovely Guaso Nyiro to meet me.

"And then, Albert thought," she added, "that he might pick up a bird or two for our dinner."

Suddenly I remembered my box of beautiful vegetables and had my men lift it out of the car. The wetting hadn't hurt the vegetables in the least (I caught myself wishing I looked half as charming and fresh), and proudly I presented them to Africa's distinguished visitors. They seemed delighted and very grateful. Each selected a large, luscious tomato and sat down, their backs propped comfortably against a tree, to enjoy what I personally know to be a feast in the African wilderness.

"The very best tomato I ever tasted," the duke said, which, of course, made me very happy. The duchess thought so too, wanted to know what variety it was, and suggested to her husband that they plant some in their garden the moment they got home.

I sat with my back to a tree opposite them—I think I munched on a stick of celery—and with practically no prompting at all told them about Lake Paradise, our gardens, Martin's work, everything, and their genuine interest made me forget how funny I must have looked with river water still running out of my clothes and boots and making little puddles all around me.

They both had seen several of our pictures in England and felt that Martin was doing a very important work, which made me very proud indeed.

At just about this time, my husband, driving the camera

truck, appeared on the opposite bank. I was so afraid he would plunge into the very hole I had got into that I tried by screeching and waving my arms to convey some sort of warning, but either he couldn't hear me or thought what I wanted to say wasn't especially important, for he drove right down my tire tracks into the river and crossed in apparently the exact same place where I had attempted so disastrously to cross. He kept right on coming, however. Either the hole had filled up or I had a special genius for sinking where there were no holes. He looked me over with the most astonished expression and said—pretty exasperatingly, I thought—"Well, gosh, what happened to you?"

I ignored that part, of course, and introduced him to the duke and duchess.

We all had a lot of fun together. Pat Ayer, their professional hunter and also an old friend of ours whom we had known in Nairobi, joined us, and we went to the Isiolo River and had a feast under the trees on our combined lunches and our vegetables. We went fishing, too. My luck held up pretty well and the little duchess caught more than any of us, but neither Martin nor the duke did very well, although the duke did catch a crab. He was pleased no end, put it in a box, covered it with moss, and took it back to camp saying he was going to keep it as a mascot. I was reminded of my small brother—though I didn't say so—who was always bringing home crawdads, turtles, frogs, and the like for his "menagerie."

The duke found Martin's cameras of special interest, and in the short time we had together my husband explained as much as was possible of motion-picture technique. He also wrote out a list of recommendations with regard to equipment for various uses. More than a year later we received a longhand note from His Royal Highness, telling us that he had purchased several cameras and was struggling to master the Eyemo, and that he was endeavoring to remember all of Martin's cautionings and instructions.

The duke and duchess, with their gift of genuine interest in and sympathy with other people's problems, had us talking by the hour of our work, and especially of our ambition to develop a great film library of Africa's vanishing wildlife. Animal

idiosyncrasies and family habits, especially those of the elephant, filled them with a sort of childish delight, and both regretted genuinely that their stay in Africa this time was too
short to permit a trip with us up to our Paradise. The duke
expressed the hope, too, that we would not neglect to include
the unexcelled grandeur of British East Africa in our pictures.

"Kenya is the gem of the empire," he said. Just as the duke
and duchess loved Kenya, so were they beloved by all the colony.

The duke was an excellent shot and altogether a perfect
sportsman, as I have found most Britishers to be, but he agreed
with us that it was far more satisfying and certainly much more
dangerous to hunt with the camera.

Frequently of late I find myself recalling one little incident
of our meeting. We were sitting out under the trees in Isiolo.

"Albert," the young duchess said, "I hear something singing."

"What is it?" her husband asked.

"Probably a mosquito," she replied.

"And what is it singing?" he asked.

" 'God Save the King,' " she laughed.

At that time, she little knew that one day her husband as
King would carry the burden and sorrow of war.

Chapter 24_____

Soon after our return to Lake Paradise, a runner came bringing a telegram from George Eastman, informing us that he, Mr. Daniel Pomeroy, and Dr. Audley Stewart were arriving in Nairobi for their long-promised visit to us. There was also a message telling us that Carl Akeley with his party of taxidermists and artists was already in Nairobi. George Eastman's coming was something to which we had looked forward for so long that we were on our toes instantly to be off and meet him.

The Guaso river, scene of my embarrassing immersion in the presence of the duke and duchess of York, decided to assert itself just about as we reached it; it was at flood stage and impossible to ford. Thinking perhaps it would subside, we camped on the bank for three days, but the high water showed no signs of abatement. On the fourth day a Boer convoy rider, carrying supplies to some distant military post, appeared with ten wagons and nearly two hundred Abyssinian donkeys.

We knew that if we were to reach Nairobi in time to meet the Eastman party we would have to move on, so Martin arranged with the Boer to pull our machines across the river by mules and a cable. It was a terrific undertaking. The stream was so swift that it was all we could do to keep our cars from being overturned and losing our supplies and equipment. As it was, however, only one machine was badly damaged.

In spite of our delay, we arrived in Nairobi a day ahead of the special train bringing Mr. Eastman and his party from Mombasa, so we got in touch with Carl Akeley immediately

317

and had an exciting reunion. He had taken a big stone house at the edge of town as a camp base, and we were overjoyed to know that he planned to remain in British East Africa for some time.

I haven't talked much of Kalowatt, our gray gibbon ape, but she had traveled all over the world with us and was so much a part of our lives that I suppose we sometimes took her for granted.

We had put up at the Norfolk Hotel, as was usual with us on our short visits to Nairobi. Martin had gone down to the lobby for a cigar, and I was busy unpacking. It was a hot night, the window was wide open, and I caught a glimpse of Kalowatt just as she leaped out onto the roof. I could understand that she would want to stretch a little after being cramped up in the room all day, and I wasn't particularly alarmed, but she was in a mischievous mood and this time refused to come back when I called her.

The slope of the roof was such that I couldn't go out after her, so I ran down into the lobby and called to Martin, and together we rushed into the street to see if we couldn't coax her down. She chattered to us, scrambled across the roof, jumped into the trees over our heads, and then back to the roof again and beyond our vision. I rushed back upstairs, thinking perhaps she had returned through the window to our room, but arriving there I found it empty. Running to the window, I arrived just in time to see her leap onto two high-voltage wires. There was a puff of smoke and Kalowatt hung limp. I screamed, ran to Martin, who was just coming into the room, and fainted.

Someone called up the power company, the current was shut off, and the little gibbon's body was removed from the wires. We wrapped it in a blanket and laid it in a chair.

"We've got to be sensible about this," I said to my husband.

"Of course we have," he said, but I saw his chin quiver, and I could fight the tears no longer. Sleep was impossible, so we took one of the cars, drove out to the plains, and paced up and down until daylight. We then returned to the hotel, got an officer's rubber-lined tin dress case, and, using it as a casket, buried our pet under a large tree in a forest reserve ten miles from town.

* * *

It took something over a week to get the Eastman-Pomeroy things out of customs and plan the first safari. We had expected to take our guests straight to Lake Paradise, but as luck would have it, the rains were early this year, and we knew that high and turbulent as the river had been on the way down, both it and the roads would be even worse by now, so on Carl Akeley's advice we decided to go to the Kedong Valley, about thirty-five miles south of Nairobi.

Martin and I were glad of a quiet interlude. Too, I felt that Mr. Eastman's physician, Dr. Audley Stewart, was glad to have this African trip open up in easy stages for his distinguished patient and friend. At any rate, it gave us all time to enjoy camp life for itself alone, and also to enjoy one another.

The name of George Eastman is high on the list of America's great industrialists, and, like others of his stature, he was extremely kind, sensitive, resourceful, and versatile. He loved to cook, and it was grand fun to see him take a turn at our clumsy little camp stove. Even Mpishi stood and watched in awe as one after another there emerged delicious muffins, corn bread, beaten biscuits, graham gems, lemon tarts, and huckleberry pie. Mr. Eastman also rigged up an ingenious device for a shower bath in our temporary camp and was proud as Punch over his accomplishment.

Mr. Pomeroy, who was a patron of the American Museum of Natural History and devoted many years and a great deal of money to building the African Hall, was fully as eager as Mr. Eastman, I think, to get to our Lake Paradise. As a matter of fact, we talked of little else as we sat around our campfire at night. The plan with regard to the African Hall was to complete the groups if possible within the next year. To that end, Mr. Pomeroy had offered to obtain the difficult kudu group, while Carl Akeley was making up the water-hole and other groups. William Leigh and his colleague Arthur Jansson, both fine artists, were to paint the habitat groups in their natural settings, and Mr. Eastman had undertaken to complete the buffalo group. I was assigned by Mr. Pomeroy to collect the impala group.

Reports came finally that the rains to the north had let up

a little, so we pushed off with our guests and long caravan of cars and trucks. We found that the Guaso Nyiro had decided to behave itself and that the road, most of the way, was passable.

To our great relief, we found everything at the lake in good order, and once more, as on so many occasions, I was grateful for our small army of loyal, well-trained employees.

We already had built several very nice guest houses, but Mr. Eastman's, we had determined, must be larger, nicer, and better equipped in every way. We had taken extraordinary pains to choose the site—too extraordinary, perhaps, for, in order to provide Mr. Eastman with the full thrill and every opportunity to photograph, we had picked the elephant trail leading to the lake, which doubtless proved not only puzzling to the big animals but at times a bit lively for our guest, as day and night the magnificent creatures lumbered by.

Our good friend Phillip Percival (Blayney's brother), whom Mr. Eastman had chosen as his professional hunter, accompanied us, and this pleased us very much, for we knew that this safari, with its many animal objectives, would be subjected to extraordinary risks to life and limb, and we felt responsible for the safety of our guests.

I doubt that there are many places of interest or scenic beauty in the world that both Mr. Eastman and Mr. Pomeroy hadn't visited, but our Lake Paradise held them when first they saw it, exactly as it did us, in a breathless, silent spell.

Reveling in my duties as hostess, I settled down in earnest to helping our native servants adjust themselves to the routine necessary for the comfort of our expanding community. I made out menus; we churned butter, cooked, and baked; and altogether our little village on the lake fairly buzzed with pleasant activity. Our guests were delighted with my fresh garden fare, which they all swore was the finest they had ever tasted, and, of course, my eleven humpbacked milk cows kept everybody well supplied with fresh milk, cream, cottage cheese, and buttermilk, to Mr. Eastman's special delight.

Every time I think of our second dinner after our guests arrived, a little chill creeps up my spine. Our dining-room windows overlooked the lake, it was a perfect evening, there were the lovely smells of night-blooming flowers and the curious blend of silence and sound of the wilderness, and we were all completely happy. I chanced to notice that Mr. Eastman's water glass was empty and signaled for one of our servants to fill it, when I saw a cobra crawling straight for Mr. Eastman's foot. Instead, then, of signaling for water, I signaled the house boy to do something about the snake, which he did promptly, and quietly, with a heavy club.

"A fine hostess you are," laughed George Eastman. "Snakes for dinner." That this was the first time a cobra had intruded into the house nobody would, of course, believe.

We organized our hunting parties these days always with a view to completing the African groups for the museum. Martin was firm about one thing, however, and I could see everybody loved him for it. He would permit no animals to be shot, no matter how fine as specimens they might be, anywhere near the lake itself.

"They all know they're safe here and that they can trust us," he said, a little defensively, the first time he laid down the rule, "and I wouldn't betray their confidence for anything."

On our fourth day out to one of the blinds, I had a fright which I didn't soon get over. Mr. Eastman was very much interested in the new, 16mm cinecamera which he had recently developed and carried everywhere with him. Rounding a clump of thornbushes, we came on an old rhino. He was grazing with that smug air of disdain for the rest of the world which these peculiar animals have, when suddenly he became aware of us. We had had no way of knowing what Mr. Eastman would do under the circumstances and were completely unprepared when he started toward the animal, taking pictures with his little camera as he went. As a matter of fact, he walked right up to within twenty yards of the ugly beast. We, meantime, stood completely frozen.

Suddenly the big beast decided to resent Mr. Eastman, snorted, lowered his head, and charged.

Never have I seen a greater exhibition of coolness than Mr. Eastman now displayed. Instead of turning and running, which anyone else would have done, he stood quietly, still facing the animal, and then when, snorting and ferocious, it was within

perhaps fifteen feet of him, he simply sidestepped it, like a to-
reador, and actually touched its side as it passed. All of which
Martin caught with his own camera.

This, of course, was not the end of the incident. The rhino,
growing momentarily more enraged, whirled to make a second
charge, when Phillip Percival's gun brought him down.

"Come along, Osa," Mr. Eastman said two or three morn-
ings later. "Suppose you drive me around today and be my little
big-game hunter."

I was delighted and proud as could be, of course, and decided I was going to make this a big day. I told myself that I'd
find some specimen for him, that I'd do something the professional game hunters thought I, being a woman, couldn't do.

We wound up with one warthog!

Mr. Eastman pretended great delight and proposed that we
go home and celebrate by baking a couple of lemon pies. If this
amazing man was intemperate about anything—he almost never
drank—it was about lemon pie. He never ate less than two large
pieces, and poor Martin, who actually disliked lemon pie, followed suit, proving to me that he could, if necessary, be a perfect host.

I've never known a man to have the downright love of a
kitchen that Mr. Eastman had, and whenever I was there, giving attention to some special dish, he was usually right at my
elbow, giving professional pointers and checking my methods
and recipes.

All these years since then I have cherished the memory of
those hours. He treated me exactly as though I were a young
and slightly unpredictable daughter and never could seem to
get over what he called my "pink-silk-dress-little-girlness," as
contrasted with my ruggedness on safari. My husband always
laughed when this came up, and said he had married me young
and trained me that way. And so he had!

The friendship and understanding that grew up between
those two always made me very happy. They were always
"George" and "Martin," but somehow I stuck to the formality
of "Mr. Eastman." On the one occasion when I did vary this
salutation, I was so ashamed I didn't know what to do.

For no reason at all, I was feeling quite hilarious as I stood over the pastry board in the kitchen putting the finishing touches to the bitter-plum pie.

"Hey," said Mr. Eastman, striding in, "that's no way to pinch that piecrust!"

"What say, Pop?" said my tongue before I could check it.

Mr. Eastman was just as astonished as I was. "Wha-a-at did you say?" he asked.

"Oh—why, I said 'Old Top.' You know, that familiar English expression."

He knew perfectly well what I had said, but his eyes twinkled, and from then on—just as a reminder, I suppose—he often addressed me as "Old Top."

Slowly but with gratifying results, the specimens for the museum groups were obtained. Martin, as always, worked steadily away at his film record. At length we decided to go down to Nairobi and join Carl Akeley on a safari in lion country, the Serengeti plains of Tanganyika.

Much as we loved Lake Paradise, we were forced to face the fact that sooner or later we would have to leave it. We had built up as complete a record as seemed possible of the animals that made it, and the surrounding country, their sanctuary. As for our elephant record, both Mr. Eastman and Mr. Pomeroy said they didn't see how it was possible to hope for greater perfection either of detail or fact.

The lion, we knew, would be our next study, and this safari with Carl would be valuable as a preliminary step.

Making an impressive array, with the Eastman, Pomeroy, and Akeley parties, Messrs. Leigh, Rockwell, Raddatz, and Jansson, and all our own following and equipment, we set out toward a section southeast of Nairobi in Tanganyika Territory. A desolate waste in the foothills at the edge of the great plains, it is a rough, practically waterless section and quite different from the northern country. While not far from civilization, these foothills are isolated by natural barriers and, at the time of our first visit at least, were considered among the best game areas in the world.

Martin and I and the Eastman party selected a campsite sheltered by a grotesque rock formation, while Carl Akeley and his hardworking little group set up tents nearby.

While we were getting our camp settled, Phil Percival and Martin reconnoitered for traces of lions and returned on the run to report a big-game migration only a few miles distant.

The next morning we were out early, and it was not very long before we witnessed one of the most amazing sights of our travels. Stretched far and wide as far as the eye could see were animals. It was breathtaking. There were tens of thousands of wildebeeste. Those who have seen but one or two isolated animals such as ostrich, zebra, or giraffe in zoos or circuses can have no conception of what it would mean to see miles and miles of unfamiliar animals. There were countless wildebeeste, Thompson's gazelle, Grant's gazelle, warthog, topi, zebra, kongoni, giraffe, hyena, ostrich, and jackal. High overhead, vultures floated in wide circles on motionless wings.

We all took pictures like mad, and it wasn't until we returned to camp that night, tired and quite beside ourselves with excitement, that we realized we hadn't seen a single lion. This was going to be something to tease Carl Akeley about, we said, and we remembered Father Johnson and his wistful longing to see "just one lion."

We had just finished dinner that evening, however, when Carl Akeley rushed into our camp.

"I've found them," he announced excitedly.

At dawn the next morning we were on our way with Carl in the lead. "I don't believe this pride has ever been disturbed," he said.

I could see that Martin was dubious; one only spoke of animals "not being disturbed" up at Lake Paradise.

We trudged for hours up the dry, rocky plains, sweating and miserable. The blazing tropical sun produced heat waves that fairly frizzled us, while fine dust rose to torture our nostrils. I could see that Mr. Eastman's physician was quite worried, but whether or not our good friend suffered particularly, he made no sign. I think his sole comment was something to the effect that the temperature was just about right for the baking of a lemon pie.

We followed Carl into a shallow depression between two hills. Here he stopped and motioned us to be silent, and a lion crossed our path not ten yards away. If it was aware of us, it didn't even bother to look around. And then, to our astonishment, eleven full-grown lions emerged.

We hadn't the remotest idea what to expect. Eleven great lions not ten yards away. All I could do was hope they weren't hungry. Martin's eyes fairly popped, and Mr. Eastman went to work at once with his 16mm cine. This reminded my husband that he also had a camera with him, and as quietly and speedily as might be, he set it up. To our amazement, the tawny beasts still paid little attention, though the click of the camera seemed to tickle their ears a little and they twitched them slightly. It was I, of course, who had to grow noisily excited. Up to now they had merely turned their heads toward us and blinked lazily; several had yawned, but at sound of my voice they faced us sharply, their muscles bulging under their shining coats. Several switched their tails and growled, and while I don't know about the others of our party, I do know that I was goose bumps from head to foot.

The lions, however, after a moment or two of consideration, seemed to conclude either that we were not good food or that we just didn't matter one way or another, so, rolling over, they stuck their feet in the air and went fast asleep.

We were all so happy we could scarcely contain ourselves, and exchanged congratulatory grins.

My husband ground hundreds of feet of film of the lovely big cats, Mr. Eastman's camera buzzed, and finally we all decided to leave, when a twelfth lion, bigger than any of the rest, meandered into the scene, eyed his sleeping companions whimsically for a few moments, then apparently decided to tease them a little. He mauled and mouthed them, every last one, until he had them all awake. The donga resounded with their growls and snarls of irritation and then, as suddenly as he had started his little game, the big fellow thought he too would like a nap, and presently twelve kingly beasts lay, feet in the air, snoring blissfully.

We tiptoed away, and selecting a shady spot under a mimosa, we ate our lunch and for two hours talked lion. I've since been so glad to have that memory of Carl; it was one of his happiest moments, I think, to be able to prove a tried and fond theory of his, that the lion will not molest man unless he is first attacked.

We were to have made another visit to the lion valley early the next day, but when we called for Carl we found him desperately ill.

He was smiling when we went into his tent, but his face looked very flushed against the white pillow, and Mr. Eastman's physician took charge immediately.

"Go ahead, Martin," Carl said to my husband. "Go ahead with your work. Get all the data and the pictures you can—through them, better than any other way, the world will come to know about animals—about lions. Sportsmen—so-called—too: I want them to know how unsportsmanlike it is to slaughter animals simply for the sake of slaughter."

He was quiet for a minute then smiled again. "An even dozen, like so many tabby cats, fast asleep on their backs, and we only ten yards away."

There was a sort of shadow over all of us after that. We didn't know how desperately ill Carl Akeley was, but somehow we were afraid. Shortly afterward, Mr. Eastman and Mr. Pomeroy left for home. I remember Mr. Eastman saying, as he was stepping on the train, "Back to the world of fraud and front." He sighed a little. "At any rate," he said, "wherever I happen to be, it's going to be nice to think of you two—your fine work together—your fine lives together. Good-bye."

Chapter 25

Carl Akeley was dead.

We had closed our Lake Paradise home and were on our way to Nairobi when the sad news reached us. Apparently recovered from the illness which had struck him down when we were together in Tanganyika, he had gone up to Mount Mikeno, in the Belgian Congo, and there, weakened as he was, had contracted pneumonia, which had ended his fine and useful life.

Martin's plan now was to make the lion his major study, and to this end he decided that Nairobi, which was a comparatively short distance from lion country, should be our headquarters. We found a lovely place just four miles out of the city, which gave us a view of snow-covered Kilimanjaro to the south and the familiar Mount Kenya to the north. The house, built of gray stone, stood well back in its several-acre plot, and the grounds, beautifully landscaped, were delightful.

The main house had eight rooms and was equipped with every modern convenience, including tiled baths, central heating, and electric refrigeration. A fine big kitchen with plenty of cupboard and drawer space assured a smooth-running, efficient household. Martin added a laboratory, of course, building it of gray stone to match the house.

We remained in Nairobi only long enough to put things in order and then left for the Chogoria Scottish Mission near Meru. For several years, Martin and I had promised ourselves that one day we should climb to the top of Mount Kenya and pho-

tograph the snow and ice as a rich and interesting contrast to
the tropical life below. We took thirty porters with us, together
with our headmen and gun-bearers, while our faithful Willys-
Knight trucks and a new "Six" carried our supplies. John Wilshusen, of whom I shall tell later, was in charge of the cars.

January 16 saw us at the Chogoria Mission on the slopes of
the mountain, and there, with the help of Dr. Irwine and his
wife, we signed on fifty extra Meru porters. On the advice of
these two fine people we sent John to Meru for blankets—nearly
two hundred, I think—and I've an idea that up to the time this
tactful suggestion was made to us, we had forgotten just how
cold ice and snow and high altitude could be.

The early part of our climb took us through forests of fairy-
like beauty, but up grades so steep that the porters were obliged
to rest on an average of every thirty minutes. These forests
were left behind us the next day, and we came to a belt of
bamboo where nothing else whatever grew—only bamboo, fifty
feet tall and so thick that almost no daylight could penetrate.
One of the many curious things about this bamboo forest was
the fact that it began suddenly and ended just as suddenly,
with perfectly clean-cut edges.

Emerging from the bamboo, we found ourselves in some of
the most beautiful country I have ever seen—great rolling
mountain plains with groves of scrub trees, all fantastically hung
with Spanish moss and with Mount Kenya towering above it in
all its rugged and almost forbidding beauty. Late in the afternoon of the third day of our climb, we crossed the timberline
and began to know what cold really was. Even inside our tents
and with blankets piled on us five and six deep, we were cold.
Sleep was impossible, and all night long we heard the men
coughing and stirring about. In the morning I saw that Martin's face was flushed and found he had a temperature of a
hundred and two, while five of the porters, it later developed,
had temperatures of a hundred and three. Martin was really
miserable; his legs and back ached, and I tried to persuade him
to abandon the plan of going on. I have an idea, although he
didn't say so, that the young duke's suggestion that we try to
capture some of the harsher but grander beauty of Kenya in
our camera was what really kept him to his stubborn purpose.

He, as well as the porters, seemed better the following day, so once more we proceeded to climb.

From this point on, the grade was so steep that we were obliged to lighten the men's loads, and the altitude was such that we found ourselves short of breath. Martin grew steadily better, however, and decided to investigate a nearby ridge for photographic possibilities. This took us on an exhausting climb of some two thousand feet—a distance not at all apparent when we started out—and by the time we returned to camp it was dark, and we were so chilled we went to bed without dinner.

When we awakened, two very sick people, in the middle of the night, I acknowledged drearily to myself that we had no one in the world but ourselves to blame. Martin now had a fever of a hundred and four, and mine was a hundred and two. I had the men bring hot whiskey and hot-water bottles, but with little effect, apparently, for by morning we were both much worse. My temperature continued to rise, I could scarcely breathe, and my husband, thoroughly frightened, sent two porters down the mountain for kerosene to stock our stoves—he was determined not to give up. John Wilshusen began now to take things in hand. He gathered together every porter he could find and, arming them with pangas, started back up the mountain in the big Willys-Knight.

That John was built of the stuff of which heroes are made was proved conclusively in the next few days. Under his direction the men chopped through dense growth, dug into the mountain, and at times almost carried the car up steep grades, and on the second day after leaving Chogoria Mission he pulled into camp, only heaven knows how, with the car. Covered with cuts and scratches, grease and oil, the porters were completely exhausted. The top of the car was nearly gone, the side-boxes had been ripped off, there was almost nothing left of the fenders, but the engine was in perfect condition.

All of this was told to me later by Martin, for by now I knew of nothing that was going on; my breathing was labored, and my husband said it was perfectly obvious that I had pneumonia.

John worked on the car all that night, and also on stretchers which he rigged up for Martin and me, and bundling us in blankets early the next morning, he had us carried out to the car. Then we started our wild ride down the mountain. A number of men had been sent on ahead to the very bad places so as to be fresh and steady for the risky job of lowering the car down precipitous drops. Ten men clung to the side as we rode, in readiness to jump off and hold the car by sheer weight of numbers if it seemed in danger of getting out of control or tipping over. Eight times during the trip it was necessary to lift us out of the car and carry us past those places where it seemed impossible that the machine could remain upright.

When we arrived at the mission, it was dusk. Dr. Irwine said that Martin had influenza and bronchitis, with a temperature of a hundred and four, while I had double pneumonia.

A little after midnight, although he had only an hour of rest, John went to Meru, where he sent a telegram to Nairobi asking for another doctor. He waited until a reply told him that a Dr. Anderson was coming, then dashed back up the mountain to the mission. Dr. Irwine decided that a nurse was necessary at once, and without a moment's hesitation John started on the 165-mile trip to Nairobi. He made it in five hours and twenty minutes, found a nurse, and was back with her in five hours. When told by Dr. Anderson that certain medicines and another nurse were required, he started on the second trip to Nairobi within a half hour after completing his first. At Nairobi, there was no nurse available, and he was forced to drive sixty miles into the country to get one.

On John's arrival this time, Dr. Anderson said that ice might help to save my life, so loyal John made still another trip to Nairobi for an ice machine. It was a hand-operated affair and John himself ran it, days on end, at full capacity, turning out ice every three minutes. Martin told me later that John had scarcely slept in eight days. There isn't a doubt in the world that we owed our lives at that time to tireless, courageous John Wilshusen.

We remained six weeks at the Chogoria Mission, convalescing, and it seems that all I remember of that fantastic experience, when my fever was high and my life in the balance, was the strange beauty of a seemingly far-off bell and the soft chant of missionaries and natives.

* * *

"Safari fever." I heard Martin chatting in low tones with Dr. Irwine outside my doorway. "I think safari fever is the thing that ails her now, and if you could give me a good nurse and would let me take her out on the plains where she could see and hear the animals and get the sun and feel some activity, I just know she would soon be all right."

In a matter of days we were installed at Embayo, an old familiar haunt of ours not far from Meru, where great herds of buffalo and elephant, and rhino in numbers were then to be found, Martin was happily busy at his cameras, and Sister Withall, my new boss, was literally teaching me to walk again.

The treatment worked perfectly, especially the sun and the activity, and in a few weeks I was able to walk and hold a gun. On the day I took up my old position beside Martin at the camera, Sister Withall sat behind us on the hood of a motorcar. A rhino spied us and began sneaking up to us. I covered him, and when he charged I had to drop him. At this, I heard a piercing scream and turned to find that Sister Withall had fallen off the truck and was completely unnerved.

"I can't believe you're here," she said in a frightened peep. "I was sure you were both of you finished."

We had to leave for the States to supervise the editing of the pictures we had taken in and around Lake Paradise. This was a two-fold task, inasmuch as the camera studies which Martin had taken to meet the scientific needs of the Museum of Natural History required one type of assembling, while those to be released through the regular motion-picture channels to defray the expenses of the safari and return money to the investors were of another type.

We arrived in New York on May 16, 1927. There was a glorious reunion with all our dear ones from Kansas, and other reunions with our friends. There was also steady, grinding work. Somewhat to our astonishment, I think, our Lake Paradise pictures gave promise of being a tremendous success, and offers for personal-appearance contracts of upwards of a hundred thousand dollars poured in. Naturally, we considered these. The sort of work we had chosen to do literally gobbled money, but just at this time—some nine months after our arrival—Mr.

Eastman came down to New York from Rochester and urged
us to go with him, at once, back to Africa. The decision
was not difficult to make. We said promptly that of course we
would go.

Our business associates thought we were crazy to turn down
such wonderful opportunities to fatten our bank account, and
said so without mincing words. I shall never forget Martin's
reply.

"At best," he said, "life is much too short for all the work
we've set out to do." I remember him smiling then. "And anyhow," he added, "I guess money isn't very important to Osa
and me."

This resulted in a chorus of protests: Money was important
to everybody. What could we hope to accomplish without money?

Martin grew very thoughtful. "The point is," he said, "that
when you live in Africa, down close to the earth and the animals, you acquire a different set of values from when you live
in the city. Living anywhere away from the city would do the
same thing, of course. And what makes it great," he smiled,
"is that Osa feels exactly the same as I do about it."

Across the world, the Johnsons filmed many diverse peoples, including the
Ituri Forest pygmies.

Pygmy drummer relays a message on the "bush telegraph."

A village deep in the mists and towering trees of the Ituri Forest

Samburu at waterhole in Northern Kenya, where water sources are few

Turkana seek shade under the tail of *Osa's Ark*.

The *Spirit of Africa* comes in for a landing at Ngornit, one of several fields that "flying safari" members constructed in remote regions.

Vern Carstens, the Johnsons, and *Osa's Ark,* larger of the two amphibious Sikorskys

Africa's two highest mountain peaks filmed from the air

Mount Kenya

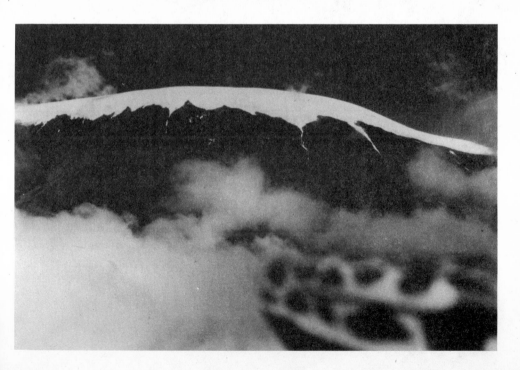

Mount Kilimanjaro

Aerial shot showing Elmolo village on the shore of Lake Rudolf

From Kenya's original Treetops, Osa searches for wildlife. Destroyed by Mau Mau twenty years later, it has since been replaced by a luxury hotel ideal for game viewing.

Checking her gun was an essential daily chore.

Four cheetah cubs make a lapful.

Solid comfort after a hard day's work at the office or a breathless simmering blind

Chapter 26 _____

We spent several delightful holiday weeks with Mr. Eastman and his physician, Dr. Stewart, in London, Paris, and southern France; Christmas Day was spent on the Riviera. During these leisurely weeks we grew to know Mr. Eastman as we had never known him before. Among his many constructive charities was one that included setting up dental clinics in different parts of the world. It was on this trip that he and Lord Riddell—at a cost of many millions—established the London Clinic, and on which, also, his gift of a clinic to the Italian government was made. His dream was that one day every child, no matter how underprivileged, should be provided with dental care.

Arrived at Cairo, via Port Said, Mr. Eastman chartered the luxurious Nile steamer *Dal,* which, with its twenty-seven state-rooms, was commodious indeed for our small party of four. Our host made certain that the chef, stewards, room-boys, and crew measured up to his exacting standards. He also installed an electric refrigerator, many cases of his favorite mineral water, and a variety of good foods, including a large supply of live chickens, goats, and sheep.

Up past Luxor and the Valley of the Kings, through the historic land of the Ptolemies and pharaohs we sailed, passing Aswan and the second cataract. On up the White Nile, we stopped at Khartoum, and there found Merian Cooper and his Hollywood crew taking scenes for the picture entitled *The Four Feathers*. We lingered for a few days in a sort of celebration at meeting in this out-of-the-way part of the world. Merian, of whom Martin and I were very fond, made a farewell reel of us, and then we pushed off into the Upper Nile. Here we passed through the land of the wild Berbers and the Anglo-Egyptian Sudan.

Breaking our leisurely trip frequently, we went on shore trips and secured some extremely interesting pictures of gazelle, elephant, and water life—crocodiles and hippopotami.

A curious phenomenon early one morning on the Upper Nile was the sight of thousands of huge Nile perch—some upwards of three hundred pounds—floating on the surface, most of them with their silver-white bellies glistening in the sun. The engineer of our boat gave it as his opinion that an underwater earthquake was responsible. At any rate, the native crew had a fine time gaffing those that were still alive and preparing for a fish feast, always a treat to them.

According to arrangement, Phil Percival met us at Rejaf with a small fleet of motor cars, and we proceeded southwest into the Belgian Congo, then east into Uganda to Rhino Camp, on the Albert Nile. Leaving the cars and taking on fifty porters and two skinners, we began a foot safari. Dr. Stewart saw to it that a sedan chair was contrived for Mr. Eastman, whose advanced age—he was nearing seventy-five at this time—made necessary some precautions to conserve his energies.

Mr. Eastman succeeded on one occasion in securing a fine elephant specimen, and on another a white rhino. Two examples were still needed to complete these groups at the Museum of Natural History.

Several weeks later, we returned with Mr. Eastman to Rejaf, in the Sudan. There he boarded the *Dal*, saying good-bye. Somehow I felt that we would never see him again, and I think he felt something of the same thing. "I think," he said in earnest, almost solemn reflection, "that this has been the happiest period of my entire life." Then, as we shook hands in a last farewell, he said, "I know you will take good care of each other. That, at least, I can always know."

Tears filled his kindly eyes. "I'm going to ship you back my electric refrigerator, Osa," he said, and disappeared into his cabin.

* * *

After leaving Rejaf, Martin and I returned to northwestern Uganda, where Martin was able to make fine pictures of the rare white rhinoceros. But what especially delighted both of us were the pictures he made of the Wambutti pygmies in the Congo, particularly those of the chief eating. We had cooked rice, of course, for our guests. The chief tipped a cup each of salt and sugar into the pot, then sat down and waited. Quickly a number of women moved into the scene, rolled the hot rice quickly into pellets which they placed on flat leaves, then took their places at either side of the chief's chair. There was a ceremonial pause in which each woman seemed to count up to ten, and in which the chief slowly opened his mouth. Then began a most exacting job. The little balls of rice were stuffed rapidly into the chief's mouth, the women working from both sides. Still other women, who probably considered themselves less privileged, stood ready to wipe away the surplus food when it stuck to their potentate's chin.

Although the grizzled gentleman swallowed as speedily as possible, his gullet became clogged every now and then, and it seemed certain to us, as we saw his eyes bulge, that he must choke to death. He merely motioned for a gourd of water, however, which still another woman had ready, washed his throat clear, and blandly opened his mouth for more pellets. This went on and on. This was a custom, we were told, that made the position of "chief" highly desirable.

While packing his cameras, Martin said, "We're coming back here sometime and make a complete record of these little people."

We then returned to western Uganda, crossed Lake Albert, and, hiring a small boat, sailed up the Victoria Nile to photograph hippos, crocodiles, and elephants. And for the first time we saw the magnificent Murchison Falls.

Working our way slowly east, we crossed Uganda and eventually reached Nairobi and our home in Muthaiga.

Lions! For a year we lived with them in what Carl Akeley had called the "lions' den," that area some five hundred miles square in Tanganyika Territory to which Carl had taken us shortly before the illness which was to end his life. We worked with lions; we ate and slept with their roars all around us. At times, and with good reason, we feared the great tawny cats, but in the end we grew, as Carl said we would, to respect and love them.

Our equipment consisted roughly of five tents, two water stills, ten motion-picture cameras, eleven still cameras, one hundred thousand feet of film, medical stores, foodstuffs, a typewriter, and even a phonograph—and guns, of course. In all, there was something like four tons of stuff, and our big touring car, together with four trucks, carried the lot.

I drove the touring car with four porters hanging on wherever they could. Martin took the wheel of one of the trucks, which carried two tons of supplies and six porters, while the next truck, equally overloaded, was driven by Urg, our newly acquired Swahili mechanic.

As we rolled into this vast and almost immeasurable domain that is the lion's "happy hunting ground," I thought of Carl Akeley's resentment against the caging of these beautiful beasts. Here, the lion has an abundance for every need, from food and air to freedom, and restraint is probably the one thing he cannot comprehend. Yet for thousands of years he has been hunted and captured and caged to satisfy the vanity of man. I am deeply in sympathy with those enlightened zoos, such as that at San Diego, dedicated to education rather than to entertainment, which are willing to appropriate sufficient ground to give their lion prizes some of the liberty and color of their native home.

Although the lion has counted more than any other factor in man's dread of Africa, man, curiously enough, is the only enemy the lion really fears. Hunters from the days of the ancient Ptolemies and earlier have ranged the plains of Africa with all manner of weapons which were too much even for the lion's magnificent strength, speed, and cunning. It has always surprised me that lions did not somehow remember, and that they would trust us at all.

Government has now reduced the menace of the hunter as much as possible by high license fees and other protections, but there is still considerable wanton killing. Martin and I have always done all we could to encourage the setting aside of game preserves, and it was one of his special hopes to see the Serengeti Plain made into a protected area where lions could be hunted only with the camera. This has now finally become a fact under the direction of game warden Monty Moore and his splendid and heroic wife.

For the most part, the lion is a thoroughly agreeable personage. He lives a most leisurely existence, loafs and sleeps a great deal, has just as playful moods as a house cat, and is just as decided a personality. He minds his own business, is very fond of his family, and takes his duties as a family protector very seriously. As a youngster, he usually attaches himself to a pride, or "gang," of young males and they roam about together, sometimes for years, having a hilarious time, sharing their food and their fun, until he finally settles down to domestic bliss and the raising of a family. When he becomes a grandfather and too old to keep up with his family and friends, he is ejected from the pride and left to roam about alone, and it is then that he often becomes a "rogue," probably a neurasthenic condition not unfamiliar to humans.

Naturally, being of the cat family, the lion is carnivorous. He kills to eat. Except in self-defense, he seldom disturbs a living thing, although I have known him to attack without provocation and have always been careful not to startle or annoy him. When attacked or wounded, the lion never retreats but fights as long as there is a spark of life in his magnificent body.

Weighing anywhere between two hundred and five hundred pounds, this massive cat has great strength combined with feline suppleness. On short spurts he can overtake almost any other animal on the plains, and a single blow of his huge clawed foot, or crunch of his jaw, is almost certain death. Many of my friends, expert shots and fine sportsmen and fully aware of the ways of the lion, have been killed or disabled or severely mauled in a moment of recklessness.

Sir Alfred Pease, the well-known game hunter, made it a rule when hunting lions to keep at least two hundred yards between himself and the beast. His friend George Grey, brother of Sir Edward Grey, hunting with him one day, failed to observe this rule and galloped to within ninety yards of a lion that had been slightly wounded. The animal charged. Sir Alfred tried heading it off and pumped several shots into it at close range, but the maddened creature, though terribly wounded, leaped upon Mr. Grey, lacerating him so cruely that he died shortly afterwards.

Theodore Roosevelt wrote: "The hunter should never go near a lion until it is dead; and even when it is on the point of death he should not stand near nor approach his head from the front."

Martin had the complacent look of a man who has just finished a large and thoroughly satisfactory meal. What he had just finished, however, was not a meal but an afternoon's photography in the midst of fourteen lions. The big beasts had been as indifferent to us as we, in turn, might have been to a couple of field mice, and while this attitude on their part gave us a comfortable enough feeling, I can't say it was exactly flattering.

My husband had exposed several magazines of film and was about to put still another into the camera.

"Well, my gracious," I said, "haven't you got about enough?"

Martin grinned at me a little sheepishly. "Oh, I guess so," he said, "but, golly, aren't they wonderful?"

He looked fondly off at the sleek, lovely animals. For hours they had boxed and mauled one another. When tired, they had slept, usually on their backs with their feet in the air and snoring mightily. They had been through this routine several times. There were perhaps eight or nine lionesses among them, but very little ill temper or jealously was displayed. In fact, a better-mannered or more amiable group—man or beast—could not be imagined.

"Of course they're wonderful," I replied, "but they've eaten nothing in hours. Suppose they suddenly decide they're hungry?"

I stepped on the starter and began backing away, whereupon one of the husky young males decided to challenge our departure. He bristled, his eyes sharpened with excitement, and he started to follow us, measuring his sinewy, menacing stride exactly to the roll of our car. There was only one safe thing to do, and that was to stop, for a lion, like any other member of the cat family, finds a retreating object almost irresistible. Martin trained his gun on the animal's great head.

Looking up at us in mild surprise that we should have stopped, and a little disappointed, I think, at our taking the fun out of his little game of pursuit, the lion sniffed at our left front tire, then bit it gently. The taste of rubber was new to him, apparently, and he wrinkled his nose, not quite sure that he liked it. Then he tried again. Persuaded this time that it was nothing he cared particularly to eat but that it might be worth playing with, he began mouthing and growling over it in the manner of a puppy with a rubber ball. The other lions moved up as if on cue and stood lazily watching this performance.

My husband looked a little anxious. "A puncture wouldn't be a very healthy thing right now," he said, his voice lowered to a cautious key. The more he thought about this, the less he liked it. "The explosion right in his teeth might make him mad, too," he added.

"How about racing the motor?" I offered.

Martin nodded. "Yes. Try it. It might distract him."

I did so. The lion forgot the tire, as we hoped he would, and, cocking his head, listened attentively. So far, so good, I thought, and pushed a little harder on the accelerator. The racing engine now gave a cloud of noxious fumes, and taking advantage of the astonished sniffs and distaste which all the lions suddenly exhibited, I backed away, jockeyed out of sight around a huge rock, and streaked off across the plain.

In order to obtain a really complete pictorial history of the lion, it became apparent that we must photograph his nocturnal as well as his daylight habits.

Fortunately, Martin had experimented at length and successfully with night camera work and knew all the mechanical requirements. Contrary to his usual procedure, however, of rigging up the flashlights and cameras and letting the mechanical devices do the work, he decided that he would probably have better results with the lion if we stationed ourselves in our car and he operated the camera himself.

The method followed was to set four flash lamps on firmly planted poles about six feet above the ground, then to fasten the cameras securely to solid platforms three feet in front of and below each lamp. These were connected with dry batteries and controlled by a long "firing" wire. The cameras, especially made for this purpose, took pictures automatically at a speed of one three-hundredths of a second when the light from the flash was at its maximum.

After setting up this apparatus, a much less pleasant task confronted us: the shooting of a zebra for bait. The guilty feeling we always had about this would have seemed ridiculous to anyone less concerned than ourselves, but the sight of the happy, rowdy little fellows always reminded Martin of his pony, Socks, and put me in a mood where I wanted to pet and certainly not to shoot them.

First, in this connection, of course, there was the ignominious business of sneaking away from camp. Assuredly, since we wouldn't admit to each other that we were sentimental about zebra, we weren't going to attempt to explain our actions to our porters.

Our routine usually followed the same pattern. Having located a herd and moved within shooting distance of it, we would glance furtively at each other, and then either Martin or I would yawn. I usually managed to get in ahead of my husband on this.

"Ho, hum," I would say. "You haven't done much shooting lately. It's about time you practiced up."

"Oh, as to that," he would reply carelessly, "as long as I'm only the cameraman around here and you're the one holds the gun, I think you should keep in practice."

"Well," I would then say, "I don't feel like shooting today. I think my head aches."

"Oh, all right," my husband would growl, "but if I just wound one of the poor fellows don't blame me."

With this he'd jerk his gun to his shoulder and pretend to take aim.

This was my cue to sigh. "Never mind," I'd say. "Let's pick out an old one or a lame one and get it over with."

Martin's look of relief at this always endeared him to me. Then we would stand for quite a long time, weighing the relative age or lameness of this zebra or that zebra. Finally one would be selected, I would shoot him, and in silence we would go back to camp. Our porters were then sent, of course, to fetch the victim of my gun and place him at a spot exactly

fifteen feet from the cameras. Ouranga always directed this part
of the flashlight operation and it was he, too, who, waiting until
it was quite dark, cut the entrails from the carcass and dragged
them about the site. He always added a mumbled incantation
to this disagreeable business and took credit for the results—if
good. Seated in our car at a discreet distance by this time, with
gun and "firing" wire ready, we sent all the porters, including
the theatrical Ouranga, back to camp.

The wretched hyenas were invariably the first to find our
zebra. Sometimes a well-aimed rock would disperse them, but
when they came in packs and seemed on the point of eating
all the bait, we were usually forced to shoot one or two to show
them we were in earnest.

"If only the lions would eat the darned old hyenas." Martin
grumbled, "everything would be fine."

"Shhh," I whispered. "I think I hear something."

"Oh, there won't be anything doing tonight," my husband
said drowsily. "I wish I were in bed." This said, he promptly
went to sleep.

The sky was overcast. There was no moon, and the darkness was black and thick and cold. I remembered how quietly
lions moved on their padded paws. I also derived what comfort
I could from the fact that we had sat in open cars many times
before, with lions all around us, and that so far we had not
been eaten.

Then I heard a tearing sound, and a chewing and gulping
and crunching and, along with this, a sort of purring growl.

I nudged Martin, but he was too fast asleep for gentle
methods to have effect. I pinched him. He said "ouch"; the
crunching, accompanied only by a deep growl, went steadily on.

"Golly!" my husband said. He turned on his electric torch
and there, sitting right in front of us and wearing one of the
finest manes I have ever seen, was surely the king himself: the
king of all the Tanganyika lions. Lifting his great head slowly,
the big animal looked disdainfully straight into our light. A piece
of zebra flesh, torn and dripping, dangled from his mouth, but
not even this could detract from his majesty.

My husband now put our flashlights and cameras into operation. The lion dropped his piece of meat, bared his teeth and

roared, and then, with an abruptness that left me trembling and my gun still pointed at his head, went back to his feast.

Others of his family joined him. Several of them were his wives, apparently, and the smaller ones might have been his half-grown sons. They were a fine-looking lot and formed a perfect picture.

"Oh, that's great! that's great!" I heard Martin whispering to himself. He pressed the button. Nothing happened. Again he pressed it with all his might, and there was no sign of a flash. Frantically he pulled the wires from the button and touched them together, but still without result.

"Well," he said, "I guess there's nothing else to do."

He was looking straight out to where the lions were feeding.

I knew what he meant, but I couldn't believe him. "What do you mean?" I demanded.

"I've got to get out there and fix it, that's all."

He was out of the car before I could stop him. I caught him by the collar.

"You're crazy," I said, half crying.

"Give me the sawed-off gun," was all he said.

So I drove the lions off the kill by throwing the powerful searchlight of our car in their faces, tooting the auto horn, and yelling, covering Martin, the while, with my gun. The lions retreated about twenty yards, and in a few brief minutes, which seemed like an eternity, my husband found the loose connection and returned to the car.

"Don't you ever do that again!" I said, practically in collapse.

Martin went straight to work, though I saw that he was shaking a little.

The lion king, having eaten his fill, apparently decided now to investigate the flashlights and cameras. He even gave one of the cameras an experimental bite.

"You let that camera alone!" my husband yelled, completely beside himself.

The majestic cat glanced our way indifferently, then began chewing at the base on which the camera was fastened. The whole thing went over.

Martin got out of the car again and began throwing rocks and anything else that came to hand. To add to the complication, one of the younger lions now decided to follow the cue of the older lion and, seizing one of the wires, tugged at it until he had torn it and several other wires from their fastenings.

We sat there throwing rocks, shooting our guns into the air, yelling until we were hoarse, but not until those two lions had pulled down every wire, battery, camera, and pole of our equipment were they satisfied. Then they strolled off, their tails waving proudly, and our night of flashlight photography was definitely at an end.

A few days later we came upon a large pride of young males resting under a cluster of trees, and we stopped to watch. They were extremely curious and began edging up to look us over. They were so playful and frisky that Martin obtained some new and very valuable film. We decided to lunch there and climbed out through the aperture at the top of the truck. Then we sat down to enjoy our sandwiches and to watch.

At the sight of our food, the lions came up close to the car and sat down like a bunch of hungry beggars. I threw them some partridge legs, which they tasted, and then licked their chops as much as to say, "Pretty high-toned food for a wild lion."

For an hour they played about us, within a few feet of the car, bit at the tires and nipped at one another, and had a rowdy time. We even called them by name (not for exact resemblance, of course): Roy Chapman Andrews, the most dapper of them; Lowell Thomas, the one who roared most; George Dryden, the one who bit the tires and seemed most interested in the rubber business; Merian Cooper, the wise and well-mannered one who kept his distance through most of the fracas. And the lions seemed satisfied with the comparisons.

Perhaps it was experiences of this sort that made us a little reckless and that had us thinking of the huge felines in terms of fireside tabbies. At any rate, we were on foot one very hot day—our camera and gun-bearers with us, of course—when we turned a sort of corner past a jagged rock and there, not twenty yards from us, was a sleeping lion.

The big creature was on his feet almost instantly and facing us. He drew his ears back, switched his tail, and snarled— three signs I didn't at all like. My husband proceeded busily, however, to set up his camera.

"I don't like his looks, Martin," I said cautiously. At the same time I signaled for my gun.

"Oh, he's all right," my husband said. "A little cranky, maybe, but just bluffing." He started to crank the camera.

Then, with a low growl, the lion started slowly toward us, his tail lashing from side to side. How at such a moment I could notice, and sharply at that, the ripple of his hard shoulder muscles under his shining yellow coat, I don't know.

"He's going to charge, Martin—I tell you he is!"

"I don't think so," my husband said, biting hard on his cigar.

The lion, crouching tensely now, stared at us in what seemed to be an all-consuming hatred. Then he charged.

Martin's hand continued mechanically to crank the camera.

The animal looked as large as a bull as he leaped toward us, mane flying, fangs bared. I seemed to be watching in a prolonged, timeless sort of daze, and then, without really being aware of what I was doing, I shot. Afterwards I couldn't even recall taking aim.

The lion seemed to hesitate in midair and then fell just thirteen feet from the camera's tripod.

To give an adequate picture of our almost innumerable encounters with lions of the Tanganyika region would require many weeks to tell. There were triumphs and disappointments. We worked long hours under the most discouraging conditions. We saw the leonine prototypes of the entire human race: the clown, the outcast, the misfit, the arrogant, the tragic, the noble, the dictator—yes, and even the flirt—and we made photographic records of all of these in their natural habitat.

Sometimes our adventures were exciting; other times they were plain drudgery. Much of the time we were happy and comfortable; some of the time, as on all our safaris, we went through almost unbearable hardships. It was the sum total that mattered to us both, however, and there was an immense satisfaction in being able to present the true picture of this noble animal to the millions of people who had thought of him as a vicious, treacherous, bloodthirsty beast.

In the middle of July we went to Nairobi to meet three Boy Scouts who, through the efforts of George Palmer Putnam, David T. Lyman, and James West, executive head of the Boy Scouts' organization, were given a free trip to Africa.

Since the Boy Scouts of the entire United States had selected these three lads for this fine adventure, our expectations, naturally, were high. When Dick Douglas, Dave Martin, and Douglas Oliver stepped from the train, however, we knew that no mere expectations could do them justice, and the five weeks they spent with us were diverting and extremely pleasant. We took them on safari with us, and they made the acquaintance of the lion, the rhino, and the elephant in their native surroundings. The porters were quite awed by the boys, not because they were white but more particularly because there was no native feat of skill at which the youngsters did not prove more proficient than the native himself.

For example, the Wakambas live by their bows and arrows, but the boys, who knew little or nothing of archery, in a contest with them soon were able to beat all comers regardless of experience and age. These young Scouts also taught the natives curious types of wrestling. When it was time, at the end of the five weeks, for the boys to leave, I think our men were almost as sorry as we were to see them go.

Chapter 27 _____

George Dryden and his son Eastman joined us in Africa in 1929. We had been to the States, had attended to the editing of our latest film and to the business details of its release, and now we were back again, preparing for the safari we had long promised ourselves into the Belgian Congo.

Sound was now a part of motion pictures, and sound apparatus would be part of our equipment when we headed for the land of pygmies and gorillas. Our personnel, in consequence, was increased, and with us from the States had come Richard Maedler, sound cameraman; Louis Tappan, in charge of sound equipment; and DeWitt Sage, an enthusiastic young naturalist and son of Henry Sage, member of the board of trustees of the American Museum of Natural History.

Preparations for a safari the size of this one were always tedious, confining, and tiring, and we hailed with delight the arrival of our dear friend George Dryden. He and his son had seen, in New York, the first rough editing of our film *Simba*, and nothing would do but that they themselves must visit the great Tanganyika "lion's den" and make the acquaintance, so to speak, of some of the magnificent cats that had been our actors in that unrehearsed drama.

This worked in perfectly with our plan to try out some of our new equipment and to familiarize the new members of our party with life on safari, so we assembled our men, and in two weeks we were on our way.

Mr. Dryden's previous adventures had been in Alaska and Canada, and in helping to build industrial and financial structures in the world of business. Africa was new to him, and business cares were left behind. That the unusually heavy rains in the Tanganyika section had turned the roads into so many bogs, that times without number we were all obliged to get out of the cars and dig and push and haul, left Mr. Dryden completely unruffled. As a matter of fact, the worse things were— and we had our days of sweltering heat, and other days when swarms of stinging insects descended upon us—the greater patience he displayed. He was a crack shot and always cool when we were in a dangerous spot, a most considerate sportsman, and we have never had a finer nor more agreeable companion in all our travels.

It was our luck, of course, just because we had bragged about the almost invariable good nature of our lion friends, that we should run into a cranky one at the very outset of our safari. My attention was distracted at the moment by something as completely inconsequential as a button hanging loose on the waistband of my khaki shirt, and it was George Dryden's gun that stopped the catapulting onset of yellow fury.

From then on, naturally, the teasing never stopped. Martin had told everybody who would listen, how "Osa held the gun," and here I had been caught napping. Something like two months later, though, my husband tweaked my snub nose and said I had redeemed myself. It came about up on the Abyssinian border.

The Drydens had extended their African trip to visit this ruggedly beautiful part of the country, and we were standing in a compact group one day watching old Boculy go through his mumbo jumbo over a piece of caked mud.

Just then a gun was thrust into my hands and, whirling, I saw a rhino—strong, sharp horns gleaming in the sun—galloping straight toward us. I shot and, luckily, he swerved before he dropped. His momentum was such that had he held to his course, he would have plowed straight into us.

My husband strutted for at least a week after that, and I was glad to see him so pleased, but, of course, I gave full credit to my gun-bearer.

Shortly after Mr. Dryden and his son left on the Uganda railway for Mombasa, there to sail for England and the States,

Martin and I started on our safari to the Belgian Congo.

Our motor fleet this time consisted of seven Willys-Knights, four of which were trucks built with aluminum sides and tops. Two of these were camera-cars especially designed for taking pictures as we rolled, and one had a microphone as part of its equipment. One of the trucks was fitted out as a complete darkroom and, of course, carried a good portion of our photographic supplies. Another truck was convertible into a sort of living quarters, with two folding beds, a built-in gasoline stove, and as many essentials to comfort as it was possible to carry, for we knew in advance that a hard trip was ahead of us.

We were to travel by rail from Nairobi to Tororo, in Uganda, and Martin had arranged for two coaches and two flatcars to carry us and our equipment. On the morning we piled aboard the little train on its narrow-gauge track, we resembled one of those small one-ring circuses that tour our own Middle West. Our party included four white men and myself, and twenty-one picked natives, including two cooks, personal servants, drivers, gun-bearers, and headmen.

The train lurched so violently on its narrow-gauge track that it seemed certain we should all be smashed to bits, and I never was able to understand how our automobiles and trucks, carefully lashed though they were, remained on the flatcars. After two days of this nerve-racking travel, we pulled into Tororo and thankfully unloaded our cars. I don't know when I've ever been so happy to get my hands on a steering wheel and to feel that, for a time at least, I could control my own destiny.

Four days of driving brought us into the wretched, barren, steaming village of Butiaba, on Lake Albert. The barge we had reserved to carry our equipment across the lake was waiting. But the *Samuel Baker*, the steamship we were to board, had been delayed.

Martin decided this would be a fine opportunity to run up to Murchison Falls for some pictures. We had been at Murchison Falls three years before, but this time we would not only record its roaring, raging sound, but capture on film the noisy, often raucous sounds of the animals in the area.

Returning to Butiaba, we completed arrangements for the shipment of our supplies into the Belgian Congo. No easy task!

Some six weeks before, we had shipped from Nairobi a hundred and fifty cases of gasoline and oil and grease for the cars, together with a hundred cases of foodstuffs, outboard motors, tents, guns, ammunition, and other supplies. This was waiting for us, and when we added to it the ten tons of paraphernalia carried on our seven cars, we found we had a veritable mountain of cargo.

Fastening our heavily loaded barge to the *Samuel Baker*, which was to tow it, and boarding the steamer, we started on the thirty-mile journey across what is said to be one of the roughest bodies of inland water in the world. Again and again the lumbering barge seemed to stand on end, and it appeared certain, as Martin and I watched it from the rear of the boat, that all our precious possessions must tear loose from their moorings and slide to the bottom of Lake Albert. At ten o'clock that night, however, we nosed into the harbor of Kasenye, and the Belgian customs officials did what they could to unknot the red tape which, of necessity, tied up our goods.

Early the next morning we headed our caravan toward the land of the pygmies. Our first goal was Irumu, main station of the eastern division of the Ituri forest. The road was very good, but it was so steep and wound in such tortuous curves that it was all we could do to make it with our heavy loads. It leveled out finally, however, and we rolled into Irumu without even a minor mishap.

After establishing a temporary camp beyond Irumu, Martin and I set out to find a suitable site for our permanent base. Nearby, two roads branched off into a V, the left prong being the Beni road near the Semliki River, and the right prong leading to Mambasa, in the heart of the Ituri forest. We decided on the Beni road and headed into the depths of the forest. After a few days we met Deelia and Salou. Deelia was a sixty-pound, bewhiskered, agile old chap whose height was something like three feet ten inches. His perfectly formed body was covered with hair, and his only garments were a crude bead necklace and a loincloth of bark. The other pygmy was Deelia's son, Salou, a fat, active fellow who stood a full twelve inches taller then his father. Both had wide-spreading nostrils and big, staring eyes. The pygmies spoke Kingwana, and Salou informed us proudly that he was chief of all the pygmies in that district.

Nearby, shifting uneasily from foot to foot but seeming anxious to impress us with a certain importance, stood a big, strange-looking native. His large head was out of all proportion to his thin body, and he wore a straggly goatee which, if anything, added to the general silliness of his appearance. He was dressed in an old, ragged mess jacket and a pair of ancient trousers which probably had once been white. We were puzzled by the fact that Deelia and Salou paused frequently to confer with him, and then we learned to our astonishment that he was none other than Bwana Sura, a headman, for whom a pygmy village had been named. A man with neither standing nor influence among his own people, he had, for some unknown reason, made himself a power among the pygmies.

Neither Deelia nor Salou could make head or tail of why we wanted to pitch camp near their village, but they set to with a will and had a place cleared for us, and soon we were comfortably installed in our roomy tents, with good beds, bathroom, and a large, pleasant, screened veranda.

Each day Deelia and Salou brought a few pygmies into camp, and at length we had a little colony of thirty. Once they became acquainted with us and confident that we would not hurt them, they were a happy lot, and fun to work with. Bwana Sura, the big native, made himself a nuisance, however, along with his father, subchiefs, and various hangers-on. Shameless as any city mendicant, the big black pointed out things around camp which he thought he should have in payment for cleaning our campsite and bringing in the pygmies. As a matter of fact, he'd had very little to do with either, and so, thoroughly impatient one day, Martin booted him out. Bwana Sura held no grudge, however, and when we needed him later, he was available.

After securing some excellent pictures of the pygmies' native habits, Martin sent for Bwana Sura and asked him to have all his subchiefs within a radius of fifteen miles assemble their subjects. My husband emphasized the fact that the little people must bring their drums and be ready for a big assembly.

Messengers from the different villages arrived about a week later and told us where the pygmies, all gathered together, could be found. As might have been expected, they were massed in the darkest depths of the forest, and it became our job to transport them to our camp where the light was good and our sound equipment was set up.

This of itself was a job to challenge Solomon, and I'm not certain to this day how it was accomplished. I give credit for much of it, however, to Martin's fine smile and persuasive powers. For myself, I cajoled and coaxed, but the pygmies were simply terrified of our cars. After what seemed hours, I managed by gentle urgings and extravagant promises to fill my car with women and children. Some forty of the little men, each desperately clutching a miniature bow and arrow, were persuaded to enter one of the trucks.

Presently the little people in my car began to sing—a sort of high, piping squeak. "Happy?" I queried lightly, feeling quite flattered. But by their expressions I knew they were singing to keep up their courage.

To coax these strange little people out of the cars was almost as difficult as it had been to coax them in, and it was only when they saw the huge "debbies" of boiled rice, together with presents of tobacco, calico, and salt, that they conferred among themselves and apparently decided that we meant them no harm.

They were beautifully formed little people, with clear skins and well-shaped bodies and heads. The only ornaments we saw were the occasional bead necklaces, and the only garments worn by either men or women were the breechclouts of calico or bark. The average height of the adults was around three feet ten inches, and their weight from sixty to seventy-five pounds.

Chief Deelia seemed to feel a little less sure of himself with so many strange subchiefs and tribesmen around, but after a while we coaxed him into starting a little dance. His son and several others joined in, two or three drummers took their positions, and in a very little while our clearing was filled with dancing pygmies. Their dance was a hop, really, and the tiny people had the look of so many dolls on strings. Even mothers with their babies strapped to their backs hopped to the rhythm of the drums, and every male pygmy clutched a bow and arrow.

One pretty, feminine show-off decided to do a solo and skipped about coyly for the greater part of an hour, much to the amusement of the rest of the women and girls. By dint of considerable patience, I persuaded some of the women to show us how they cooked their rice and bananas, and Martin coaxed the men into a friendly boxing match. The last ended in a free-for-all, but, fortunately, there were no serious consequences.

Biologically and psychologically, these pygmies of the Ituri forest are very like those we found on the island of Espíritu Santo in the New Hebrides group. They are shy and elusive and constantly on the move, with the darker, remoter parts of the forest their favorite habitat. Their possessions are limited to crudely made bows and poisoned arrows and a couple of clay pots; their homes are the barest of shelters that can be put up in a few hours and as easily scattered, leaving no trace.

The domestic life of these people is clean, wholesome, admirable. We could learn but little of their courtship, although we managed to photograph a wedding, and were told that once a man took a mate, he did not part from her. As far as we could find out they had no religion, and gave no thought to the hereafter and very little more to the present.

Theirs, it might be said, was a Utopian existence, for they showed neither hate, greed, vanity, envy, nor any other of the dominatingly unpleasant emotions of our so-called civilized world. Each man plays his pleasant game of life, with no desire to interfere with, and caring little about, the conduct of his fellows.

As long as bananas are available to them, however, it must be admitted that there is one vice to which they yield. Drunkenness. Martin found most interesting their method of achieving this state. It was, simply, to gather a lot of overripe bananas, carry them to a hollowed-out log, dump them in, and mash them. Five days were sufficient to turn this pulp into an evil-smelling, acrid mess which, for alcoholic content, must have been potent indeed, for we have seen whole villages—men, women, and children—drink a little of the beer and go on a hilarious spree.

A fact which has puzzled many scientists is that once the breath of life has passed from the body of these tiny people, they seem to vanish from the earth. No one, to my knowledge, has ever found a burial ground, and one scientist whom we met while in the Belgian Congo said that he had searched for years hoping to find a skull which he might study, but that he had never found one. More, he said that he had given up all hope of finding one.

Martin and I tried to learn from these diminutive blacks what they thought of death or whether they had any thoughts or beliefs of a hereafter, but they seemed not to understand what we were talking about. They lived, apparently, only in the present, and tomorrow didn't exist.

At the end of several months among the pygmies of the Ituri forest even my exacting husband agreed that our film and sound recordings probably were as complete as we could hope to make them. On the day that he reluctantly made this decision, we had upwards of five hundred of the tiny actors in our camp, and with all their good nature, they were growing somewhat petulant. They were unaccustomed to the burning African sun and longed for the chill dampness and constant twilight of the forest. Too, our white rice and sugar and salt, which at first had been such a treat, now palled on them, and they longed for their usual diet of spinach-like grass, grubs, flying ants, and a bit of monkey or elephant meat now and then.

On the morning that we told them they could go, they danced and screamed with joy. Lining them up, we gave each a little bag of salt, a handful of beads, a half yard of cheap calico, a package of tobacco, a box of matches, and, to their delight, a guest cake of pink soap, on which we saw them at once begin to nibble. By night there wasn't a trace of pygmy. They were gone like small black shadows, back to their native forest.

Chapter 28 _____

"This is going to be fine! I remember saying enthusiastically to my husband and to DeWitt and our sound men—to the world in general, in fact. "I love this!"

Martin smiled. He looked wonderful, not in the least tired, even though our pygmy trip had been so trying and the preparations for this safari into the high haunts of the gorillas had been filled, as always, with tiresome and irritating details. I had tied a new red bandanna around his throat just before we started out and he appeared very gay.

We had outfitted at Rutshuru for our safari up Mount Mikeno. Those is charge of this government station had cooperated to the fullest possible extent in helping us stock up with food supplies and to find the hundred and fifty or more porters and guides necessary for our undertaking.

It was an invigorating day;—bright, not too hot—when at least we were at the foot of Mount Mikeno, ready to start our climb. I remembered many times afterwards how I had looked up those steep slopes, thick with jungle forests, and thought how much I was going to enjoy the lush growth after the hot, bare plains of Tanganyika.

The mountains seemed to rise almost straight up, and, we had been told at Rutshuru, it was twenty-one miles to the saddle at the top. I saw Martin looked up there often as we climbed, with a deep sort of thoughtfulness in his eyes; for that was where Carl Akeley lay in his last sleep.

At noon on October 10, we arrived at the Lubenga Mission,

an outpost of religion ruled over by five jolly White Fathers and four sweet nuns, who devoted their lives to the spiritual and physical welfare of the native blacks. The settlement was made up of many low, rambling, but attractive buildings, which housed workshops of various kinds, schools, dwellings, and a large church. Lovely gardens of flowers and vegetables lent a pleasant, rustic touch to the whole. The fathers put a comfortable, three-room rest house at our disposal and were extremely generous with their fruits and vegetables.

Lubenga is located on the side of Mount Mikeno, at the edge of, but not within, the Parc National Albert. The White Fathers were earnest in their praise of Carl Akeley for his efforts in persuading the Belgian government to set this land aside as a game reserve and gorilla sanctuary.

The good White Fathers were deeply interested in Martin's work as a whole and in this undertaking in particular, but they were dubious, too.

"It is true," they said thoughtfully, "there are many gorillas on the higher slopes, but Mount Mikeno is not kind to strangers." Quickly then, the friar who was speaking amended this. "The weather is often very unkind," he said.

Gaily, as always, and unmindful of gloomy warnings, we set out on the next morning with a hundred and fifty or so porters carrying our equipment, and our guides leading the way to a temporary base.

"Couldn't sleep last night. . . . All worn out. . . . Our nerves on edge. Making pictures of gorillas isn't what it's cracked up to be."

This is an item under the date of October 23, taken from my diary.

Gorillas were all around us. We heard them feeding, thumping their barrel-like chests, and screaming invectives at us, but by the time we had climbed through the cold mists and rains and thick, sopping jungle growth to where we had heard them, they were gone, usually, beyond our view.

I wished passionately that I were back on the warm—yes, and barren—plains of Tanganyika.

"It's all perfectly silly," I mumbled to myself as I slipped and slid. The high altitude cut short my breath. "Even when we do catch up with a gorilla, the light's no good and we can't photograph him."

Almost invariably, of course, just as I'd finished some such demoralized mumbling, a gorilla would show himself, the sun would break through the mist, and my husband would manage to get a very nice picture.

We reached a plateau, finally, perhaps a quarter of a mile in width.

"This is wonderful!" I said, standing erect for the first time in hours, with my feet planted firmly on the nice, flat earth. "Why, I could keep on going forever here!"

I was soon to change my mind, however. The undergrowth, reaching to my waist, was so thick and laced with such tough vines that to walk through it was impossible.

Both Martin and DeWitt looked completely baffled. Our men looked discouraged. Our headman, Bukhari, however, looked enormously pleased with himself and with the world as he found it. I watched him in a sort of stupefied astonishment as, suddenly, his head disappeared beneath the surface of the matted growth and then reappeared almost instantly some twenty feet away. The effect was similar to that achieved by an underwater swimmer, who goes down in one place and comes up suddenly in another.

Dramatically, he revealed his discovery to us. He had found a tunnel through the impenetrable growth, a tunnel made by the huge gorillas.

"Fine!" shouted Martin. "Good old Bukhari!"

My husband bobbed out of sight into the tunnel. DeWitt and the men followed, and I, perforce, did likewise.

I think, incidentally, that I should make mention here of the fact that whenever our sound men, Richard Maedler and Louis Tappen, seem to have been lost somewhere in the narrative, it is because they were either back in camp or down at the mission, or, equally likely, back at Rutshuru, doing what they could—and heroically—to repair the delicate mechanism of our sound equipment. These men, to put it approximately in their own words, had had to turn into a pair of nurses. Martin said, and often, that the honor of making the first sound pictures in Central Africa and the Belgian Congo really belongs to Dick and Lou.

Mostly on hands and knees, for days on end, we trailed the big gorillas through their dank, green passageways. These led, of course, straight to both feeding grounds and nests, and, when a few good pictures were secured, aching muscles didn't matter in the least.

The favorite foods of these hairy monsters, we found, as we pursued them on all fours through their tunnels, are the slender shoots of scrub bamboo and a wild, bitter celery.

My first encounter with one of the Mount Mikeno apes had me just about as frightened as anything that had happened to me in years. It was on a Sunday morning. Martin had decided to sleep a little later than usual, and I thought it would be nice to surprise him at lunch with some wild celery. The sun was shining fitfully and, encouraged by its cheeriness and warmth, I wandered perhaps a quarter of a mile from our plateau camp. Standing in the middle of a celery patch, I had just stripped a stalk down to its white, tender heart and taken an experimental bite. Its bitterness, worse than quinine, astonished me, somehow, and I spat it out with accompanying noises. Suddenly, then, I heard a loud grunt just behind me and, whirling, found myself face to face with an enormous gorilla.

"Nagapate!" I yelled, for no reason at all, and ran for dear life.

Martin had missed me, and I ran squarely into him not fifty yards away.

"What's that about Nagapate?" he asked, quite puzzled.

When I had caught my breath, I tried to explain. For some reason, the sudden appearance of that black face had reminded me of that terrifing experience on our first trip to Malekula.

"He just made me think of Nagapate, that's all," I said crossly. My husband was laughing at me. As a matter of fact, at that moment, with my fright still upon me, it would have been very easy for me to believe the gorilla capable of any and all the stories of kidnaping and general ferocity attributed to him. That the big animal had made no move to touch me didn't occur to me until much later.

A fine subject for my husband's camera and sound equipment, but maddeningly elusive, the gorilla is the largest of all ape species. He weighs from four hundred to six hundred and fifty pounds and stands from five-and-a-half to six feet tall. His head juts almost neckless from his enormous, hairy torso, and his long arms and bent legs propel him along at amazing speed. The treetops, where he would like occasionally to travel about, won't hold his great weight, and he is forced to stay for the most part on the ground. Here he runs in packs of varying size.

Martin had succeeded finally in securing pictures of the big fellow eating and a mother gorilla caring for her young, but it seemed to me we were weeks catching them at the job of making their beds.

Stationing ourselves in hiding in what we hoped would be a likely place, we finally saw and recorded the entire procedure. It is simple enough, and just as crude as might be expected.

First, the gorilla advances upon a spot which, with much chest pounding, he declares to be his own. Then he squints suspiciously in all directions, ready, apparently, to take on all challengers.

The big fellow's next move is to sit down right where he is and pull the tall grass around him. This he laces in some manner over his head, achieving a sort of cage, then he reaches outside for whatever leaves, moss, or tender grasses happen to be about. Carelessly these are tossed about, to sit on, lie on, or eat—the whole business is very haphazard—and the moment the sun has dipped below the horizon, he is asleep. At sun-up he is awake and off, leaving his nest in an unspeakably filthy condition.

For some reason wholly incomprehensible to Martin and me, Bukhari was suddenly possessed of the conviction that the Alimbongo Mountains would be a far better place in which to pursue our gorilla hunts. The good fellow was persistent, and since Mount Mikeno, with its thick undergrowth, had presented so many difficulties, the matter of persuading us was relatively easy. Before we left, however, we climbed to Carl Akeley's grave.

It was a hard, steep climb. A cold drizzle had set in, and at every step our clothing slapped soddenly against our bodies. Just as we reached the saddle, the sun broke through the low-hanging, forbidding clouds. The mountaintops, green jungles, and yellow and purple veld showed in wide-swept, lavish proportions. We were glad Carl could rest in a place of such peace and majestic beauty.

We pitched camp close to our friend's resting place and remained long enough to make some much-needed repairs. The cement slab was in perfect condition, but the stockade needed rebuilding. While the men were doing this, I planted hardy ferns and vines all about and left, on the grave, a large wreath of the wildflowers that Carl had loved.

First, we headed for Kibondo, a village on the slopes of the Alimbongo Mountains. Steep grades and many hairpin turns made our progress slow, but the roads were smooth and hard and we arrived with our mass of equipment in good shape.

Kibondo is some eight thousand feet above sea level, and its intelligent, energetic natives, some three hundred in number, devote much time to their well-kept truck gardens. The surrounding country has a thick jungle growth very like that of Mount Mikeno, but the many well-packed trails made travel through it comparatively easy for us.

Contrary to Martin's pessimistic expectations, we learned from the natives that gorillas were to be found everywhere in the district, and that while the villagers had a wholesome respect for the big apes, they accepted them as a part of their everyday life. For this reason, doubtless, they were puzzled to understand our interest in them, and, naturally, we didn't try to explain.

With an unremitting persistence that surprised even me, Martin set about inquiring into the alleged ferocity of the gorilla. What truth was there, he asked over and over of every native we met, in the stories so generally accepted in every part of the civilized world, of women and children being carried off by the huge anthropoids, and of men being killed by them? In all instances, the natives shook their heads and even eyed us a little suspiciously because we could put credence in such tales.

"Why should gorillas carry off women?" said one. "Women

are made only to carry firewood, plant gardens, and build houses, and gorillas don't have fires, houses, or gardens!"

I began to see that as my husband put these questions to the villagers, there was even more behind his inquiries than an explorer's interest in his subject of the moment. I was soon to learn what this interest was.

"I'm going to take one of these big fellows back with me to the States," he said one day. "I think it's about time all those stories of the viciousness of the gorilla should be debunked."

"What?" I demanded, remembering the trouble we'd had getting even friendly Bessie back to the States.

Martin was lost in thought. "I'm going to give the folks back there a chance to see the gorilla, how big he is and strong, and yet how he never uses either his size or strength to hurt a single living thing."

With his usual thoroughness, my husband went about obtaining a permit from the Belgian government that would allow us to capture one of the enormous animals. While waiting for this permit to arrive, we moved easily with our equipment over good trails to where the animals were and made a fine record of them in both pictures and sound.

"Well," I said dubiously, "I suppose you know what you're doing."

My husband had the coveted permit tucked safely in his pocket and had arranged with the village headman, Chief Pawko, to supply us—for a price—with native hunters. It had rained all morning of the "big day"—that was my name for it—but the sun came out nicely by noon, and it was then that Chief Pawko presented himself. With a large manner, he said that he had brought with him several hundred brave huntsmen and a great pack of gorilla hounds.

What we found on inspection was a self-conscious group of about seventy-five blacks who shuffled uneasily as we looked them over. The dogs, half starved and mangy and numbering exactly six, were led about on leashes and wore wooden bells.

The chief hastened to assure us that these were trained hunting dogs—the best anywhere—and that in no time at all they would track down a gorilla and hold it at bay until his men had made the capture.

During all this, Bukhari came closer to laughing than I had ever seen him. Dewitt, Lou, and Dick looked skeptical, and I took my cue from Martin.

"Of course they can," I said, sort of generally. "Why not?"

The chief and his men stood about then, apparently a little uncertain how to start, so Martin led the way up a familiar mountain path. Some twenty minutes later we struck a gorilla trail, and Chief Pawko, who was both plump and oily, instantly looked smug. His men jabbered like mad, and the dogs set up a dismal howling. This seemed to us to be a very odd way to capture any sort of wild animal, and Martin spoke to the chief about it.

Chief Pawko was ready with an answer. He explained, very learnedly, that since the gorilla was used to both natives and dogs, it paid no attention to them. My husband seemed about to say something but changed his mind and forged ahead.

Chief Pawko's general idea seemed to be to keep after one gorilla even though there might be others about, so for two hours we struggled up mountain slopes and down again, sometimes on hands and knees, and always to the accompaniment of yelling natives, yapping dogs, and the clatter of wooden bells.

On and on we plodded, with our quarry keeping well in the lead.

Suddenly Pawko stopped and held up his hands. Now was the time! The natives spread out in a semicircle. The dogs—on leash all this time, of course—were brought to the center of the circle. The excitement was almost more than I could stand. I was even convinced by now that the chief knew what he was about. Chief Pawko gave a sudden and dramatic signal. The dogs were turned loose. There was a mighty canine chorus— and the dogs bolted for home!

"Aw, nuts!" said DeWitt, and left for camp.

Completely undaunted, Pawko next divided his hunters into two groups, sending one into the jungle and putting the others to work clearing out a hundred-yard patch of undergrowth.

We waited, gloomy and detached.

After about two hours we heard the stalkers closing in; they made a wonderful noise. Chief Pawko's black eyes darted brightly from Lou to Dick, to Martin and me. He looked very proud.

Yelling at the tops of their lungs, the stalkers crept hope-fully into the clearing. Their disappointment as they stared about showed plainly that they had expected, as a result of their ef-forts, to see the clearing full of gorillas.

Chief Pawko, still undaunted, had another plan which, ac-cording to his lights, was simply colossal. He told it to his men. They also thought it was colossal. During this, we left and went back to camp.

My husband's permit from the Belgian government to cap-ture a gorilla was pushed out of sight in one of our traveling bags, and the subject was dropped. Martin wanted a few more pictures and sound effects of the big animals, and we went about getting them in the usual way.

Some two weeks later we had finished a good day's work and started down the trail on the Alimbongo slope about five miles from camp.

"Well," Martin said, "I think our record of gorillas is about complete. I don't know of another thing we need. Do you?" he asked.

"Not a thing," I replied promptly. I was a little tired of go-rillas after these many months, and besides, I was looking for-ward to going home to the States.

Suddenly, around a bend in the trail, we came upon a pack of comparatively young apes headed by an old silverback. He was enormous, standing well over six feet tall. With no partic-ular reason that I could figure out, we started in pursuit and soon were all running back up the mountain.

The huge silverback acted as a rear guard for the pack, and our chasing after them had put him in a state of diabolical fury. He charged and retreated, pranced on stiffened legs, screeched with frenzy, and pounded his enormous chest. Suddenly, how-ever, he seemed to grow tired not only of us but of his job and, leaving the trail, struck off through the matted undergrowth, cursing as he went.

The rear guard gone, Martin rushed the pack. All but two ran off screaming. The two laggards, also screaming, lost their heads and scrambled hand over hand up a somewhat isolated, sixty-foot tree.

"Wonderful!" my husband exclaimed. "That's perfect! Great!"

I knew then that my husband had not forgotten his permit to capture a gorilla.

The methods he applied were both efficient and effective. First, every tall tree within jumping distance of the one containing the gorillas was cut down. Next, the ground under this tree was cleared of undergrowth in a complete circle for a space of a hundred feet. Dick and Lou were stationed at the sound camera and apparatus, and I took another camera from a different angle. My husband sent some porters to the cars for tarpaulins and blankets. I admired the way—in spite of his excitement—that he seemed to think of everything.

"You, DeWitt," he shouted above the screech of the frightened apes and the bedlam in general, "when the tree falls, you grab one and I'll grab the other."

DeWitt eyed him wildly. "Me?" he said.

Martin had turned, however, and given the order for the waiting blacks to apply their axes to the trunk of the lone tree. "All right," he said, "start cutting her down."

DeWitt looked anxiously at his bare hands and rubbed his cheek. Clearly, he was wondering how he'd come out in an encounter with a gorilla's claws and teeth.

The sharp blades, meantime, were biting quickly into the tree trunk, and, tardily, DeWitt's doubts also assailed my husband. The pair of gorillas, while young and obviously frightened, were far from being babies and were indubitably powerful.

"Hey, DeWitt," he shouted, "we'd better borrow the fellows' coats. Put on as much as possible." Then, off to one of the blacks, "You," he commanded with an anxious eye on the tree, "get the gloves out of the cars—driving gloves!" With this hasty padding, both Martin and DeWitt took on the look of deep-sea divers.

Automatically I cranked the camera and felt sorry for the two apes. Sweethearts, I decided from the way one seemed to be trying to console and protect the other. The female would be the one doing the protecting, of course.

The tree cracked a signal and tottered with momentary uncertainty. Martin, I saw, was jumping up and down.

"All set, DeWitt?" he yelled.

DeWitt nodded vaguely, his mouth open, his eyes fixed on the apes in the top of the swaying tree.

The tree crashed. Bukhari threw a tarpaulin over one slightly stunned gorilla and trussed it up. Three other blacks, working under his command, trussed up the second gorilla, and it was all over before Martin and DeWitt, in their heavy paddings, could move from where they stood.

Bukhari strutted with pride from then on and appropriated the right to say how the two animals should be transported to camp, how they should be cared for, and, very particularly, how and by whom fed. The fact that we had two gorillas and one permit was also a matter of simple solution for him. Just ask for another permit, he said in his best Swahili.

Actually, by the time we left the Congo, we had three gorillas. For as we started our return trip to East Africa, we met a group of natives carrying a very sick baby gorilla. I insisted on stopping to look, and just then the infant opened his eyes. Turning to Martin, I said, "We have to buy this poor little baby."

Martin didn't argue. "All right," he said, "we'll straighten things out with the Belgian government somehow."

It was not quite as simple as that, of course, but after a number of cablegrams to Brussels, we received the necessary permits to take the gorillas with us.

The gorillas attracted much attention to Nairobi. Congo and 'Ngagi, for so we named the two gorillas we had captured, adapted themselves to captivity, and are now happy citizens of the San Diego Zoo. Snowball, as we called the baby gorilla, regained his health and now lives at the National Zoo in Washington.

Osa works at typing, despite companionship of primate friends.

Only the smaller Sikorsky was suitable for Bornean river travel. Renamed *Spirit of Africa and Borneo,* it now sported the symbolic Oriental eye on its prow. Here the plane is surrounded by expedition personnel.

The Johnsons' houseboat with the *Spirit* in tow

Mother and child orangutans aloft

Proboscis monkeys

Juvenile

Adult

Gobong glides sleekly through nipa-palm backwaters as the Johnsons search for proboscis.

Osa talks with one of the primitive Raumanau tribesmen.

Martin greets Tenggerese men.

Muruts welcome Martin and Osa and their great flying bird.

*Chapter 29*_____

The plane made a smooth, three-point landing on the new flying field at Chanute; the folks were there to meet us, Father Johnson and Freda among them; and I was so happy I was beside myself. We had been tied up in New York editing our latest picture, *Congorilla,* and this was our first trip home.

My father looked at me approvingly, then beamed at Martin.

"I see you've done what I told you to, Martin," he said. "You've taken good care of our Osa."

My husband seemed preoccupied. He was looking off toward the plane on which he had just come from Kansas City. Then he looked at me.

"Do you like flying?" he demanded.

"Why—yes. Yes, I guess so. It gets you places in a hurry. We wouldn't have been here until day after tomorrow."

"I asked if you like it." He seemed impatient.

"Well—" I temporized. "Of course it's pretty high up. Do you like it?"

"No," he answered shortly. "I don't."

Later that day I was in my grandmother's room; she was showing me some wonderful new quilts which she had made for our next safari. Mama brought in some beautiful sweaters which she had knitted, two for Martin, two for me. Martin came in, his face sort of puckered.

"I suppose a person in a plane over Africa could see quite a lot," he said.

"Martin, you mean—?"

"You know, all the places we've wanted to explore and couldn't reach?"

"Oh, yes, Martin, of course!"

My husband was gone before I woke up the next morning. He had left a note.

"I'll be with Vern Carstens over at the flying field," was all it said. Vern, the manager of the airport, already had a reputation for being one of the best pilots in Kansas.

Father was with me when I read the note.

"Well, Osa," he chuckled. "If you're going to keep up with Martin this time, you'll have to grow yourself a pair of wings."

Vern worked with me for quite a while, putting me through my paces in 180- and 360-degree landings; shallow and steep banks; turns, spirals, stalls, and spins; wind and temperature and all manner of emergency tests; navigation and meteorology; and ultimately announced that I was ready for a solo flight. My husband had already "graduated."

The day was set, and when I arrived at the airport with Martin, all our folks were there, as well as half the population of Chanute, waiting to see me make my debut as an aviatrix.

I grinned mechanically at everyone. Neither my father nor mother seemed very happy, but Grandma beamed and Martin gave me a close hug. "You'll do just fine, honey," he said. "I know you will."

I got off the ground without mishap and soon found myself floating in a circle two thousand feet in the air—all by myself. Around and around I flew, putting off the dread moment when I should have to land.

Gritting my teeth, finally, I pointed the nose of the plane downward. The ground came up with terrific speed and, hitting it, I bounced thirty feet in the air. As I had been instructed, I gave the ship "the gun" and found myself circling the field again, two thousand feet up. My second and third tries at landing were exactly like the first. I bounced and was off. Everybody was staring; Martin and Vern were waving their arms. I'm not quite certain to this day how I managed finally to land the plane without having it bounce off the ground again, but land I did, and sat there for a minute marveling at my good luck.

I do remember that Vern was the first to reach me. He was livid.

"Is that the way I taught you to fly?" he yelled. "Coming into the field with your tail in the trees and just missing the telephone wires!"

I wanted to tell him I thought I was lucky to get down at all.

"What was the matter with you anyhow?" he continued. "I thought we were going to have to shoot you down!"

I'm reasonably certain that we didn't go to the Sikorsky plant that bright spring day in 1932 with the idea of buying anything, but the fact remains that when we left we were the proud owners of two beautiful planes. Powered by supercharged "Wasp" motors, they were a ten-seater and a five-seater, both amphibians.

Martin decided that the larger plane should be named *Osa's Ark,* and had it painted with zebra stripes, and we finally chose the *Spirit of Africa* as the name for the second plane, and painted it in the color and design of a giraffe's spots. The interiors, like our different cars, were adapted to safari need, and quite efficiently, I thought. Most of the seats, for instance, were removed from *Osa's Ark* to make room for equipment. Two light-framed but comfortably upholstered sleeping bunks were installed. We had a tiny washroom, a little gasoline stove with two burners and an oven, a compact outfit of pots and pans, a set of dishes which nested into an extremely small space, and a supply of food staples. Every inch of space was utilized for storage, under the bunks, under the seats, and overhead, and there were baggage compartments forward of the cockpit. One unipod camera mounting specially designed by Martin was installed to facilitate his aerial photography, and I designed a very complete typewriter desk, for I had just received an assignment to do a book and some magazine articles.

This was to be an air safari to Africa. As pilot, we had with us our good friend and flying instructor, Vern Carstens. The Sikorsky factory "loaned" us test-pilot Captain Boris Sergievsky and mechanic Al Morway to assist in delivering the planes to Nairobi. Arthur Sanial and Robert Moreno were in charge of the complicated sound equipment, and Hugh Davis was to assist my husband with his laboratory work.

Inasmuch as we had already approached our home in Nairobi from the east coast via Mombasa, and from the north via the Nile, we determined this time to come up from the south for a glimpse of Rhodesia and South Africa. On January 23, 1933, we and our planes disembarked from the *City of New York* in Table Bay at Cape Town. After the usual unraveling of red tape, we assembled our planes, which were then lifted into the water. From there we took off and flew to the airport.

After a week of checking and testing the airplanes, we were ready to head for Nairobi. Martin and I rode in the big plane, with Boris at the controls and with Davis and Morway as passengers. Vern flew the smaller plane, carrying Moreno and Sanial. We were proud, of course, of our efficient-looking ships, with their gleaming propellers and bright new paint, but I couldn't help grumbling a little at the charge of $750 which we had had to pay for the twenty-four-hour storage of the planes on the quay!

Our 4,400-mile flight from Cape Town to Nairobi over the rough mountainous country was not particularly pleasant. We had implicit faith in Boris and in Vern, but the best pilot in the world could very easily, and with small blame, crash in territory such as this. The fogs seemed always with us; there were neither "beams" nor friendly fields; and even our maps, we found, were fantastically inaccurate.

Further to complicate matters, due to the difference in loads and speeds, our ships could not fly together. Towns were widely separated, and, all in all, the problem of gasoline was seldom absent from our minds.

The *Spirit of Africa,* too, was a great anxiety. A smaller and slower ship than the *Ark,* she was proportionately as heavily loaded, and the problem of fuel for Vern was an even greater one than it was for us.

Time after time we lost our way in the fog, frequently, it seemed to me, just as our gauge was in swift descent. I remember the relief we felt as we landed in a small town named

Broken Hill, which lay midway between Cape Town and Nairobi. Vern had already landed and refueled, fearing he might
have to begin an aerial search. Happily, we took on gasoline
and consulted maps. Mpika, we decided, would be our next
stop. It was only a three-hour flight and both planes were starting out with a five-hour supply of gasoline; obviously, there
was nothing more to worry about. We waved cheery good-byes
and promised to meet at Mpika.

Two and three-quarters hours passed very pleasantly for us.
This time we were almost smug in our certainty that not only
would we find Mpika in a few minutes, but that we would land
with a good two hours' surplus of fuel in our tanks. Vern had
dropped behind two hours before, but that was usual. The fog
had cleared, and this alone was enough to give us confidence.
No Mpika appeared, however, and soon we found that we had
been traveling something over three hours and a half.

Still another half hour joined eternity.

Finally, Boris turned back in an attempt to find some land-
mark, but all we saw below were mountains, deep canyons,
cataracts, rocky streams, and an occasional village.

We all chattered with a sort of brittle gaiety now, and glued
our eyes on the gas gauge. The needle and the "zero" line soon
met. I saw a mountain shaped like a face with the mouth wide
open and had visions of dropping into it. The gauge by now
indicated empty—completely empty.

Then Boris spoke—for the first time, I think.

"I've been doing some figuring," he said, "and according to
my calculations we have just about enough gas in the pipes
and carburetor to last us four minutes."

Our eyes flew to the clock. Martin reached across and gripped
my hand.

"Whatever happens, Osa—I sort of feel that you'll be all
right for a long time yet." He looked at the clock. Two minutes
had gone. "You know what the English always say—we've heard
them thousands of times here in Africa—"

"You mean—'carry on'?" I heard myself saying.

"That's right."

He looked at the clock and just sat there. The boys in the
seats behind hadn't said a word. The four minutes had passed.

It was going on to five. Any minute now, I thought, we'd hear the sputter of the dying motor.

The thought made me angry. Martin and his work—our bright shining plane—fifty thousand dollars' worth of cameras and specially ground lenses stowed in the tail—

Boris zoomed for altitude to give me a better range with the binoculars, hoping that we might see Mpika in the dim distance.

"A lake," I cried, as I spotted a blue dot in the forest below. "I know it's a lake." I prayed fervently.

All were incredulous, then Boris shouted, "I think she's right," and headed for the spot. A lake it was, but perhaps six or seven miles distant.

Boris set the amphibian down in a beautiful landing on the tiny lake's smooth surface. Examination showed that there was just enough gasoline for fifteen more seconds of flying time.

To my astonishment, I saw that this was no lake in a jungle swamp; it was a private lake, with smooth banks and beyond that a wide stretch of close-cropped lawn, and beyond that, a house. Not a house, a mansion!

Recovering from the shock and surprise, I found that we were being greeted by Lieutenant Colonel and Mrs. Stewart Gore-Brown. They took quite as a matter of fact our descending upon them so unceremoniously and offered us the hospitality of their lovely home. Having retired from the British army, the colonel found this Elysian spot and had literally hewn an estate out of the jungle, even making the bricks of the buildings from the native clay. Their magnificent coffee plantation was one of the finest in Africa.

We were anxious about Vern, however, and our first concern was to get some gasoline from somewhere and push on to Mpika, wherever it was.

These heavenly people—and I shall always think of them as such—not only knew exactly where Mpika was but also supplied us with the gas to get there. We had overshot the place, apparently, in our swift plane.

Vern, we found to our great relief, had arrived hours before in good shape.

*   *   *

In Kenya Colony, a hundred and seventy-five miles or so south of the Abyssinian border, there lies a valley which separates the rugged Mathews Range from the equally rugged Ndoto Range.

Difficult to reach by ground, nevertheless we had managed to make our way through to this mountain-enclosed plain while at Lake Paradise. We felt that in a concentrated area, reasonably sheltered from winds and teeming with game, we could make some very interesting studies from the air, and decided on Ngornit, a desolate native village which actually was very little more than a name, as our base camp. Sanial and Moreno took fifty blacks and went on ahead to clear the shrubs and level the ground for a landing field.

While these preparations were being made at Ngornit, Martin had much to occupy him at Nairobi. There was a hangar to be built at the Nairobi landing field; there were lenses and cameras to be cleaned, adjusted, and tested; and there was sound equipment to be assembled. My time was full, of course, with the purely housewifely duties of airing our long-closed Nairobi home, and also with purchasing and packing supplies for our air safari.

Two months after our planes were first set down in Nairobi, the *Ark* was lifted off the ground by Vern and headed for Ngornit. Three hours and twenty minutes later we circled the big white cross which Sanial and Moreno had had outlined on the ground of our wilderness airfield. A "sock" gave us our wind direction and, as usual, Vern made a perfect landing.

Martin and I never did get over our astonishment at the freedom which our planes in Africa gave us. We called them our "seven-league boots." Mountains, jungle, plain were a vast panorama beneath us; great elephant migrations, herds of thousands, also great flocks of white herons and countless giraffe and plains game were spotted one moment from the air, and the next moment were being recorded by our cameras. We were able to land in ordinarily inaccessible places where white people had never been, and here saw natives of strange, remote tribes.

And Lake Paradise—loved by us, I think, above any place on earth—we saw cradled in its mountain lap, a sanctuary for the animals for hundreds of miles around, a sanctuary for our memories.

The south tip of Lake Rudolf was only an hour by air from our camp at Ngornit, and we set out early one morning, with Vern at the controls, to learn more of this curious and desolate body of salt water. One hundred and eighty-seven miles long, extending deep into the Abyssinian border, its shores are as barren and pocked as the craters of the moon, and from the look of the few stunted trees we saw, it is swept by hot, fierce, unending winds.

Fifty miles from the southern end of Lake Rudolf there is an island inhabited by natives known somewhat vaguely as the Elmolos, natives who, according to legend, believe themselves to be the only people in existence, and their island, set in apparently limitless stretches of water, to be the entire world.

In an hour and a half from Ngornit we were flying over this tiny speck in the rough, salty lake. Vern circled several times, then shook his head.

"Can't land," he said. "Too rough."

My husband wasn't to be convinced until he had looked through the binoculars and seen the breakers on the beach. Reluctantly he admitted that it was a little rough, and he had to content himself with taking photographs from the air.

I think we must have flown to Rudolf from Ngornit a dozen times, hoping to descend in the waters near the little island, but Vern refused to take the risk in a sea which, apparently, was always rough.

We flew on north over the lake for perhaps seventy-five miles and came to what on our map was indicated as Center Island. Perhaps ten times the size of the island inhabited by the Elmolos, we saw, as we flew over, that it was uninhabited and had three little lakes on it, all in the craters of extinct volcanos.

Vern circled, eased gently onto the water on the lee side, and taxied to a stretch of sandy beach. Shouldering our cameras and guns, we climbed over bare, volcanic rocks to the shore of one of the stagnant little lakes. Herons by the hundreds waded sedately among the water plants near the banks and flew noisily overhead, and crocodiles, more than we had ever seen— sometimes three deep—lined the shores.

We took pictures of everything. A little tired, after a bit, my husband sat on a jutting rock, swung his foot, and said that we might come here to live sometime. I blazed indignantly and said I thought the place was horrid. Nothing grew on it; there was even something wrong with the sun, the way it looked, all white and bald. And the heat, with the funny, dry bite that it had—and the wind! Why, the wind alone would be enough to drive me crazy, I said.

Just then I saw a puff adder under the rock within an inch of his swinging foot. At the same instant Vern came running and yelled, "Come on! The wind!" We ran, and forgot about the puff adder.

Hauling, pushing, struggling, we turned the plane about against the wind and, soaked with salt water, climbed in. The waves were running frighteningly high, but Vern, cool as always, started the motors. Our ship stood on its tail one moment and crashed on a wave the next. Slowly Vern opened the throttle; faster and faster we hit the waves until they were like triphammers pounding us to pieces.

Then the pounding stopped. We were in the air.

Something about that horrid lake seemed to fascinate Martin. Another day we landed in a quiet cove on the mainland. I opened the hatch and looked out at the bleak shore.

It was just about as desolate a place as one could find in the world. Only an occasional tuft of dried, wiry grass broke the nothingness of the place. The scenery had all the qualities of a surrealist painting.

Martin, I saw then, was looking intently off. Twenty curious-looking naked natives were peering at us over a slight rise above the beach. Presently, showing no fear and very little curiosity, they came down to us. They paid no attention whatever to our plane but seemed to find us very amusing; our white faces and hands in particular, though our clothes, too, seemed to strike them as being pretty silly.

Our native interpreter said they seemed to be of the Turkana tribe, and Martin and I concluded that as a result of some tribal battle, probably, they had wandered many generations before to this dismal place.

We had seen other Turkanas, but none quite as fantastic as

these. Their long, kinky hair was plastered with mud and tallow and molded into the most ingenious forms. Bulk and height
seemed very important in this peculiar type of ornamentation,
and we learned that the dead, just before they were buried,
were shorn of their hair that it might be added to that of surviving relatives. Additional mud and tallow were required, of
course, to make the dead man's hair stick, and the shaping and
molding that followed brought about coiffures of such bizarre
design and abstract quality as would delight a sculptor of the
modern school.

Other uncomfortable ornaments worn by this strange tribe
of Turkanas were disks of wood the size of a man's hand,
hanging from holes in their noses. And as if this weren't enough,
plugs of ivory or wood were thrust through their lower lips. An
intriguing feature of this plug was that a little clever manipu-
lation with the tongue could give it quite an animated look. It
could be pushed out, pulled in, or wiggled.

We opened a saltine tin for lunch, and I handed it to one of
the men to pack away. But the natives had spied it. The food
did not, apparently, interest them, but that shiny piece of tin—
to my astonishment, I soon beheld the most of it dangling like
a new jewel from the nose of a strutting dandy.

What little we could see of the skin of these people appeared to be a good, healthy brown, but the daubings of mud
and alkali which had been applied gave it a very unhealthy
look.

My husband thought these people were marvelous and declared enthusiastically that we would remain right where we
were for a few days.

Vern took the plane up in the air so he could land on the
hard-packed sand of the beach. Martin and I watched the natives closely to see what their reaction would be to the big ship
as it went into the air. To our complete astonishment, there
was no reaction whatever. They were equally unimpressed when
the plane roared to a landing within a short distance of where
we stood. The only thing that interested them was the broad
shade spread by the wings. Running under it, they decided it
was wonderful and almost fought one another for a place in it.

We had no trouble at all persuading several of these blacks

to get into the plane. Martin, Vern, and I were all set, however, for some excitement when the ship lifted into the sky. There was none whatever.

A small village appeared below us perhaps half a mile from the shore. A few cattle, poor things, stood in the blazing sun. Martin asked our native interpreter to point out a cow to one of our passengers.

"That is not a cow," our Turkana passenger said emphatically and in some surprise. "A cow has legs."

We saw his point after a few minutes. He could not, of course, see the cow's legs from the air.

Our interpreter next pointed out a tree.

Again the Turkana shook his head; his mind was made up by this time that we were very stupid people.

"That," he said, "is not a tree. You look up to see a tree, and you can walk under a tree. That is not a tree."

Chapter 30 _____

We had moved our camp three hundred miles from Ngornit, when a runner brought word from Trubee Davison, president of the American Museum of Natural History, that he, his wife, Dorothy, and Pete Quesada, a U.S. Army pilot, were on their way to Nairobi. Would we, the message went on, help them collect four elephants to complete a museum group started by Carl Akeley some years before?

I doubt that we've ever broken camp more quickly or with greater eagerness.

Upon the Davisons' arrival we made a survey and selected the Tana River as the best place at the moment in which to secure the elephants.

This was Mr. Davison's first visit to Africa; he wanted a more intimate view of the country than could be had by plane, so he went with the caravan of trucks. This caravan carried the supplies and hunting equipment, as well as seventy-five porters. Ten skinners also were added to the expedition to take care of the pelts.

Giving the trucks several days to reach the little government post of Garissa, the rest of us followed by plane. Pete Quesada flew the smaller of our two planes, the *Spirit of Africa*, with Dot Davison and a native cook as passengers, and Vern piloted *Osa's Ark*, carrying Martin and me, together with our heavy load of camera and sound equipment.

The selection of the Tana River proved to be excellent. It seemed to us that elephants were moving everywhere, and we

392

were all confident that we'd have the four specimens to complete the museum group in no time at all.

The Akeley museum group already had a large bull, together with a lesser bull, a cow, and a baby. The museum
wanted to enlarge the group to a small herd, still keeping the
big bull dominant. What really was needed was a collection of
fine specimens just a trifle under full growth.

Every morning for days we were up early and on the trail
until dusk, searching for the right specimens, but without success. Studying a distant herd through his binoculars one day,
Trube exclaimed delightedly that our luck had changed; there
was at least one of the lot that seemed the exact size needed.

We had followed the herd for more than two hours when
our trackers came back and reported that the beasts had turned
around and were headed toward us. Excitedly we agreed that
the first kill should be Dot's.

We waited, and I was proud to see how cool Dot was as the
herd approached. Presently she took careful aim—I had told
her about the little place in the forehead the size of a dollar she
must try to hit—and fired.

At first the fine animal seemed only wounded and gathered
himself for a charge. She fired again, and the elephant fell where
he stood. The rest of the herd stampeded.

My husband, whose first interest was always his camera,
decided he must now have some more aerial shots of the various fine elephant herds in the district. I went with him and
we had rare luck with light, groupings, and the closeness with
which we were able to swoop down over the big animals and
photograph them.

Trubee and Dot's experience that day, however, was the
one that took the spotlight when we gathered around the
campfire that night. Trubee, it seems, had taken on a charge.
Dot was using an Eyemo camera. As the big pachyderm charged
head-on, Trubee made a crack shot with his elephant gun; the
recoil threw him off balance, he fell against Dot, and the pair
went down in a heap. Elephant, gunner, and cameraman—all
flat—was something new in elephant hunting.

Within another week, Trubee and his party had secured the
four nearly grown specimens required, but we couldn't let them

go back to the States without introducing them to Carl Akeley's Tanganyika lion country. Sending our men on ahead several weeks in advance to make camp, we flew in the *Ark* from Nairobi—Dot, Trubee, Martin, and I—with Vern at the controls.

Flying low over some of our old hunting and camping grounds on the Serengeti Plains, we saw every species of animal in unbelievable numbers.

We were curious, of course, to learn what some of our old lion friends would think of the plane, and the next day after we were settled in camp, we had Vern taxi the *Ark* up to the edge of a bushy donga.

I remained in the plane; Martin set up his cameras and sound equipment at an advantageous spot; our men dragged some freshly killed bait around the place, then tied it with a thirty-foot rope to the camera-car.

The lions soon appeared. One of them I recognized, from a previous safari, as our magnificent friend with the beautiful mane and kingly air. They indulged in the usual cat pranks of tugging at the bait and jumping and riding with it and were quite unconcerned when their dinner was hauled to within twenty feet of the plane and left there.

Our regal friend looked the ship over in a critical but rather disdainful fashion, then carried a piece of meat to the shade of one of the wings and sat down to enjoy it. I noticed that he was a trifle past his prime now, and that a few gray hairs sprinkled his muzzle.

Several of the other lions wandered about the plane, only mildly curious; then I noticed a big, sleek, taffy-maned fellow approaching from the donga. Switching his tail, he stalked about the ship and kept up a continuous growling.

Opening the hatch, I talked to him, telling him to be quiet. I was perhaps head and shoulders out of the plane at the time. Looking off toward my husband, I waved my hand. A contortion of alarm crossed his face, which was my warning. Dropping down, I slammed the hatch shut over my head and in the same instant the lion crashed heavily against the safety glass.

This annoyed me. It seemed entirely uncalled for, and picking up the first thing that came to hand, I opened the hatch carefully and threw it with all my might. It happened to be a package of pancake flour and burst in a most satisfactory white cloud on the lion's nose. Instantly his head and mane had the look of a powdered wig. Bewildered and enraged, he stalked off.

I'm sure that Dot and Trubee were, at first, of the opinion that we were "showing off" our lion friends when, as on many occasions, we drove close to them. We'd been in camp only two weeks, however, when Martin and I came on our guests out on the plain in their car taking pictures of thirteen lions, none of which was more than thirty feet away and some of which were as close as fifteen feet.

Regretfully, we finally saw the Davisons off. We flew them in *Osa's Ark* from Nairobi over the Great Rift Valley and the mountains inland to Kisjumu, on Lake Victoria, where they caught an Imperial Airways flying boat to London.

In the months that followed, we established a camp on the slopes of the majestic Mount Kenya. This was on the plateau, six thousand feet above sea level, known as the Nanyuki district, and the space we cleared for our landing field was close to the lovely dwelling and gardens of our friends the Raymond Hooks.

From here, one bright morning, we set out in the *Ark* and circled over Mount Kenya peak, which, directly on the equator, rises 17,040 feet above sea level. It was exciting to realize that we were the first people to see Mount Kenya from the sky, and Martin secured some fine photographs, thereby satisfying one of his fondest ambitions and bringing to the public in close-up the detail of those majestic pinnacles of almost terrifying beauty.

Great snow fields lay beneath us, and slow-moving glaciers. We looked down into deep craters and yawning crevices, while steep, barren peaks seemed within reach of my hand. It was piercingly cold. Below, on the slopes, were patches of color which we knew to be wildflowers: gladioli, red-hot-pokers, violets, a creeper resembling a pansy, everlasting flowers, and scores of blooming trees ranging in color from vermilion to canary-yellow and white. Down lower, we saw the belt of bamboo through which we had once climbed, and lower still, endless forest-covered slopes and foothills that descended into blue shadows and melted into the plains.

Here and there we spied a frozen lake, and then suddenly,

just below us, we saw the mission where both Martin and I
had been so desperately ill, and where, but for John Wilshusen, we probably should have died.

Martin's pictures and sound effects on this trip were among
the most beautiful taken on all our air safaris.

There followed a flying expedition to the Belgian Congo over
the Ituri forest, and we thought of Stanley's slow journey through
this district, fighting starvation and fever as well as hostile natives. Writing of this journey, Stanley later said: ". . . for one
hundred and sixty days we marched through the forest, bush
and jungle without ever having seen a bit of green sward the
size of a cottage chamber floor. Nothing but miles and miles,
and endless miles of forest."

One hundred and sixty days of torture—and we were covering the same route by air in a few hours. Here was another
of Martin's visions of camera conquest finally realized.

We visited our Ituri forest pygmy friends, registered their
fear and surprise at "Mungu [God] drop out of the sky," and
photographed more of their delightful dances and festivals.

We finally persuaded some of them to ride through the sky
in the *Ark*. Their singing within the closed compartment of the
plane was an ear-splitting experience and probably relieved their
feelings, even though it did the reverse to mine.

Next we chose a campsite on the northern slope of Mount
Kilimanjaro. The highest mountain in all Africa, it thrusts its
peak 19,324 feet into the sky. My husband wanted to fly over
the peak, but Vern, a daring yet cautious pilot, would not risk
the down drafts which he knew would exist about the vast ice
fields. He did consent, however, to take us above the clouds to
circle and photograph for the first time the glittering, snowcapped crest.

That flight is perhaps my most vivid memory of Africa, for
it marked the last safari to that glorious country which my husband and I were to take together.

My health had given me much secret concern for some time
now, and it became necessary for me to return to the States as
soon as possible.

Martin and Vern made a very comfortable bed for me in *Osa's Ark,* and after many good-byes to our friends in Nairobi, we headed for Tororo, in Uganda, where, after taking on gas, we left for Juba, in the Sudan.

Here we came upon a spectacle which seemed to us to be both a fitting conclusion to our long work among the elephants and a reward for the years of patience with them. Thousands of the great beasts were moving in the bush below. We circled them and saw more and more on every hand. Martin, beside himself with excitement, hurriedly set up his cameras and, as Vern flew again and again over their backs, as low as he dared in that treacherous terrain, Martin spun out thousands of feet of what we concluded to be a migration, and one of the greatest and most dramatic we had ever seen.

As the totos scurried under their mothers legs and the families ran together for protection, the big bulls lashed at us, showing their magnificent ivory and their equally magnificent courage.

Noon of the next day found us in the horrible heat of Malakal, and that night we slept in Khartoum. In ten hours we had covered a distance that, with Mr. Eastman only a few years before, had taken us seventeen days by Nile boat.

The following day saw us flying over the ancient temples of Egypt and the Valley of the Kings. We spent the night in the sumptuous hotel at Luxor, and the next day we took to the air again for Cairo. Here we were forced to remain a week to obtain the necessary permits to fly over the Italian and French colonies in North Africa.

Wherever we stopped we were required to go through the same tiresome maze of red tape, answer the same questions, and submit to the same inspection by officials. At Mersa Matruh we were even asked if we had any coffins aboard!

We skimmed along North Africa, stopping at Bengasi, Tripoli, and Tunis, where we were required to fly a weird and complicated course to avoid seeing their fortifications. Winging our way across the Mediterranean, we touched Sardinia, Cannes, Lyons, and at last Paris, and then crossed the Channel to London.

After only six days in the English metropolis we were aboard the S.S. *Manhattan* with our planes, bound for New York.

We had flown more than sixty thousand miles over African jungles, and thanks to Vern Carstens, his flying skill, and the care he gave our planes, we made the entire trip without mishap.

Chapter 31 _____

The next few months in New York had a shadow over them. I was only just out of the operating room when word came of my father's death. He had been killed in his engine cab on what was to have been the last run before his retirement.

My grief, together with my somewhat slow convalescence, weighed upon my husband, and I insisted, finally, that he go to Medical Center for a thorough physical checkup. He had been in the hospital for only a day when I saw that a checkup was not what he needed.

"I'll tell you what we could do," I said. "We could go to Borneo."

"Borneo!" he shouted. "That's the idea! With our new cameras and sound equipment, and with one of our planes—why, that'll be great!"

"That's just it! With one of our planes, we'll be able to land on the rivers way back in the interior and get the most wonderful pictures we've ever made!"

Martin's eagerness grew by the moment. "You're right, Osa! Why, with our plane we'll even be able to move in on the proboscis monkey and his whole family and photograph him right where he lives!"

"Yes, and maybe we can fly over Mount Kinabalu—the highest peak in Borneo! Nobody's ever done that!"

"Absolutely, and think what we'll be able to get with our sound equipment, all the noises in that thick green jungle, the language of the natives, the music!" He was thoughtful for a

399

moment. "I wonder," he said, "what effect British discipline has had on the headhunters since we were there?"

"We'll go and find out," I said with mounting excitement.

"That's what we'll do," my husband said. "This time we'll be able to fly to the headwaters of the Kinabatangan River. Won't that old chief be surprised to have us drop in on him from the air!"

My husband left the hospital on the spot.

There followed several months of busy preparation and then, once more, we were headed for the open sea.

I think my most cherished possession is Martin's diary of this trip. In it, among other things, he wrote: "Osa and I were now all excited . . . we were on the last lap of our journey . . . Sandakan only a few hours away . . . our home for the next year.

"We followed the course of the Papar River to its headwaters, the Crocker range of mountains, and were flying at about eight thousand feet . . . at our north we passed the desolate peaks of Mt. Alab, now we were in jungle country entirely . . . no signs of huts or villages. . . . We had been so engrossed in the marvelous scenery below that we failed to notice the approach of a long line of storm coming in from the direction of Sandakan . . . big black clouds started forming about us . . . for minutes at a time we were flying blind from cloud to cloud . . . the sky became darker and darker, a long stream of lightning forked from the clouds ahead and we could hear the report of thunder above the hum of our engine . . . and in a moment we were closed in . . . rain beat on our windshields, we could not see the tips of our wings. . . . Jim turned our nose upwards to be on the safe side in case there were any mountain tops in our way. Gosh! what a feeling, here we were over the heart of Borneo jungles in a storm . . . flying blind, no place to land with a desolate broken country below us and mountains on all sides.

"Two hours from the time we left Labuan we sighted the waters of Sandakan Bay. . . . Jim brought the plane down on the smooth surface . . . and we were home."

* * *

Fourteen months were spent in the land of rivers and jungles, and once more we returned to the States. We had been back nearly three months, and there was still a good tan on Martin's face and hands, and he was lean and buoyant and strong. More, there was a deep happiness in him, for the critics everywhere were hailing the photography of his new Borneo picture as quite the best of his career. The explorer in Martin had long ago been satisfied; the artist, until now, had not.

"You know?" he said smiling, "I think you and I are just about the two luckiest people in the whole world."

"Anyhow, I know I am," I said. He was being general while I was being specific, which is so often the way of a woman.

We had flown to Salt Lake City from the East the night before. It was a bright, crisp winter afternoon, and we were taking a cab at the hotel for the Mormon Tabernacle, where we were to lecture with the Borneo picture.

Martin fumbled at his tie as we rolled through the city's wide, clean streets.

"Do I look all right?" he asked anxiously.

"You look wonderful," I said firmly, re-straightening his tie. "You always do."

He chuckled. "Something about lecturing before kids always reminds me of that time I pulled a boner in the high school at Independence."

"You mean you're nervous?"

"Well, kind of. Can you believe it," he said, a little awed, "that we have an eighty-seven-thousand-dollar lecture schedule ahead of us?"

"I think it's wonderful," I replied.

The cab pulled up at the side entrance of the beautiful Tabernacle. Entering the anteroom, we could already hear, even beyond the closed doors, the buzz of children's voices. Nine thousand, we were told.

"Nine thousand!" Martin gasped. "Gosh, I hope they can all see the picture." Then he added quickly, "Osa, since this is our first lecture—when you've finished your part, what do you think of going out and sitting with the children and listening to their comments? We'll find out that way what they like best."

An organ prelude suddenly surged through the Tabernacle

and out to the anteroom where we stood ready to go on the platform. I was so happy I shivered a little. When the music was over, my husband took my hand and led me out on the platform. The faces of nine thousand schoolchildren looked at us as we were introduced. I made my introductory address and then Martin began to talk in the lovely, simple way he had.

"When Mrs. Johnson and I first went to Borneo seventeen years ago," he said, "our photographic equipment was old and clumsy and the heavy expenses soon wore a big hole in our pocketbook. You can imagine," he confided, "what a sad condition that was for a pair of ambitious young camera-explorers."

Our audience of youngsters laughed, sympathetically.

"As a matter of fact, about all we got with our poor old camera on that first trip was a picture of some elephants. We probably wouldn't have got that if the big fellows hadn't chased us up a tree. Oh, yes, some buffalo charged us." He paused to think a moment. "These, and a lot of crocodiles, and some natives clear up at the headwaters of the Kinabatangan River, just about completed our film record of Borneo on our first trip. The beauty of Borneo we could not capture with the cameras of those days, and so you see," he said, looking thoughtfully out at his audience, "we had to go back."

Our picture now appeared on the screen.

"There's the boat on which we sailed from New York," my husband explained. "A Dutch cargo steamer named *Kota Pinang*. A nice little boat. That was August thirteenth, 1935, and we had with us the finest camera equipment, and our pocketbook," he chuckled, "was strong and fairly well filled."

Martin glanced off at me and smiled, and then continued: "That chap you see standing near the gangplank is Jim Laneri, a Hartford lad and one of the best pilots in the world.

"Oh, yes, I meant to tell you. The plane we took with us was the *Spirit of Africa*. We added *and Borneo* to her name and painted a Chinese 'eye' on her prow for safe passage. Along with *Osa's Ark,* she took us over sixty thousand miles of African plains, mountains, and jungles. There she is now, all crated and being hoisted aboard."

My husband was turned a little toward the screen; the light from it flickered across his face.

"On September twenty-sixth," he went on, "we docked at Balawan, on the northeastern tip of Sumatra, and flew the rest of the way to Sandakan, in British North Borneo. Sometimes Osa took the stick; sometimes I did."

Martin then highlighted the picture by telling of our plane trip across the Malaccas to Port Swettenham, from there down to Singapore, and then east across the China Sea, escorted by a Royal Air Force flying boat. He told, too, of our dropping down at Kuching for much-needed gas; of our meeting with the Rajah and Ranee Brooke of Sarawak, and of our tilt with two converging thunderstorms when we attempted to fly overland from Kimanis Bay to Sandakan.

Borneo, in all its wild beauty, was there on the screen for all those quiet, eager children to see.

"That," my husband said to them, "is Mount Kinabalu, the highest peak in British North Borneo. In a moment we shall fly over her. The natives call her the 'Chinese Widow.' On the day we photographed her, she wore, as you shall see, a ruff of white clouds around her throat."

Next, Sandakan Bay, as we saw it from the air, was spread upon the screen, a rich panorama of sea, mountains, rivers, jungle, and cloud-banked sky.

An astonished little "ohhh" went up from the boys and girls in the audience when they saw the jungle camp which we had built deep in the interior of Borneo. Covering a cleared space the size of four city blocks, it comprised twenty houses and cabins, a laboratory, and a hangar for the plane.

Flowering trees overhung the river nearby, and the jungle all about us was alive with brightly plumaged birds, monkeys, and apes.

"It was like living in a great zoo," Martin said with a sort of wistful reflectiveness. "Oh, and those white flowers," he added. "This will interest you girls: They are orchids, and Mrs. Johnson counted five hundred blooms on one spray."

Ecstatic "ohs" and "ahs" went up from the feminine portion of our audience.

My husband laughed then. "Don't get it into your heads that life in the jungle is all orchids," he said. "There are millions of insects, most of which bite, scorpions, centipedes, and every kind of snake you can think of—bad ones. Why, there's even a snake that flies. Oh, yes, and in a minute you'll see a tree-climbing fish. Oysters grow on trees in this fantastic country, too," he added.

Some more "ahs" went up from our audience when the picture showed Borneo's sun bear, a little black fellow with a whitish-gold horseshoe on his chest. They also loved the droll, fluggy lorises, or "night apes." Owl-eyed and stump-tailed, lorises looked for all the world like living toy gnomes.

Martin paused and grinned at me, then addressed his big audience again. His manner was that of a person talking to just two or three little neighborhood boys and girls.

"Now, I know you're going to laugh when we come to the pictures of the proboscis monkey," he said, "for even when he's sad, this fellow with the long nose has a comical look."

A shout went up from the youngsters when the long-snouted monkey and his family appeared.

"The way you see him there," my husband went on, "the whole business of moving into his home, and photographing him, appears very simple. But he is a shy fellow and you'd never guess that we spent four months winning him and his family over." He smiled. "I give Osa credit for most of that," he said.

The picture ran to its close, presently, by showing us and our plane back at Singapore as the guests of the sultan of Johore.

Then the houselights went on, and the children rose and applauded. My husband took my hand and drew me to the center of the stage, and we bowed together. He looked very, very happy.

We were on our way in a cab back to the hotel. Martin was still smiling.

"It's all nonsense," he said.

"What's all nonsense?"

"This thing about cake. Not being able to eat it and have it too. We've been doing it all along."

I was thinking about something else, about how hard he'd had to work on this Borneo trip, and never a word said about it.

"What I mean," he said, "is that we've had the fun of going to places like Borneo, and then of coming back and showing our pictures, and sort of living the fun all over again."

"Yes, I know," I said.

"Why," he continued enthusiastically, "I ate my cake once again for every youngster in that audience this afternoon."

"Yes," I said, "but there's one thing wrong with this whole business. You never tell anybody how hard you worked in that horrid, steaming jungle."

"Well, gosh, you worked just as hard as I did."

"I haven't stood, bathed in sweat, for hours and hours over developing tanks, and over cameras and sound machines that were all corroded. I haven't seen the work of months—twenty thousand feet of film—lying under my hands, ruined by mildew!"

My husband pulled his lips in while he thought about this. Then he grinned.

"Maybe not," he said, "but you had the work of managing things—helping win the confidence of the natives and seeing that I had good food, too, and taking care of me and keeping me from having fevers."

"That was my job, and it isn't important now. But that beautiful picture. It is beautiful, the critics all say so, yet it looks as if you photographed it as easy as pie."

"Oh, well, it's been fun, too. Even the hard part has been fun." He sighed with an intense satisfaction.

We had had dinner sent up to our room and were just sitting down to it when the hotel phone rang. The clerk said that two little girls were in the lobby and wanted to interview us for their school paper.

"Why, sure," my husband said. "Send them right up."

"Here," I said impatiently. "At least have some soup while it's hot."

There was a light rap at the door. I opened it, and in walked two rosy-cheeked schoolgirls. They carried brand-new notebooks and freshly sharpened pencils.

"We're writing an article for our school paper," they said in a lovely bird-like duet. "You see, while we made a lot of notes on your lecture this afternoon, we need a few more details."

"Well, fine," said Martin. "I hope you'll make a special point of mentioning that proboscis monkey. He was one of the chief reasons we went back to Borneo."

The blue-eyed girl dismissed this at once. "First," she said,

"we want to know more about the Rajah of Sarawak at Kuching, and your dinner with him and the Ranee."

"Oh, I see—well—"

"We know, of course, that he is the White Rajah, the third
generation of the Brookes to rule—"

"That's right."

"Did you dine in a palace?"

"Well, maybe you'd call it a palace." My husband grinned.
"Anyhow, it was a very nice house."

"Palace," said the blue-eyed girl firmly, and wrote it in her
book.

"You see," Martin put it, "we'd had no luck at all on our
first trip to Borneo—with the proboscis monkey, I mean,
and—"

"What else happened at the palace?" The blue-eyed child
was now looking at me.

"Well," I tried to think. "We went to the grandstand on the
parade grounds and witnessed a most interesting pageant.
Troops drilled, natives wrestled, wild men from the interior
danced and pretended to fight."

"Oh, that's wonderful!" said the brown-eyed little girl. They
both scribbled like mad. "And did you sit in the grandstand
with the Rajah and his lady?" she asked. "As their guests, I
mean?"

"Yes. Yes, that's right," Martin replied with a longing look
in the direction of our fast-cooling dinner.

"And," put in the brown-eyed girl, "about the Sultan of Johore?"

"Why, he gave a banquet for us at the palace," I said. "It
was really very nice. He was most gracious."

"Did the sultan wear a crown or a turban, and were there
a lot of jewels in it?"

Martin looked at me. "He wore regular dinner things, didn't
he, Osa?"

"Turban with jewels in it," firmly said the blue-eyed child.

"That proboscis monkey—he's a rare fellow, and I think—"
My husband tried again.

"And about flying the way you did over those jungles?" asked
the brown-eyed one. "Weren't you afraid?"

Martin was uncertain. "Sometimes, of course," he said. "But, we had done so much flying—sixty thousand miles over Africa and all—"

"Yes, but in that storm. What if you had had to make a forced landing?"

My husband was quite earnest. "Oh, we'd have managed somehow, I guess," he said.

"But all those wild people and animals and snakes, and things—what about those?"

"It wouldn't have been any fun, of course," Martin smiled, "but when you fly over countries where there are no regular air routes, landing fields, or radio beams, you just have to— well, sort of take those chances."

"And, of course," I added, "we had a wonderful pilot and a very fine plane."

"Oh, yes," my husband said. "While you're about it, you might put down there that we flew thirty thousand miles over Borneo."

The two little girls seemed suddenly aware of our fast-chilling dinner, and took a hurried and embarrassed leave.

"Don't forget about the proboscis monkey!" Martin called after them as they ran with sudden shyness out the door.

We were at the airport the following morning at six o'clock to catch the plane for Burbank, California, and, as Martin had said, it might as well have been the middle of the night.

"I wish we had thought to get the names of those two little girls," he said.

"I was just thinking the same thing," I said. "Why couldn't we write to the school board at Salt Lake?"

He nodded. "I'd like to send them some photographs of the proboscis monkeys. Those two cute babies, clinging to the limb. Glossy prints, you know, for illustrating their story."

I laughed out loud at that. "You and your monkeys!" I said. Then, on second thought, "Let's send them a picture of the sultan, too. They'd love that."

Martin grinned. "Sure," he said. "With a turban on."

"Sweet, weren't they—so eager to do a good job of reporting."

"Yes," he replied. "Grand youngsters."

"Do you know what I've been thinking?" I asked suddenly.

"Well, I can make a guess." My husband studied me earnestly. "You mean, buy a home?"

I nodded. "Just a little one."

His face puckered anxiously. "That's something you've always missed a lot, isn't it?"

"Yes, but we've had each other, and that's what really makes a home, isn't it?"

He squinted reflectively. "I wonder just how one goes about this business of adopting kids? he said.

"Oh," I said, talking excitedly and fast. "I didn't know you'd thought any more about that, but I've found out just what to do. And about the house: We could have a little place in the country, couldn't we, with room enough for the pets?"

"Sure, and the children could play with them."

We were boarding the plane.

"That's a fine idea," he said. "I like it." He smiled.

There was the sound of the motors starting. Slowly the plane swung 'round and rolled down the runway.

Martin looked toward me, still smiling.

I shall always remember that smile.

CRASH FATAL TO MARTIN JOHNSON

Game Hunter's Wife Most Badly Hurt of 11 Plane Survivors

LOS ANGELES, Jan. 13 (By International News Service).—The second victim of a Western Air Express passenger plane crash, Martin Johnson, world famous big game hunter and explorer, died here today.

Eleven others, including Johnson's equally famous wife, his companion on many of his adventure trips, were injured.

Some of the political names for areas visited by the Johnsons have changed. The names used by Osa Johnson have remained in the text and on the maps, but the modern names are noted below with those known to Osa.

Belgian Congo—Zaire
British East Africa—Kenya
British North Borneo—Sabah
Lake Rudolf—Lake Turkana
New Hebrides—Vanuatu
Rhodesia—Zambia (north) and Zimbabwe (south)
Ruanda—Rwanda
Urundi—Bwandi

Index

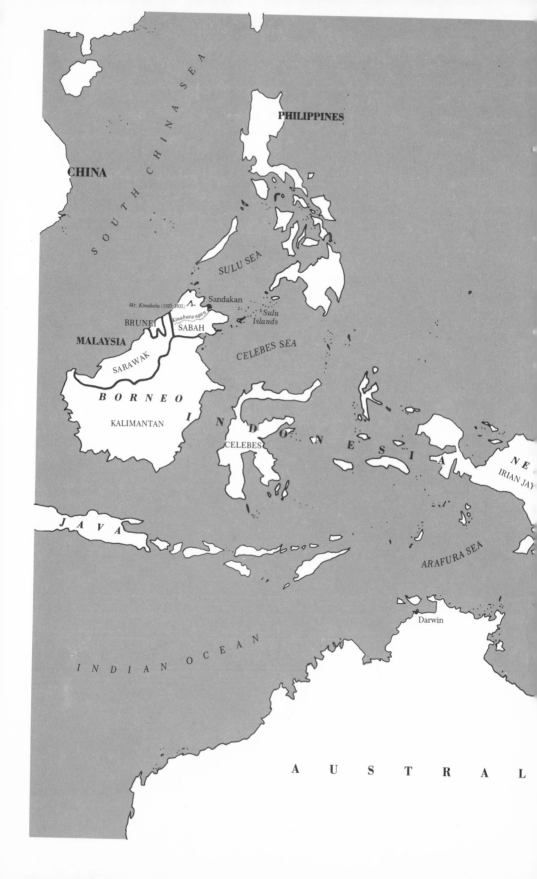